So We Live:
The Novels of Alexander Baron

Alexander Baron in 1956

So We Live:
The Novels of Alexander Baron

Edited by Susie Thomas,
Andrew Whitehead and Ken Worpole

Five Leaves Publications

So We Live: The Novels of Alexander Baron
Edited by Susie Thomas, Andrew Whitehead and Ken Worpole

Published in 2019 by Five Leaves Publications
14a Long Row, Nottingham NG1 2DH
www.fiveleaves.co.uk
www.fiveleavesbookshop. co.uk

ISBN: 978-1-910170-61-8

Printed in Great Britain

Contents

Introduction

Susie Thomas

In our blood we know an axe can fall on
us at any second. So we live. We live.
(*The Lowlife,* 1963)

On 4 December 2017, the centenary of Alexander Baron's birth, a group of his admirers met in The White Hart on Stoke Newington High Street to celebrate his work. Baron's novels explore the life-and-death issues facing ordinary people — war, politics, identity, sex — with a compassion and humour which won him huge renown, at first. Although he could engage readers with his deft characterisation and story-telling he lacked the one talent a novelist needs to stay news: an ability (or willingness) to turn himself into a brand. We formed The Baron Six to spread the word: the novelist Anthony Cartwright; the Second World War historian Sean Longden; the academic and researcher on Jewish literature Nadia Valman; the journalist and historian Andrew Whitehead; the writer Ken Worpole, who interviewed Baron in the early 1980s; and me. Each of us has produced articles and prefaces about his novels before coming together to work on a book about him. The first hurdle was what to call it. The title caused sleepless nights as we devised ever more convoluted subtitles in an attempt to do him justice. In desperation we settled on key words, City, War, Lowlife, although we hoped we would discover the answer in Baron's own writing. Finally, Ken Worpole found the title in Baron's 1963 classic, *The Lowlife. So We Live* occurs in an exchange between the Jamaican immigrant, Joe de Souza, and the narrator, and evokes Baron's philosophy as a novelist. As Baron's son says, "It has a gentle Yiddish resonance: it's a defiant affirmation of life, but could equally express a shoulder-shrugging fatalism". Drawing on his novels, screenplays, and memoir — published and unpublished — this book will demonstrate what is distinctive about Baron's work and why he is still worth reading now.

For the birthday celebration, Ken Worpole devised a tour of the streets that Baron walked and recreated in his novels with so much attention and affection. (If you would like to follow in his footsteps Andrew Whitehead has developed "A walk round Baron's manor", with a map by Nancy Edwards, which you can find at the end of this book.) From The White Hart we went to Coronation Avenue, the scene of the 1940 bomb disaster that killed more than 160 people, many Jewish. We passed by the former Apollo Cinema, which sometimes used to show Yiddish films; and which was given an Ottoman makeover when it became a mosque for the local Turkish community in the 1990s. Then we made our way to Foulden Road, where Baron grew up and which appears as Ingram's Terrace in *The Lowlife*:

> When I was a boy, these houses were occupied by superior working-class families, who kept them in beautiful condition. … Now most of them are tenements. The street is still clean. … All is quiet and decent. Negroes have come to live, more every month. And Cypriots. The Negroes are of marvellous respectability. Every Sunday morning they all go to the Baptist Chapel in the High Street. You should see the men, in beautiful pearl-grey suits and old-fashioned trilbies with curled brims, the big women full of dignity, and the little girls in white muslin and bonnets. It slays me. They are the Victorian residents of this street, come back a century later, with black skins.

The Baptist Chapel is now next to the Aziziye Mosque and Baron would have been delighted that there has never been any sign of hatred between the neighbours. Our next stop was the former Simpson's factory, built in 1929, which at one time employed up to 3000 garment workers; the sort of place where the narrator of *The Lowlife* — "Harryboy Boas (two syllables, please)" — puts in a few shifts as a Hoffman presser when he's down on his luck at the racetrack. He's not one of those "goomps" who believe in the virtue of labour but it's warm, "wisecracks and practical joking go on all the time", and the bonus is a shag in the basement with any of the women workers who are up for it: "like lighting your cigarette from a stranger's".

The celebration ended with a tasty meal in the Bos Cirrik restaurant, which reminded me that Baron's novels are full of descriptions of food and that Barbara Hardy's comment on Dickens fits Baron to a T: "eating and drinking are valued by him as proofs of sociability and gusto, but more important still, as ceremonies of love". As we discussed our favourite novels, I also thought of Baron's cryptic "Note on My Work", found among his papers at Reading University, in which he expresses his gratitude to the critics and academics who have paid attention to his books before he complains, with wonderful curmudgeonliness, that they have missed the point: "my novels have always been looked upon as unconnected works and, most of them, as realist essays upon London life or upon war." Baron's admirers have been divided into two camps: it's as if the fans of the London novels are drawn to the radical, the outsider, and assume the war novels must be patriotic and conformist — the antithesis of everything Harryboy represents. The war novels have mainly been read by historians who express little or no interest in *The Lowlife*, or the London anarchists' favourite, *King Dido* (1969). But Baron's novels are all recognisably by the same hand; connected by "the presence of history" and a "visionary exploration of the theme, 'where are we going?'" ("Note on My Work"). The chapters in this book are by diverse hands, but we have kept in mind the need to make connections between his books. To this end, Sean Longden's discussion of the Second World War novels follows Baron's veterans back home as they struggle to adjust to civvy street in *With Hope, Farewell* and *Rosie Hogarth* (1951).

With the exception of the country house novel, *Gentle Folk* (1976), it is history from below (conscripts, women, and lowlifes) that informs Baron's stories, as characters attempt to be masters of their fate in the face of war, clashing ideologies and tribalism. Baron also wrote two novels about the Spanish Civil war and its aftermath, *Franco is Dying* (1977) and *The War Baby*, which he saw as central to the conflicts of the twentieth century. As he said in the interview with Ken Worpole: "Spain is everything that's happened in the earth in our time." *The War Baby* will be published for the first time in 2019 by Five Leaves. It is really now, after years of semi-obscurity, that we need his novels as Europe fragments once again and extreme nationalism has returned with a vengeance.

As a respectable old man, living in a quiet quarter of north London, Temple Fortune, Baron looked back on his early years, when he belonged to a Dalston gang that got into fights. As he told Ken Worpole: "In the street when I was a small kid, I used to tell stories. I wasn't very good at a punch-up. Story-telling gave me my status." In *The Lowlife*, it's the narrator's sister, "fat Debbie", who is the fighter: "she ran with a gang of rough boys, … she ruled those boys, … and I worshipped my heroic big sister". Baron never went in for the razor blade in the potato, to borrow Claud Cockburn's phrase, not even when Mosley's Blackshirts tried to rule the streets of Whitechapel when he was a teenager. In his (as yet) unpublished memoir, *Chapters of Accidents*, Baron recalled "it was the way of Gandhi" that defeated the fascists at The Battle of Cable Street. But as a Communist, a Jew, and a feminist, who carried Baudelaire's *Les*

Fleurs du Mal with him into battle, he knew a good fight when he saw one. His novels are powerful testaments against oppression and it's not just what he wrote about, but his voice — direct, intimate, compassionate and savage — which speaks to us today.

The war novels drew on Baron's six years in the army which, according to his discharge papers, left him suffering from "psychoneurosis". Written in a white heat, and published in 1948, *From the City, From the Plough* rapidly became a bestseller. On its publication, V.S. Pritchett said "this is the only war book that has conveyed any sense of reality to me"; Randall Stevenson has compared its significance to the First World War classic, *All Quiet on the Western Front*; and Brian Sewell was reduced to tears when he read it on the tube for Radio 4's *A Good Read*. According to the leading military historian, Sir Antony Beevor, "Alexander Baron's *From the City, From the Plough* is undoubtedly one of the very greatest British novels of the Second World War and provides the most honest and authentic account of front line life for an infantryman in north-west Europe."[1] So why have so few people read it in recent years?

One answer would be that the story of the Second World War has been told more dramatically in films. (The golden age of twentieth-century war literature seems to have been the First World War.) It could also be, at least in England, that Second World War novels have more kudos when they are written by and about the officer class. Baron told Ken Worpole that most British war novels were written "by the kind of intellectuals to whom the army was an agony… an awful experience, sleeping with thirty-five ruffians. The officers didn't seem to have the Robert Graves touch. Graves, Sassoon, knew the Tommies were the men getting the rough edge of the stick." Perhaps surprisingly, Baron did not include Evelyn Waugh in this reckoning: although he considered him a political "reactionary", he praised Waugh's *Sword of Honour* trilogy as a "magnificent" illumination of a whole complex of human problems ("On Being English and Jewish"). With the exception of Waugh's trilogy, cynical American war novels seem to have more appeal for readers today: give me Mailer or Heller, I hear you say. John Williams suggests that the British no longer want to think about the Second World War: "We find it hard to accept that all those old men you see with medals… are heroes — no more or no less than a Guevara or a Mandela" ("Swords to Ploughshares"). So Orwell's *Homage to Catalonia* is considered a

---

1 Email from Antony Beevor to Susie Thomas, 8 January 2017.

classic while Baron's war trilogy has struggled to stay in print. But, as the conflict recedes into greater historical distance, there are signs of a renewed interest — and recent films, *Dunkirk* and *Darkest Hour* — may foster a desire to return to literary representations. The Imperial War Museum is reprinting *From the City, From the Plough* in September 2019, which augurs well. It would be great if the trilogy could be published in one volume under the title Baron envisaged for it: *Men, Women and War.*

For the most part Baron's soldiers aren't Officers and Gentlemen: nor are they heroes; they are conscripts, with no control over whether they live or die; their only choice is whether they can hang on to some human decency and sense of beauty, or not. Halfway through that first novel, the London "doggy boys" from the racetracks and a bunch of "country bumpkins", march past Mont Pinçon towards the end of D-Day: "there were roses growing in the Norman hedges, pink, wild roses…. A rifleman stopped to pick a rose, and fixed it in the netting of his helmet. All down the ranks men stopped to pluck flowers." Within the space of five pages there are "dozens of bloody little battles"; some of the soldiers, whom Baron evokes so vividly, survive the barrage but many do not: "nothing stirred in the field but the petals of the pink hedge roses which fluttered in the helmets of the dead".

It is striking that Baron, while on the side of the ordinary soldier, is never sentimental or jingoistic. Towards the end of his third war novel, *The Human Kind* (1953), a drunken doggy boy recounts his conquests in a bar:

> "This tart. Every night, regular as clockwork, along she come with her shopping-bag. Into me tent she come, then off she went to the swillbins…. I made her earn it. Something for nothing, that's all they want."

The "tart" is fourteen, starving, so "thin you could put your fingers round her waist", but the soldier is proud of being British: "'Wops and Wogs, all them niggers and Chinks,' he shouts, 'Scum o' the earth!'". Flowers of evil, flowers of pain.

Baron was not only a great novelist of the ordinary infantryman but of the women as collateral damage. This emerges most powerfully in the second volume of his war trilogy, *There's No Home* (1950), which draws on Baron's experience of being billeted for two months in Catania in 1943. John Williams' afterword to the novel quotes from a letter that Baron wrote home during this brief respite from the fighting:

> I'm just reading Jane Austen's *Northanger Abbey*. The book is a real refuge from the sweat and slog of this life, with its calm unruffled style, its early nineteenth-century heroines and its storm in a teacup adventures. As a matter of fact I am always staggered when I think of Jane Austen. Here was a parson's daughter, born in the country a century ago, educated at home, never seeing the outside world – yet she saw right through the social stupidities that she lived amongst, and the snobbery and shallowness of the minor rural gentry.

I wonder if Baron knew Rudyard Kipling's story, "The Janeites", about soldiers in the First World War who secretly read her novels in the trenches. Perhaps his practice of indiscriminate reading on a vast scale had led him to the Poet of the Empire, as it later allowed him to appreciate the reactionary Evelyn Waugh. Williams explores how Baron applied the clear eye that he admired in Jane Austen in order to evoke the domestic life of a small street in one Sicilian town and its female residents. All of the women have lost men in the war and are hungry for life. At the heart of the novel is the developing relationship between Sergeant Craddock and a local girl, Graziella, who falls in love with him. When the soldiers are ordered to move on, the affair is doomed. As Williams says: "it is a measure of Baron's talent that, in the end, we don't know who to pity more — the men heading into the horror of war or the women left behind. Out of an instinctive empathy with women as well as men, Baron has fashioned a novel that is at once masculine and feminine, a war story and a love story, an affirmation of the human spirit and a tragedy".

Graziella makes another appearance in Baron's *The Human Kind*. These vignettes might seem like off-cuts from his earlier war novels, but Baron's use of the first person here allows him to dig deeper into some aspects of his experience. In "The Indian" he tells us that he decided to tell the story of Graziella and the soldier as it "really happened" and not as he had described it in his novel, *There's No Home*. The substance of their relationship doesn't seem that different: the girl and the soldier are both initially inhibited about getting together, in comparison with the enthusiastic coupling that is going on all around them. The major difference is in Baron's account of how they overcame the barrier to intimacy through the figure of an Indian soldier. As he walks down the street towards them Graziella is frightened of him and Baron is surprised at this racial prejudice: there are lots of American Negroes billeted in the area and "there was

A photograph of an unnamed Italian woman found among Baron's papers after his death — perhaps the model for Graziella in his novel *There's No Home*

neither aversion nor that self-conscious generosity towards them which is as offensive as hatred". Some of the women are attracted to the Negro soldiers because they were "the finest-looking and the most unfortunate". But it was the opposite with the Indians, for reasons Baron cannot fathom since they behaved with "a more mature courtesy than any other troops I have ever seen". The Indian soldier is nineteen years old and has left behind three children (while he fights for the British Empire); he wants to hold Graziella's baby as consolation and Baron persuades her to agree despite her fears. It's after this moment "that they became lovers". I can't think of a better hymn to multiculturalism.

It seems that Baron was busy taking notes and shaping stories throughout his war service. He sent "Toy Shop" to his then girlfriend, Nell, who sent it to the *Daily Worker* where it was published. (A facsimile is included here after Chapter Two.) He later reworked this story, which appears as "The Music Box" in *There's No Home*. Baron also started a monthly paper for his platoon, *Pioneer Parade*, which he edited for several issues, putting his earlier experience as a journalist to the army's benefit. We have included a copy of the cover of the first issue, in which Pte J.A. Bernstein (as he was then known) promises it's "going to be a paper that's written by its readers".

Baron later recalled that his publisher, Jonathan Cape, threw a party to celebrate *From the City, From the Plough*:

> It was a beautiful summer evening. I set off on the 73 bus from Hackney. I've always been very shy and was all the more so after the war. I was very badly shaken up by then. I finally got off the bus at King's Cross and I walked through Bloomsbury. Then I saw a pub and I thought: "I'll buy some Dutch courage." So I stopped and had a double whisky… I arrived at the Cape offices, and I stood on the opposite pavement and looked up at the windows of the first-floor room where they held the parties, and I heard this sort of babble of well-bred, high-pitched conversation. My heart sank and I turned round and went home. ("Swords to Ploughshares")

Reading this now it's hard not to think: get back on the bus and go to the party! Although Baron published fourteen novels, he never felt at home in the literary world; he did not give readings, attend book launches or belong to a coterie. But perhaps it was not only class consciousness that left him standing on the pavement, looking up at the sweetshop window. As he told Jeb Nichols, he "had a kind of childhood sympathy for the outside character", which never left him ("Seeing Life"). Born Joseph Alexander Bernstein on 4 December 1917, his father was a Polish-born furrier who came to England as a child. Baron described his father as a "great self-improver": "when I was a very small boy he bought an atlas and neither one of us knew how to decipher these coloured patches. I remember him bending over this thing and myself kneeling on the chair next to him, working it out together". His mother, Fanny, née Levinson, was a "good and serious reader" who led a "solitary life with books", which her son later shared with her. Baron and his younger sister, Ida, made weekly trips to the public library and by the age of fifteen he had read Marx's *Capital* and Shaw's *Intelligent Woman's Guide to Socialism* as well as novels, history and poetry. He later said: "I think the greatest education is indiscriminate reading on a vast scale" ("Seeing Life"). He won a scholarship to Hackney Downs grammar school but he turned down a place at the University of

London, in part so that he could contribute to the family finances but also at the urging of the Communist Party. As he later recalled: "very heaven it was to be a Young Communist at this time" (*Chapters of Accidents*). As a sixteen-year-old schoolboy, he was sent on a political mission to Paris, where André Malraux bought him lunch and Louis Aragon questioned him. He joined the Labour Party League of Youth and became assistant editor of *Tribune*. When the Labour Party crushed the League of Youth because of its radicalism, the Young Communist League made him editor of their fortnightly paper, *Challenge*. He recruited for the party, stayed up half the night writing the paper and revelled in his secret life.

Baron enlisted at Islington on 25 July 1940, having been turned down by the RAF because of his poor eyesight, and fought in the Sicilian, Italian and Normandy campaigns. This wasn't the derring-do of boyish dreams but back-breaking, if dangerous, drudgery. He was promoted to corporal and was recommended by his commanding officer for promotion to officer, but was turned down presumably because of his political affiliations. A few months after the D-Day landings, as the army moved into Belgium, he began to suffer from nervous exhaustion. He was repatriated and sent to a training camp in Ireland to train recruits, where he was knocked over by an American truck and hospitalised. On his demobilisation he asked for a typewriter, on which he wrote *From the City, From the Plough*, and so Alexander Baron the novelist was born. At the beginning of the war, Jewish soldiers were encouraged by the army to change their surnames in case they were caught by the Nazis but he had refused to do so, which makes his later abandonment of Bernstein all the more surprising. Perhaps, having fallen out of love with the Communist Party, he wanted a new identity; a public break from the past. As Andrew Whitehead explores in Chapter Two, Baron became profoundly guilty about the deception he practised as a member of the CP, especially that he had been one of a handful of YCL leaders who were nominated to go underground if the Party (which at this time opposed the war) was outlawed.

Baron was in a bad state when he returned to his parents' house in Hackney in 1946. He credited his friend Ted Willis with finding him a job as editor of the journal *New Theatre*, which was associated with the left-leaning Unity Theatre. Baron also became a Director of Unity Theatre and he later recalled that he used to get home every night about midnight, then sat down and worked for three hours on his novel

("Seeing Life"). The success of *From the City, From the Plough* in 1948 allowed Baron to give up his job at Unity and complete his war trilogy: *There's No Home* was published in 1950 (American title *The Wine of Etna*) and *The Human Kind* in 1953. The latter was filmed by Carl Foreman under the title *The Victors* (1963). Foreman, a Jewish American who had been a Communist in his youth and was blacklisted by Hollywood in the 1950s after appearing before The House Un-American Activities Committee, must have seemed an ideal collaborator. But Baron was disappointed that Foreman turned the London doggy boys and the country bumpkins into American GIs. It was a box office flop. Later, Baron developed his own screenplay, *The Poor Bloody Infantry*, but it was never filmed.

Baron was up to his neck in history: as a Bolshie, a soldier and a Jew. He began by considering himself an English novelist above all: saturated in English literature from Chaucer to Thomas Hardy and dedicated to recording the experience of the working class. But as time went on "Jewish preoccupations, obsessions, and symbols" took possession of him. Although Baron said that this "wound" became central to his writing, he struggled to find a "way of coping with it in literary form" ("On Being English and Jewish"). Chapter Four charts his attempts to grapple with this theme in the articles and stories he wrote for the *Jewish Quarterly* between 1953 and 1963, two of which are reprinted in this volume: "The Anniversary" (1953), which recounts his attendance at a commemoration for the mass deportation of the Jews from Paris in 1942, and a written interview with Jacob Sonntag in 1963 entitled "On Being English and Jewish".[2] In his first fiction dealing with Jewish themes, *With Hope, Farewell*, the protagonist, Mark, is torn between his fury at anti-Semitism and his hatred of the vulgar, East End community from which he longs to escape. On his return from service as a fighter pilot in the Second World War, Mark is doomed to

---

2 Nick Baron speculates that his father's attendance at the Paris commemoration may have been in connection with the French side of his family: "... he had a French cousin, Charles Burzstyn, whom he met (perhaps stayed with) on his visits to Paris both before and after the war. Charles and his father, Jacques, both fought in the Resistance. But, of course, a large number of their family, whom [my father] would have got to know in the 1930s, perished in the camps. I think the French side of the family played an important part in my father's early years — even though this is not mentioned at all in *Chapters of Accidents*."

humiliating work as a salesman and his sense of betrayal culminates when his wife suffers a miscarriage because of a fascist rally in Dalston. What will it take for this hatred to stop? the novel seems to scream. It took Baron a long time to find a way to get this story off his chest. In the meantime, he moved between Paris and London until his marriage to Delores Lopez-Salzedo in 1960. They had first met when they were both involved in Unity Theatre. Salzedo had written a play, which had been staged in some regional theatres; she also had a successful career as an advertising copywriter and later wrote several well-received radio plays.

His next novel with a Jewish theme, *The Lowlife*, also discussed in Chapter Four, is a unique and compelling novel of Holocaust commemoration mapped onto the streets of Hackney. The tone is self-deprecating and intimate; sometimes tough and occasionally deeply tender. This doggy boy gambles compulsively and at every opportunity: "show me a way of losing money and I will try it". Fantasies of wealth and largesse lure him on: "All the schnorrers will be round you and you will hand out loans like an emperor". But Harryboy also knows that gambling has more to do with the death instinct than with winning: "The gambler is the one who goes on with no peace, no release, till he has annihilated himself".

Baron believed it was the writer's job "to be the spectator who hopes he can see more of the game" ("Seeing Life"). He saw how Englishness was changing and how this was resented; he also perceived female strengths which were usually invisible to male writers at that time. From the prominence given to the women in the war novels, through *Rosie Hogarth*, to Marcia in *The Lowlife*, his female characters are striking. Baron claimed that his interest in women's role in society was not a conscious theme and certainly did not come from his background in the Labour movement, which was reluctant to take it up. As he told Jeb Nichols: "nobody was more reactionary than the Trade Unionists". Whatever the origin of his feminism, he recounted an extraordinary story of holding seminars in the middle of the Second World War: "I can remember one instance in Normandy when the soldiers were in their slit trenches having a rest for a day or two and we got them all into a barn — no officers, and we had a huge discussion about women: Should they receive equal pay? Is it wrong to see them as sex objects?" ("Seeing Life"). His enduring fascination with both women and history resulted in *The Golden Princess* (1954), set in the time of the Spanish conquest of Mexico, and *Queen of the East* (1956), based on an episode concerning Queen Zenobia of Palmyra from Gibbon's *The Decline and Fall of the Roman Empire*. Both these historical romances were also prompted by the desire to achieve financial independence by writing potential Hollywood blockbusters. MGM bought the Mexican novel but it was never made into a film and Baron decided that writing with an eye on the market, even if it focused on female characters, was not for him.

Rosie Hogarth, set in the working-class area of Chapel Market, Islington, follows a returning soldier's struggle to fit back in to civilian life and his relationship with the eponymous heroine. For most of the novel he is tortured by the belief that she makes her living as a prostitute before discovering that she is an undercover Communist. Rosie's father condemns her bloody cold hard arrogance before telling her: "'You really think yourself better than those you want to lead.'" This sounds like Baron's verdict on his younger self; and Andrew Whitehead argues that two later novels, *Seeing Life* (1958) and *The In-Between Time* (1971), reflect Baron's anguished attitude to his earlier life as a closet Communist.

King Dido, the subject of Nadia Valman's Chapter Five, signalled a return to his outlaw traditions. It's a gruelling account of life in an East End slum: Dido pits himself against a policeman — the state — and the policeman wins. Baron was probably looking back at *The Siege of Sidney Street*, one of his earliest successful film scripts, about an anarchist uprising, but the novel is also resonant today, in the time of Black Lives Matter. Baron conceived of *King Dido* and *Gentle Folk* as a representation of the two nations in 1911: the Siege of Sidney Street twinned with the Coronation. *Gentle Folk* is also a satiric portrait of H.G. Wells, the anti-Semitic socialist, with a kindly nod to the country house novel tradition in which E.M. Forster was working in the early twentieth century.

In the final chapter, Anthony Cartwright explores how the extraordinary series of London novels that Baron produced in the 1950s and 1960s focuses on the central characters' dilemma "of how to live and where to live". Baron's preoccupation with housing touches a nerve that is still raw today. Kit Caless and Gary Budden's *Acquired for Development By...: A Hackney Anthology* (2012) takes its title from *The Lowlife*: "And as I came away, I saw on a board that epitaph to all our yesterdays, 'Acquired for Development By....'" As Caless says: "It was striking to read something written half a century ago, by a writer from Hackney, that seemed entirely relevant and fitting to the current situation we found ourselves in."[3] In this volume Cartwright brings Baron crashing up to date as he connects the Grenfell tragedy with working-class struggles in *Rosie Hogarth, The Lowlife* and *King Dido*. Cartwright casts a novelist's eye on Hackney then and now and, despite many reasons to rage against gentrification, finds hope in the everyday, as Baron would have done.

Baron's last published novel, *Franco is Dying*, is narrated by an ageing former Communist who returns to the battlefields of the Spanish Civil War. As a young man Baron had wanted to go to Spain but it seems the CP put the mockers on it. *Franco is Dying* is as gripping as a thriller by Graham Greene but by this time Baron's readership had dwindled. It's hard to know why this should have been the case. One answer must be that he failed to promote his work; another, that novels written from the point of view of the outsider are likely to remain outside the canon (think women, minorities, the working class) until they are rediscovered.

Fortunately, he had a parallel career in television. Baron began by writing original dramas for ITV's *Armchair Theatre* in the 1960s, which he considered the televisual equivalent of the short story. The first plays are in classic Baron territory: *Clip Joint People* (1960, recording now lost) is set in Soho, while *The Hero* (1961, another lost recording) is set in the East End rag trade.[4] Although *Late Summer* (1963) takes place in a hotel in the South of France out of season, the main characters are Londoners. Helga (played by Constance Cummings) and David (John Stride) have escaped Hampstead, where the "shame" of their affair made them feel "like lepers". She is old enough to be his mother, but gradually we realise that this is not a Terence Rattigan story of an older woman buying the affection of her younger lover. At the heart of *Late Summer*, as in *The Lowlife*, is a lost child. Helga is still punishing herself because her son died twenty-three years earlier in Vienna, and David, the angry young writer, is the age Bruno would have been had he survived. The couple are like "two human animals preying on each other"; her parting words to him at the end of the play are to "get down to your writing".

---

3 Interview with Kit Caless, *Yeah! Hackney*, 28 March 2012 (https://www.yeahhackney.com/acquired-for-development-by%E2%80%A6-a-hackney-anthology-interview-with-kit-caless/).

4 Billy Smart, viewing notes for *Armchair Theatre Archive*, Volume 4 (2018). This volume includes *Late Summer* (1963). The screenplays can be found in Baron's archive at Reading.

Baron wanted to reach a wide audience with his original screenplays, but they might not have provided a reliable source of income on their own. According to Stephen Durbridge, who was his agent from the 1970s until Baron's death in 1999, he hit the jackpot when he was commissioned to write several episodes of the television series *A Family at War* (1970–1972), set in Liverpool, and he went on to adapt literary classics, including *The Secret Agent*, *Oliver Twist*, *Jane Eyre* and *Vanity Fair*. The IMDb credits Baron with thirty-two screenplays — a considerable body of work — but Durbridge says that writing for television at this time was "backroom-boy stuff"; it paid the bills but there wasn't much interest in making film adaptations of his novels.[5] The Italian producer and director, Mario Zampi, made a bid for the rights to *The Lowlife* shortly after it was published but he died later in 1963: another screenplay bit the dust.

It must have been bitterly frustrating for Baron in the 1980s to find himself in literary limbo: one day you are (almost) as famous as Byron and then in a blink of a literary-critical eye your new novels and autobiography languish in the slush pile. He spent his last years working on a history of Communism: only Baron could have beat on, boat against the current, borne back ceaselessly into the past. This wasn't simply an exercise in nostalgia but rather a continuation of his working through of history and the attempt to answer the question: "where are we going?" He must have been cheered when a series of writers made their way to his door to pay homage — most notably, Ken Worpole, John Williams and Iain Sinclair — writers who weren't embarrassed by his focus on class. Ken Worpole spearheaded the resurgence of interest in Baron's work and in Chapter One he draws on the interview he recorded with him in 1983. (An edited transcript of Baron talking to Worpole, "A city should be accumulated memory", appears after the first chapter.) Sinclair included a cameo of Baron in the film he made with Chris Petit, *The Cardinal and the Corpse*, and he wrote the introduction to the reissue of *The Lowlife* in 2001: "Here it is, the book, the place, the story. Enjoy".

Andrew Whitehead, Ken Worpole and I, the editors of this volume, hope you enjoy this celebration of Baron's novels, the first of its kind, and we hope that there will be other books on his work in the future.

---

5   Stephen Durbridge to Susie Thomas, 27 November 2017.

Acknowledgements

I would like to thank Iain Sinclair for sending a copy of Baron's interview with Jeb Nichols, "Seeing Life".

Sources and Further Reading

Baron, Alexander. 1948. *From the City, From the Plough*. Black Spring Press: London, 2010.

Baron, Alexander. 1950. *There's No Home*. Afterword by John L. Williams, Sort of Books: London, 2011.

Baron, Alexander. 1951. *Rosie Hogarth*. Introduction by Andrew Whitehead, New London Editions: Nottingham, 2010.

Baron, Alexander. 1952, *With Hope, Farewell*. Jonathan Cape, Five Leaves: Nottingham, 2019.

Baron, Alexander. 1953. *The Human Kind*. Pan Books: London, 1957.

Baron, Alexander. 1963. *The Lowlife*. Introduction by Iain Sinclair, Black Spring Press: London, 2010.

Baron, Alexander. 1963. "On Being English and Jewish" in *Jewish Quarterly*, 10:1, pp. 6-10.

Baron, Alexander. 1998. "Seeing Life." Interview with Jeb Nichols in *Words*, December 1988, pp. 2-7.

Baron, Alexander. 1997. *Chapters of Accidents*. As yet unpublished typescript held at the University of Reading.

Hardy, Barbara. 1970. *The Moral Art of Dickens: Essays*. Athlone Press.

Stevenson, Randall. 1986. *The British Novel since the Thirties*. University of Georgia Press.

Williams, John. 1994. "Swords to Ploughshares", *Independent*, 11 June 1994.

Chapter 1
A Dark Horse
Alexander Baron on Becoming a Writer

Ken Worpole

'Story-telling gave me my status'

On 7 June 1983 I interviewed Alexander Baron at length at his home in north-west London. He traced his urge to write to his early years when he belonged to a Dalston street gang that played football, and occasionally got into fights with other street gangs. "In the street when I was a small kid, I used to tell stories. I wasn't very good at a punch-up. Story-telling gave me my status. I could sit down on the kerb, with the others all around me, and tell them a story." From this brief anecdote — and from remarks made in his unpublished memoir, *Chapters of Accidents* and the autobiographical elements of his novels — it is clear that Baron returned time and again to his early life in Hackney, and the pre-occupations, personal and political, which took hold of him there.

The area of Hackney which formed the young writer — principally the neighbourhoods of Clapton, Dalston, Stoke Newington and Stamford Hill — contained a large, but mostly secular Jewish population. Many had advanced out of poverty in the East End ghettoes of Whitechapel and Stepney, and were later to advance further geographically and socially to the suburban respectability of north and north-west London, as did Baron himself. For much of the twentieth century, however, the borough was not only one of the two principal Jewish areas of London — the other being Tower Hamlets — but it also possessed a larger Jewish population than found in most other cities of the world, with some 100,000 Jews resident in Hackney by the 1950s according to historian Rachel Kolsky.[1]

Baron's parents were Jewish (his father came to England from Poland at the age of thirteen), and regarded themselves as free-thinkers. Starting married life in a single room in Abersham Road, Dalston, after the First World War, they moved to two rooms in Sandringham Road nearby in 1923, when Baron was five years old, soon after finally settling for life at 6 Foulden Road, Stoke Newington, where they took a mortgage on a terraced house with a basement. Barnet Bernstein, Alexander's father, was an avid reader of books of popular science, while his mother,

---

1 Kolsky, 2017, p.105.

With his parents, Fanny and Barnett Bernstein.
Images from Alexander Baron's archive at Reading are included with the kind permission of Nick Baron. We should like to thank Nick and the Kelmanson family for permission to include personal and family photos. Copyright remains with the image owners.

Fanny (surname Levinson before marriage) went weekly with the young Alexander to the local public library, where both were assiduous borrowers of fiction. It was a very bookish, working-class home where, as Baron once described in a letter to me, "We all took turns in reading *The Good Companions* aloud." Dickens was admired above all others. The young Bernstein adored his parents and sister, Ida, and described his primary school years as "the happiest of his life"; he further regarded his time as a scholarship boy at Hackney Downs School — where "most of the boys were Jewish" — as marking a period of great security and intellectual fulfilment. Yet he later wrote that by the time of his early adolescence he had gained a reputation within the family for being something of "a dark horse": intense, private, self-willed.

Many secular Jewish families at this time identified with left-wing causes, and some played a major part in the growing influence of the British Communist Party, particularly in East London, as Andrew Whitehead documents in Chapter Two. The adolescent Baron was soon swept up in this political milieu, joining the Labour League of Youth as a fifteen-year-old schoolboy, but soon showing an equal interest in the more fiery world of Communist militancy, an affiliation that was to cause some distress to his family, as well as to Baron himself afterwards. This became a major theme of his fiction: the divided personal loyalties caused by participation in the febrile, clandestine politics of the 1930s.

Throughout this early period Baron was writing poetry. "It still seems to me," he wrote in another letter, "the most essential mode of using words." In addition, though, were short stories, essays, and political journalism. At school he had steeped himself in Romantic poetry, French symbolist literature, and the novels of Dickens, Priestley, Gorky, Dostoevsky. At the age of sixteen, still a schoolboy, he was sent to Paris by the Communist Party — though ostensibly in the name of the Labour League of Youth — to an international left-wing youth forum where he was taken to lunch by André Malraux and Louis Aragon. At the age of seventeen he met and became a close friend of Ted Willis, the playwright and television screen-writer, later ennobled as Lord Willis. In time both worked for a variety of left-wing and theatrical magazines and periodicals.

The aim of this chapter is to explore the relationship between Baron's early family life in the world of secular Jewish Hackney, his love of reading, his attachment to socialist politics (and the political and ethical dilemmas which resulted from this attachment), and how these experiences were constantly revisited in many of Baron's novels which often return, however briefly, to this formative, semi-clandestine political and cultural setting. This milieu has also been illuminated, for example, in Raphael Samuel's study, *The Lost World of British Communism*, which, like Baron's *Chapters of Accidents*, is both memoir and apologia — as Samuel's wife, Alison Light, later admitted. It is in Alexander Baron's fiction, however, that this evocation seems most heartfelt and accomplished.

Home, school and youthful politics

"The last time that I have ever cried"

Although Baron much preferred his days at Shacklewell Lane Primary School, his literary and political interests began to coalesce after he won a Junior County Scholarship to attend Hackney Downs School (also known as the Grocers' Company's School, then a selective fee-paying grammar school). As he wrote in his memoir: "I started at Grocers' — Hackney Downs School — in September 1929, on a Junior County Scholarship. I wept when I had to leave Shacklewell; the last time, as far as I can remember, that I have ever cried." From the end of the First World War until the end of the 1960s, up to half of the grammar school's intake came from Jewish homes, according to Rachel Kolsky, though Baron himself recorded that "By the time of the Second World War, when the population of Hackney had changed, most of the boys at the school were Jewish." At this time the majority of the pupils were fee-paying according to Baron, though by the time he left he thought that nearly half of all pupils were on free scholarships.

Baron was not the only writer to emerge from Hackney Downs School to make a name in the literary world; Harold Pinter (b.1930) did so too, a decade later. Both held the school in high regard. Not so Steven Berkoff (b.1937) however, another former pupil. In his autobiography, *Free Association*, Berkoff described it as "a ghastly school", one in which he felt humiliated by the effects of its harsh streaming system. He left before his fifteenth birthday: "I had been propelled out of Hackney Downs with all the speed the Headmaster and I could summon." Roland Camberton (the pen name of Henry Cohen, b.1921), the author of two lesser known novels, *Scamp* (1950) and *Rain on the Pavements* (1951), had also been a Hackney Downs pupil four years after Baron, and like him and Pinter had contributed early poems to the school magazine, *The Review*. Baron stayed in touch with Camberton, and also got to know the Stepney-born writer,

Emanuel Litvinoff well, another chronicler of East End Jewish poverty and communist idealism.

Over the years the school also produced an illustrious cohort of academics, scientists and broadcasters, many later excelling in life as a result of the education they received at Hackney Downs that, to its credit, served most of its working-class Jewish pupils well. Two other significant artistic figures to emerge from Hackney Downs School were Abram Games (b.1914), the distinguished graphic designer, whose Second World War and Festival of Britain posters are regarded as amongst the finest public graphic art produced in the twentieth century, and Leon Kossoff (b.1926), the renowned painter, still alive.

This large Jewish population was, when it first arrived in Hackney, predominantly working class, invariably poor and prone to periods of unemployment or casual work only. Hackney was then still a major industrial borough, with over 2000 factories registered in 1938, many involved in cabinet-making, shoe-making, the garment trade, food production and large areas of light industry still busily employing thousands, in some factories the majority of whom were Jews. Simpson's factory in Stoke Newington Road, only a hundred yards away from Baron's home in Foulden Road, and the manufacturers of DAKS clothing, at one point employed more than 2,000 workers on the one site. Baron, Games and Pinter all had parents who worked in the "rag trade". When Baron's father, a skilled furrier, bought 6 Foulden Road in Stoke Newington at the beginning of the 1930s on a twenty-year mortgage, he set up a workroom in the basement where "after supper, he was down there until late every night doing private jobs to supplement his

With his sister Ida at the back of
6 Foulden Road

factory pay." The family also let two rooms to tenants to help pay off the mortgage.

Such life experiences inclined many to left-wing politics and causes (as well as secularism), sharpened by a growing Fascist movement's focus on East London's Jewish population as its principal target of abuse and intimidation. East London's Jews quickly learned to fight back. Indeed Hackney's Jewish population was almost certainly over-represented in local politics, with many active in the Labour Party or Communist Party, as well as in the trade unions serving the borough's industrial sector.

Baron's success at both schools was strongly supported by his home life. "We were a reading family," he always emphasised:

> My father sat at the table over his improving books and gave me Upton Sinclair's *The Jungle* to read. We all listened raptly every week to the dramatized serials of classic novels on the radio. But my mother and I and my sister too, as she grew older, were off into a world of imagination that was beyond my father's reach. We had discovered the public library. We brought home our books in a shopping bag every week. In the next ten years I must have read getting on for two thousand books from the library.

In these few sentences, intimations of the career to come can be discerned, as well as a foreboding sense of growing away from his family, particularly his father. The Bernsteins' keen enjoyment of dramatized versions of classic books surely influenced his decision later on to try his hand at adaptation of classic novels for radio and television professionally, and with great success.

Not only was the young would-be writer already moving beyond his "father's reach", it was at this time he also realised that his mother possessed a keener imaginative intelligence than his father, though this was never allowed to be acknowledged within the family. It seems that Fanny, as well as Ida, Baron's much-loved sister, were regarded by Barnet Bernstein as outside the realm of intellectual life, a position that angered the son deeply.

It is significant that Baron's first political pamphlet — written in the early days of the war as a serving soldier, and after reading Engels' *The Origin of the Family* — was, he recounts in his memoir, "on the Woman Question... the first piece of independent writing that I did in the army." As demobilisation approached at the end of the war he held discussions amongst his fellow soldiers on attitudes towards women. Baron was particularly exercised as to why the language used by so many men about women was so violent and degrading, even bestial at times. When describing his great war trilogy, he summarised the novels as being "about the lives of men and women in the war", which marks his work out from that of so many other war novelists at the time, in books that only dealt with what men did and felt.

At the age of thirteen things came to a head when he refused to agree to a barmitzvah — the important Jewish ritual ceremony which marks the passage from boyhood to manhood — greatly upsetting his parents and wider family. Not only was he becoming detached from his family, but he had become a refusenik and a source of great concern. Years later he was told by a friend: "We were all afraid of you then."

> Were my parents frightened of me? And the rest of the family? What was there in a quiet, polite, well-behaved child to intimidate them? Perhaps a sensed intensity. Perhaps I was set apart as the clever one.

> As the years went on I myself became oppressed by the notion that I was set apart from people around me. I puzzled to understand their goings-on. They often seemed to look upon me as, in the words of one friend of long acquaintance, a dark horse.

At school he later admitted to a degree of over-confidence and waywardness that began to concern his teachers:

> Essays had to be handed in but I could turn off an essay in no time… I was soon deep in my own private explorations. After dabbling in Spanish for a term I started to teach myself German. I trawled the public library for books on politics and economics. In the school library I read Fielding, Smollett and Sterne, essays and novels by D.H. Lawrence and Aldous Huxley, Clive Bell and Roger Fry on art, Voltaire, Montesquieu, Rousseau and whatever else took my fancy — Hakluyt, Anson's *Voyages* — everything but my set books.

When not at school Baron was not at home either. "I spent most of my evenings roaming the borough from one Speakers' Corner to another, listening to the political orators. On the wide roadway at the corner of Ridley Road, after the market stalls had been packed away, a dozen revolutionary sects put up their platforms. The tinier the group the more fire its orators breathed."

As a teenager (left) with his parents and sister (right) on an outing to Margate — the man to the right of Baron and the child whose hand he is holding have not been identified

The older schoolboy, now fifteen, remained unimpressed by such firebrands, as he was when attending meetings of the Hackney Independent Labour Party, despite being intrigued by the appearance of some of its male activists: "Its militants were the attraction. They were all Jews of the pugnacious kind, with angry red faces that sprouted either stubble or bushy beards, great mops of uncombed hair and lumbermens' shirts unbuttoned to the waist to show hirsute chests and hanging over crumpled grey flannel trousers." What finally galvanised his political loyalties were the meetings of the Friends of the Soviet Union (FSU) held at the corner of Amhurst Road next to West Hackney Church, a stone's throw away from Foulden Road.

"I believed everything the FSU speakers told me," he wrote later. What he was told and at the time sincerely believed — along with millions of others in Britain and across the world — was that nobody was out of work in Russia, nobody was on the Means Test, and, when not happily working, millions volunteered their labour to work on vast construction projects such as the White Sea Canal or in Siberia out of sheer joy and belief in the future. Years later the world was to learn the true story of the Stalin era when hundreds of thousands died in conditions of slave labour on such projects, along with the millions who died of starvation, at times deliberately orchestrated. Yet there was one more great achievement of this new society, according to the young FSU member who recruited Baron: "Oh yes, and they've got Free Love all over the place there."

In 1933 he joined the Labour League of Youth (LLY) where not only did he find a political home (if only temporarily), but also a comradeship and warmth which marked him, and his writing, for the rest of his life. In *Chapters of Accidents* he recalls that:

> In the summer of my sixteenth year I brought a friendly band of boys and girls into the house and my parents learned that these were members of the Labour Party which I had joined. This was harmless enough. The young people were nicely dressed and polite and my parents were glad to see me making friends.

It is this group whose activities provide the brief idyllic scenes of weekend cycling and camping trips up the River Lea into Hertfordshire, which form "Strangers to Death", the prologue to his grim collection of war stories *The Human Kind* (1953), which Sean Longden treats incisively in Chapter Three of this book. Based on a number of real such outings, this opening idyll also evokes an early intimation of young love and incipient sexual awakening. This was a brief Eden before the fall, and provides a shocking contrast of mood and setting to the atrocities and death that follow, and from which Baron perhaps was never able to recover his early idealism. Like so many others, Alec Bernstein's experience of war marked him for the rest of his life.

He was later to write of this year in the Labour League of Youth:

> I now look back on it as the only time in my political life when I was genuinely happy. The members were an ordinary decent lot… who came from the same background, who accepted the conventions of respectable working-class life even in the ways they broke them and who were open and unguarded in their speech. It was a contrast to the Communist Party milieu in which I came more and more to spend a parallel life.

In the Labour League of Youth Baron met Ted Willis (later Lord Willis, playwright and originator of TV series *Dixon of Dock Green*) "and we soon teamed up". Together they produced the LLY journal, writing most of the copy between them. "We'd spend all night, sitting in this little office we'd acquired, writing articles. The most important ones in our own names and all the rest under names which we made up." In this way, by his own admission, Baron learned to write.

Baron's enthusiasm for clandestine politics was sealed when in 1934, still sixteen and at school, Willis knocked on the door of Foulden Road and gave him a £5 note and a message from a Communist Party apparatchik, John Gollan, to attend a meeting in Paris at a certain address. This turned out to be the conference of French young communists where he was introduced to André Malraux, then a major international literary star, who befriended him, and later introduced him to Louis Aragon. Such occasions would have turned anybody's head. Whilst still ostensibly a Labour League of Youth loyalist and organiser, he was now deep inside the Communist Party.

Nevertheless, it didn't take him as long as many others to realise that both the leadership and programme of the Communist Party were entirely subject to decisions made in Moscow. These often involved embarrassing political about-turns, along with a growing numbers of denunciations and ruthless betrayals. Such betrayals were most evident amongst those volunteering to fight in the International Brigades in Spain — in fact Baron hoped to be one, but was instructed by the Party otherwise — and often resulted in the summary execution of volunteers thought to have minds of their own, on the instructions of Moscow. Long after his own defection, however, he retained a warmth and admiration for many of the duped but idealistic Party members he once knew.

> The East End Jewish Communists were to me a type apart from other Party people… I liked the warmth and animation of the comrades I met and the excitement with which they spoke. In my grandfather's earlier days there had flourished in the East End a Jewish, Yiddish-speaking labour movement of great ardour and idealism and I felt something of the same spirit in the Jewish comrades I met, cutters, pressers and girl machinists from the workshops, cabbies, market traders, shopkeepers, typists, warehousemen, doctors and lawyers and not a few prosperous self-made businessmen.

Part of this sense of immersion in a viable political culture came from the fact that, as Raphael Samuel pointed out, Jewish East London was only one of three parts of Britain — the other two being the South Wales coalfields and the Fife coalfields — where the Communist Party became almost naturalised or normatively credible. Baron's politics were certainly complex — and he knew it. His early idealism was genuine, almost naïve, and for a while he appeared almost insouciant to the menace posed by Moseleyite fascism in Hackney in the 1930s — though he is honest to a fault. In 1983 he described to me the political milieu in which he first found himself:

> There were stray branches of the Communist Party, a couple of hundred members. There were equally large bands of cheerful boys and girls who formed the Fascists. We had a curious relationship with them. On duty it was all knuckledusters and off-duty we used to fraternise — like British and German troops in 1914. We all knew each other by name. In fact, one of our fellows started going out with a fascist girl. We had long political discussions with them and asked them, wonderingly, how could they believe all this stuff. It never affected the majority of people.

This would have been around 1933. This wish to understand rather than hate those with other views is portrayed in a scene of a fight between Moseleyite youths and members of a Jewish wedding party in his 1952 novel, *With Hope, Farewell*. The hero, Mark Strong, fuelled with drink from the wedding (and partly based on Baron himself), feels sorry for the young Fascist he physically assaults in the rout, a sentiment that is repeated in his 1971 novel, *The In-Between Time*.

Such easy-going tolerance was to change dramatically after the nationalist uprising against the elected Spanish republican government in 1936. The situation in Germany further worsened with the murder of Jews and socialists on the streets, culminating in Kristallnacht in 1938, when the plight of the Jews finally became evident across the world.

Fascist militancy re-emerged in Britain after the war, particularly in Hackney, for a brief period taking even more violent forms than was evident in the uneasy pre-war truce that Baron remembered. *With Hope, Farewell* portrays an organised group of Jewish ex-servicemen coming together to combat the Mosleyites by force — which happened in real life and became known as the 43 Group — which the fictional Mark Strong declines to join. It is the violent street melée between fascists and anti-fascists near Ridley Road that precipitates the hero's wife's miscarriage, in a novel that concludes with its main character on the brink of breakdown and despair, although in the very last scene he joins forces with two railway workers sent by their union to defend a nearby synagogue (in reality Walford Road Synagogue), and finds a degree of reconciliation in that act of solidarity. In his 1971 novel, *The In-Between Time*, Baron revisited this period in his life, concluding:

So he simply remembers, with a blend of sadness, relish and incredulity, those few weeks in which he had found out about women, volunteered for a war, looked down into the great divide of our age, silently acknowledged paternity of a child that was not his own, been beaten with a stick, and seen what a confusion life is of comradeship and betrayal, tenderness and cruelty, courage and cowardice, and love that can be a benison or an affliction, all a-change kaleidoscope fashion in the same people, in the species.

A small buff envelope

When I came out of the army, I was interviewed by a committee. They said, "How can we help you?" And I said, "I want a typewriter."

Although war had been declared in 1939, Baron, still then working for the Communist Party, remembers the summer of 1940 as a golden time — until "the Germans attacked in the Low Countries and within days the entire allied front had collapsed." He was in love, and he had found a new cause: fighting fascism as a soldier. Two weeks after Dunkirk he had received a phone call from the Special Branch arranging to interview him. Why had he not been called up for military service? Baron was nonplussed, for he had registered to "join up" as soon as war had been declared. He could only think that he had been blacklisted by another branch of the security services, and said so, while also insisting he was keen to join the army as soon as possible. "A week or two later I arrived home one night and saw a small buff envelope propped up on the mantelpiece. I knew what it was and felt a great drench of pleasure." Within weeks he had been called up into the Pioneer Corps, and the "days of youth and blood", as he calls them in his memoir, began.

In Sean Longden's chapter we are given the fullest account we are ever likely to have of Baron's tumultuous and traumatic experiences out of which the definitive chronicler of "the poor bloody infantry" emerged. Once demobilised, however, Baron's former years of clandestine political activity gave way to writing about his experiences of war, in which he had been engaged in ferocious and bloody campaigns in Italy and Normandy. A series of novels were written and published in quick succession: *From the City, From the Plough* (1948), *There's No Home* (1950), *Rosie Hogarth* (1951), *With Hope, Farewell* (1952) and *The Human Kind* (1953), all of which are discussed in greater detail in the chapters by Sean Longden, Susie Thomas and Andrew Whitehead.

Baron had found yet another great cause after communism and the unexpectedly warm comradeship he found as a fighting soldier: he was now a writer.

He started his first novel in the second half of 1946 and "finished it in the Spring of the following year." Two friends, Ted Willis and Roger Woddis, encouraged him to send it to a publisher, and gave him the names of three publishing houses. "The first two wrote nice things about it but turned it down. The third was Jonathan Cape." He had submitted the manuscript under the *nom-de-plume*, John Masterman, but it was Cape himself who pointed out there was already a writer of this name, and suggested he make up another name. "He invited me to pick another of not more than five letters so that it could be printed in fair-sized letters across the spine of the book. I took Baron from a shop facia." Thus Alexander Bernstein became Alexander Baron — and was known as such ever after. Cape also thought that the manuscript's title, *The Fifth Battalion*, was too prosaic, and required something more poetic. It was Cape's wife who suggested *From the City, From the Plough*, a brilliant piece of literary alchemy.

And so one morning in May 1948, with the publication of *From the City, From the Plough*, Baron, like Byron before him, awoke to find himself famous. Six weeks after publication the novel was already in its sixth impression: the most heartfelt and moving fictional representation of the common soldier in the heat of battle in the Second World War to be published, then and since.

He returned to the modest, terraced house at 6 Foulden Road purchased by Barnet Bernstein many years before; it was to be Baron's home for nearly thirty years, apart from his time in the army. It was the locus of his life and his sense of what it was to be at home in London, to feel secure and to belong. He adored Foulden Road, and always would for the rest of his life, long after leaving it, moving to Brighton in 1961, having the year before married Delores Salzedo (b.1928), and subsequently to Golders Green in 1972, where he lived for the rest of his life. This modest terraced street was the setting for his most celebrated novel, apart from the war trilogy. This was *The Lowlife*, published in 1963.

> When I came back from the war, I had no home. I'd been knocked about a bit and was quite unwell for some time. And was very glad to go back to Hackney to stay with my parents for a considerable time. It was then that the seeds of *The Lowlife*, so

to speak, were planted... During the day spent a lot of time walking the streets. And continued, even after I'd left Hackney, to become a kind of ghost haunting a whole borough. Then gradually there took shape in my mind the idea of a novel, refracting some of the life I'd witnessed in my wanderings. I began to see through the eyes of a character who was very much on my mind, who attracted me. And who, like me, had been formed by this place but who remained, in a sense, something of an outsider.

In 1983 he was happy to admit that: "*The Lowlife* is Foulden Road, completely. I've always had a great love for Foulden Road." He went on to say that he often thought of buying the house back, later on, as a place not only to provide a room to write in, but which he "would have arranged for some nurses to live in" as a gesture of gratitude to the streets and people who helped create some of his happiest years.

Nevertheless, to begin with, the writing did not come easily — or at least as easily as it later seemed. Not only was he still in some kind of shock — what today would be called post-traumatic stress disorder — he was still a literary novice, although he later admitted that his political journalism had given him some fluency. Furthermore, his communist experience had left him "in a constant state of alert", as Raphael Samuel once described the tutored mentalité developed in Party cadres: everything possessed significant meaning, and cried out to be understood. In a letter from Foulden Road, dated 30 August 1949, to his Unity Theatre comrade, Muriel Walker — then in Italy working as a production assistant on the film *Vulcano*, directed by William Dieterle and starring Anna Magnani — he confessed:

As for me, I have never worked so hard in all my life. I had hardly finished one novel and put it to the press when — while I was resting and wondering which part of the Continent to grace with my presence — I went mad about yet another, and started on it. It will take me at least till November, and as it is a very long, complex and delicately-woven story the labour is quite heart-breaking. I write and write, round the clock, tear up, revise, polish passages again and again, go to bed at one in the morning and — after lying awake for an hour — return to the typewriter at two o'clock and work on till daylight.

Whilst completing the war trilogy, his mind began to consider other themes, and he started to think about the "new world" emerging as a result of the "post-war settlement". There was now work for almost everybody, a national health service, new clothes, new consumer goods and money to spare for eating out and, most importantly, "going up west".

Going up west

"I continued, even after I'd left Hackney, to become a kind of ghost haunting the whole borough."

From the 1930s onwards, but particularly after the Second World War, the lure of Soho and the West End for aspiring writers, political activists, jazz-loving bohemians, fashion-conscious young Jewish men and women from Hackney and the East End was magnetic. It is the principal theme of memoirs and novels by Bernard Kops (*The World is a Wedding*, 1963) and Roland Camberton (*Scamp*, 1950 & *Rain on the Pavements*, 1951), but it also features in the work of Simon Blumenfeld (who ended up a show-business journalist haunting the West End's theatreland) and Willy Goldman, as well as in the plays of Pinter, Wesker and Steven Berkoff (whose plays, *East* and *West*, symbolised this new cultural axis).

In Hackney after the war Stamford Hill was becoming the centre of secular Jewish life, particularly amongst young people. Jewish youth clubs rubbed shoulders with amusement arcades; there was the E & A milk bar, the ornate, monumental Regent Cinema, a variety of hairdressers and barbers' shops, and plenty of men's and women's clothes shops too, where the latest styles were on display. But there was politics once again. "This area became my university for the next half dozen years," wrote Steven Berkoff (b.1937) in his autobiography, *Free Association*, recalling "many evenings in the E & A milk bar putting the world to rights with road-sweeper turned philosopher, Ralph Levene."[2]

In 1959 a Jewish couple called Rita and Benny Isen opened a shop at 282 Stamford Hill under the name R&B Records and, according to Malcolm Imrie, "were among the very first to release Jamaican music in Britain: ska and rock steady, and blue beat."[3] The shop became "a mecca for young blacks from Hackney, of course, but also from the rest of London and well beyond." In the "swinging sixties" the traffic between Stamford Hill and Soho was in both directions. Young Jews, blacks, and

2 Berkoff, 1997, p.30.
3 Imrie, 2010, http://themodgeneration.com/profiles/blog/ska-mods-and-stamford-hill.

white musicians and their followers, began to share the same tastes and intermingle. Later on ingenue singers and musicians such as Helen Shapiro (who had her first Top Ten hit in 1960 at the age of fourteen), along with Marc Bolan and Malcolm McLaren, met up in the Jewish youth clubs of Stamford Hill, keen to make it big in the music world, and ended up making the pilgrimage to Denmark Street in Soho on the No 73 bus.

Another Hackney-born Jew and later music journalist, Thomas Horace Whitmer, has written about the "arty, intellectual boys at the Stamford Hill Boys Club, who are reading books written by French existentialists like Jean Paul Sartre and Albert Camus and US Beat writers such as William Burroughs, Alan Ginsburg and Norman Mailer" who later style themselves the Modernists, and only listen to black American jazz and blues.[4] They wear "grey or pink crew neck sweaters, Church's brogues or chisel-pointed shoes with moccasins for casual wear, slimfit slacks tapered and sans turn ups, college boy hairstyles of the Perry Como or Pat Boone type, brilliant yellow or baby pink button-down shirts, suede or knitted ties." British mod culture was born here, the child of the fashion-conscious Jews represented in Baron's remarkable return-to-form novel, *The Lowlife*, published in 1963, and the novel for which he is perhaps best-known today.

Baron would have observed this scene in his excursions around Stoke Newington, Clapton (home of one of London's most popular dog-tracks) and from his pre-war visits to and from the flat of John Gollan, one of the Communist Party's most senior organisers, who lived in Stamford Hill. His awareness and fascination with the Jewish interest in smart clothes, European literature, gambling and nights out on the *qui vive* is famously there in *The Lowlife*, and in the pre-occupations of its central character, Harryboy Boas. The novel marks a high point in Baron's literary career, a critical celebration of this new era, but with several darker undercurrents swirling beneath the surface.

The Lowlife proved a great success, and film rights were optioned. Sadly no film ever got made, but the book became a cult novel of London life, and remains so to this day. Harryboy welcomed the arrival of West Indian and African immigrants to his neighbourhood, adding to the melting-pot, and *The Lowlife* was ahead of its time in portraying the iniquities of anti-Semitism and racism head on.

---

4 Whitmer, 2016, p.85.

Again it is Thomas Horace Whitmer who proves the most assiduous chronicler of the tenements, terraced streets, council blocks, industrial mews, sweat-shops and busy streets of post-war Hackney, still inhabited by:

> ...the secular Jews who populate the streets of West Hackney, Stoke Newington, Upper Clapton, Dalston and Lordship Park throughout the 20th century but now live elsewhere; gamblers, betting touts, racing and boxing men, gangsters, dippers, thieves for the most part, invisible among the Jewish furriers, tailors, caterers, doctors and tens of thousands of anonymous, decent working-class Yiddish citizens they live among.

Of permanent fascination to Baron the novelist was the admixture of speech resulting from this polyglot world of Yiddish and Cockney, later augmented by African and Caribbean dialect. "I don't know if you've noticed it in East End life," he once asked me, "the humour, the ironic expression which is as much East End as it is Jewish. They spoke the same language. East End boys, if they had dark hair, you couldn't tell from Yiddishers... These characters radiate the will to live." In the army he found that some indigenous East End recruits knew more Yiddish words than some of their Jewish comrades. In a letter in December 1983 mentioning Harold Pinter, he wrote, "I've always held that the so-much-discussed speech idiom of his early plays is really that of Hackney in its melting-pot years."

In *The Lowlife*, finally Baron put to rest the internal conflicts he felt about his Jewishness, which Susie Thomas's chapter details so convincingly, and he did so by returning to the terrain of his childhood. In the world of Foulden Road he remembered the golden summers of pre-war Stoke Newington, the weekend camping expeditions along the River Lea with his band of young comrades, his first falling in love, the complex mixture of terraced streets, small industrial mews, clothing factories, parks, synagogues and cinemas, bicycle shops and cafes, that formed the lost domain of his adolescence, and which his fictional alter ego, Harryboy Boas, twenty years later refuses to leave. For in its new iteration, as a lively multi-racial neighbourhood, offering the same opportunities to young Afro-Caribbean and Asian immigrants it once offered to young Jews, it had not diminished in time but had been renewed. Sometimes you can go home again, and in *The Lowlife* the young Alec Bernstein did.

Sources and Further Reading

Unless otherwise indicated, all direct quotations attributed to Alexander Baron come from his unpublished memoir, *Chapters of Accidents*.

Baron, Alexander. 1949. Private letter to Muriel Walker, by kind permission. 30 August 1949.

Baron, Alexander. 1983a. Transcript of interview with Ken Worpole at Baron's home, 7 June 1983.

Baron, Alexander. 1983b. Personal communication. 8 July 1983.

Baron, Alexander. 1992. Transcript of interview for film *The Cardinal & The Corpse* with Iain Sinclair and Chris Petit.

Baron, Alexander. 1997. *Chapters of Accidents*. Unpublished memoir.

Baron, Alexander. 1969. *King Dido*, with an introduction by Ken Worpole. New London Editions: Nottingham. 2009.

Baron, Nick. 2016. 'Bohemian Rhapsody', *Jewish Renaissance*. April, 2016.

Beckman, Maurice. 1992. *The 43 Group*. Centerprise: London.

Gubbins, Sean. 2017. 'Simpson's — a Cut above the Rest', in *Hackney: portrait of a community 1967–2017*, edited by Laurie Elks. The Hackney Society: London.

Imrie, Malcolm. 2012. *The Mods of Stamford Hill*, http://themodgeneration.com/profiles/blog/ska-mods-and-stamford-hill

Kolsky, Rachel. 2017. 'The Bobov Sect takes over Egerton Road Synagogue: the changing Jewish community in Hackney', in *Hackney: portrait of a community 1967–2017*, edited by Laurie Elks. The Hackney Society: London.

Samuel, Raphael. 2006. *The Lost World of British Communism*, Verso: London.

Whitmer, Thomas Horace. 2016. *In Groves And Along Lanes*. Drake Bros Publications: London.

Worpole, Ken. 2008. *Dockers and Detectives*. Five Leaves Publications: Nottingham.

Worpole, Ken. 2013. 'Alexander Baron: *The Lowlife*', in *London Fictions*, edited by Andrew Whitehead and Jerry White, Five Leaves Publications: Nottingham.

"A city should be accumulated memory"
Alexander Baron talking to Ken Worpole

Some time towards the end of the 1970s I started work on a book on patterns of working-class reading and writing in twentieth-century Britain, subsequently published by Verso as *Dockers and Detectives* in 1983. A revised edition came out from Five Leaves in 2008. Alexander Baron's work cut across two of the principal themes of that book — the fiction of Jewish east London and novels which dealt with life in the armed forces during the Second World War — both deeply inflected with issues of class, geography and representation. For these reasons I was keen to interview Baron himself, which I did in June 1983, and still retain fond memories of meeting this unassuming, thoughtful man, and I am grateful for the intensity and detail of his recollections — and the precision with which he recounted them, which was continued in our subsequent correspondence. That interview developed into a lifelong interest in Alexander Baron — particularly in the relationship between the overlapping versions of his own life and experiences and those of the protagonists in his novels — an intriguing fascination which many other readers share. It tells us that a perfect fit between life and literature is impossible, thankfully so.

This is an abridged and edited transcript of the interview.

K.W.

Ken Worpole: When did your family first move in to Hackney?

Alexander Baron: When my parents were married in 1916. Before that, my mother lived in Spitalfields and my father lived in Bethnal Green. When they got married, they settled in one room in Abersham Road, near Ridley Road. I was born in December 1917. And then the first thing I can remember is when my parents moved to Sandringham Road, where we had a bigger room on the top floor with a little scullery. There was only me and my baby sister, a tiny baby then, and my parents.

We ate in the scullery — with an old stone sink, and the old hip bath hanging up. But when I was about five, my Dad had saved up enough to put a deposit down on a house in Foulden Road, which is in the borough of Hackney but is colloquially Stoke Newington. And of course in those days you couldn't afford a house unless you had a tenant. So he let the upstairs. And I think at one time he tarted up the basement and made it quite habitable and I think they let that too. Anyway — I lived the rest of my life, up to the beginning of the war, in Foulden Road.

What was your father's work?

He was a fur cutter. He worked in a factory in the City.

Did your mother work at all?

Before her marriage she worked — it must have been somewhere near the docks, a canvas and cordage factory.

Would you have said that Sandringham Road and Foulden Road were specifically Jewish areas at that time?

Well, Foulden Road wasn't. There must have been more Jews living on Sandringham Road, but it wasn't a Jewish area. All I can remember — I would then have been about three years old, one of my earliest memories — was a little gang of boys I played with in the street. I know that they weren't Jewish. There were two schools nearby, one where I think a lot of the Jewish boys went, a bit prissier. And then the rough school in Shacklewell Lane. And my Dad said: "Let him go to Shacklewell Lane and rough it a bit. Do him good." And it was the happiest time of my life. I cried when I left there, it was a wonderful school. In Shacklewell Lane I lived in the homes of my school friends. And the teachers were splendid teachers.

What age did you go there?

Well, I went when I was five. And I got what was then called a Junior County Scholarship. And I was eleven when I moved on [to Hackney Downs].

Did many others go on from Shacklewell or were you one of the exceptions?

Not in my year. In those days, my father had fairly steady work — except during the slump, you know round about 1931. Of course there were some other bright boys but I may have been the only one whose parents let him

42

go on. In fact, the same thing happened when I was at Hackney Downs, a few years later, when I'd taken what was then called the Higher School and I'd got a place at college. And I felt so kind of inferior to the boys in my street who I'd played with who were all going off to work at fourteen. Then not only did the parents want the kids out very often, but the boy or girl wanted to be earning money at fourteen. Especially the boy he wanted to be wearing long trousers and buy his Woodbines — and to be a man. So, in my year I was definitely the only one who went on to [Hackney Downs]. There may have been one or two who went on to Central School.

You talked a bit about the kids on the street. Do you have memories of the gangs, and the games that would be played on the street?

Very vividly, you see — Foulden Road was a kind of step up the social scale. It was quite Dickensian, because all the people who lived there seemed to be craftsmen and skilled workers. Clerkenwell was not far away — traditionally a great centre for craft trades or small-scale engineering, watchmakers and die-stampers and people like that. Nearly everybody in the street seemed to be really respectable working men. The doyen of the street, who lived a few doors away, was a messenger in a government ministry — he was at the top of the social scale. And there was an old man, really out of Dickens, one of those clerks who sat on a high stool in a basement somewhere and could write the Lord's Prayer on the back of a sixpence — which he did for us. There were lots of children and very little traffic in those days. The street looked nice because everybody kept their houses nice and clean — you know the old business about scrubbing doorsteps.

Every year they used to come and tar the street and lay it with yellow gravel — a great event in our lives, really a Spring festival. You could smell the tar and the steamrollers came. And the games. First of all, there was a gigantic hopscotch boys and girls played on. The girls tended to go off on their own and play indoors and lead their own lives. The boys used to roam around, this is five upwards. There was still a lot of horse-drawn traffic in the Twenties, and a lot of horse troughs. We either used to wait by a horse trough and get a lift out into Epping Forest and catch tiddlers. Or we'd hang on behind — and then you got some little bugger on the pavement shouting: "Look behind you, mister."

My Dad was a great one for the open air, parks and so on. He'd come home from work in the evening and say: "I want a breath of fresh air!"

— because his lungs would be full of fur, you know. And we'd get the 69 bus to Wormley. People would come out from the East End and Dalston for a day at the weekend or for a drink in the evening. And we just used to have a bus ride out to Wormley and a walk up in the side lanes and really felt we were in the country and then come home — oh, ten o'clock. What I remember about later on in Foulden Road — and this is a great mystery to me how it worked — was the street football league. In every street, the kids made up a football team. And I don't know who did the negotiating or what but we had a match virtually every Sunday morning. We played home matches on Hackney Downs — and we went as far afield as London Fields one way, and Hackney Marshes the other.

The other ritual was the street fight. Somebody would come along and say: "We're having a fight with Miller's Terrace on Saturday." And it was more show than blood, if you know what I mean. I was a weedy little —. My mum was always telling me to look after my glasses. But then you'd have one of the ritual street fights — nobody got hurt very much but a lot of fun was had. It really sounds like medieval village football without the football.

We did go round collecting horse dung and selling it at the front doors at a penny a bucket. Because there was plenty of it — good for the garden. The other thing — a late confession — there were posher streets where we used to cut the flowers in the front gardens. Very neatly, we'd just take half-a-dozen tulips, and then go round selling them on front doors.

When you went to Hackney Downs, it was a grammar school — it was very selective, it was run on fairly authoritarian lines —

Well, Hackney Downs was a good school when I was there. I had plenty of reasons to be grateful to it. There was a good bunch of masters — though I haven't got the fierce loyalty to it that I had to Shacklewell. But on the whole I was sorry to leave and a bit afraid to go out into the big world. I reckon I got quite as good an education as they got at public schools.

I once considered writing a novel about my schooldays. I realised it would be, in effect, a comic novel. I would be taking the mickey out of myself, of course, as well as the school. But the masters — a couple of them were comic characters. The headmaster, whom I admired very much — but I always thought he imagined himself as the head of Greyfriars. He used to also wear a mortarboard and walked about

44

swishing his gown. And there were whackings, but they were very rare. On the only occasion when I got whacked — I got four in a form whacking — it was great fun. I thought: this is just like the *Magnet*.[1]

Wasn't it unusual that it was a very English sort of grammar school whose population was mainly Jewish?

Well, it wasn't when I went there — it was just changing. I went there in 1929. Before then, Clapton, which was its immediate catchment area, and all those streets on the other side of the Downs, they seemed to be the quarter of well-to-do, old fashioned Hackney tradesmen, people who could afford to send their sons because it was mainly a paying school, and they just took a small quota of scholarship boys. In my year, thirty-three scholarship boys applied. My Mum I remember took me with fear and trembling for the interview. And I think it was the first year they took all the thirty-three applicants. And I think from more-or-less the time I went onwards — it sounds like I was leading the tribes of Moses into the desert — the proportion of Jews in the school seemed to grow until it was very noticeable.

Something I'd forgotten — in the street when I was a small kid, I used to tell stories to kids. I wasn't very good in a punch-up and this gave me my status because when we were swapping comics or reading each others' quizzes and so on, I could sit down on the kerb and the others all round me, and tell them a story.

Which you made up?

Which I made up, yes. But I probably drew material for them from the masses of books that I read. Both my parents were exceptional in this. My father, although he came to England when he was twelve, had perfect English in which nobody could detect an accent. And he was a kind of old-fashioned Victorian type, self-improver. He would read books of popular science. My mother — and it was completely unlike the other women — loved reading. I remember my mother sitting reading *Pride and Prejudice* which she'd discovered in the public library — she was loving it — and a couple of the neighbours coming in and saying there:

---

1 The *Magnet* was a weekly boys' paper best known for stories set in a fictional public school, Greyfriars, attended by Billy Bunter.

Alexander Baron at fifteen

'Good lord, look at her, a schoolteacher'. And she definitely passed this on to me. She had no guided taste in books, but she would get *The Good Companions*. She read aloud passages — the whole family loved that.

The Priestley novel?

The Priestley novel, yes. I've still got a sentimental affection for old Priestley because the first novel I read on my own was *Angel Pavement*, which was a much better novel. I always have loved London. From childhood I used to roam about. All kids had the freedom of the streets then. I used to imagine the past of London and medieval London and so on. I don't know if Londoners still love London. A city should be accumulated memory. When so much has been bombed and torn down you are really killing memories that people need.

So when did you think of writing your first novel? Before the war?

No. I thought of writing my first novel, in my daydreams, when I was quite a young boy, whether I was twelve or thirteen — I even knew the title, so awful I could never repeat it. But I made no attempt to write fiction — except for a couple of poems in the school magazine — until after I left school.

I had a place at King's College, London.[2] I wanted to be a historian. The history master wanted me to take a history scholarship at Cambridge. And all I could think of was to become a schoolteacher, maybe teaching history. I and a pal of mine suddenly sort of sickened of it and said: "Well, for God's sake, let's go out and get a job instead." We were about seventeen-and-a-half. I hadn't got the courage to get a job in a factory, because my father had worked in a factory all his life. His hands were calloused from holding this particular knife that they used. So we both got jobs at the LCC.

Then I joined the local Labour Party. I soon became prominent in Labour politics. I was in the Labour League of Youth — I was soon running [the branch] and the adjacent one was run by Ted Willis. We soon teamed up and got a kind of Militant Tendency going — but with a small 'm' and a small 't' — in that part of north London. And very soon we were running the journal of the Labour League of Youth. The circulation was boosted from 2,000 to 30,000–50,000 in a good month. And we were writing most of it between us. This would be about fourteen pages so we'd spend all night sitting up in the little office we'd

---

2 In his as yet unpublished memoir *Chapters of Accidents*, Baron says it was University College, London, that offered him a deferred place.

acquired, writing articles — the most important ones in our own names and all the rest under different names which we made up. And I had several years of this kind of Labour journalism. I don't know to this day whether journalism is corrupting if you want to be a writer or if it gives you a kind of fluency of thought and words.

I simply had no time to think of writing novels until July 1940, when I was called up. I remained in the army until the spring of 1946. All the time there, I was seeking experience and knowing exactly what I wanted to do — I wanted to write a novel about the war. When I came out, you were interviewed by a committee who said: "What do you want to do? Can we help?" And I said: "Yes, I want a typewriter." There was then a twelve months waiting list for it. And they got me a portable typewriter straight away and I just went home.

Went home?

Yes. I was quite ill for the first two years after the war and I went back to live with my parents. And then, as I got better, I began to quite often stay more and more with friends. Actually, Ted Willis, a man of many enterprises, started a theatre magazine — which was very successful in its time. And he made me the editor. I used to work in the office until at least half-past eight at night and then go home and have supper and I worked on *From the City, From the Plough* at nights. It was partly something I had to get off my chest. And partly that after the war, the first few novels to get published were all by officers — or Penguin New Writing, which was a great influence at the time, had a lot of stories by the kind of intellectuals to whom the army was an agony. And they wrote about it in this way — this awful experience you had to go through, sleeping in a hut with thirty-five ruffians. That kind of thing.

I just read these books and I thought that nobody was writing about — the soldiers were the nation in arms, they were the whole people, they were the young men of the nation. I was on the left then. I think there was a political intention — I sat down and hammered out this book. But it was also, I think, therapeutic. I wasn't in the thick of the war all the time — but I was in some fairly big actions. Towards the end of the war I had two fairly hefty concussions and I think that was why I was pretty ill for a period after the war. And it may be that writing this novel really put me on my feet.

With Hope, Farewell — I like that very much as a novel. It seems to be almost autobiographical. Was it not unrealistic to have a young Jewish person become a fighter pilot?

Well, Denis Norden was a pilot in the RAF.[3] And I remember Rebecca West, during the fascist riots just after the war near Ridley Road; she referred to a couple of young Jewish flying officers with DFCs and pilots' wings — "like young princes", she put it — watching silently. Two personal friends of mine, Jewish boys, were killed in the RAF. You've no idea, in the early days of the aeroplane, how air mad, air minded was the phrase, hundreds of thousands of boys were. Until I became interested in politics I spent all my time at aerodromes, studying planes. In fact, on the first morning of the war, I went to try and join the RAF. But nothing less than perfect sight was OK then and I was turned down.

I don't know why, but after writing the other ones, I felt I had to write a Jewish novel. I had to get something else off my chest. I don't want to go into it too much here, but I've always had a great personal rebellion against the idea of a separate Jewish entity. My father and both my grandfathers were freethinkers and so am I. I'm an atheist. I never wanted to live within this defensive world called the Jewish community. I had no real impulse to write a Jewish novel.

I'm surprised that you liked it because the story of that novel is a strange one. I liked certain episodes, mainly the flying ones. The description of the boy's first flight when he's small is — I flew in an old pre-1914 aeroplane when I was ten-years-old and that still remains I suppose the most exciting experience, wonderful experience, memorable experience of my whole life. I wrote this novel, was totally dissatisfied with it, and then I had some very bad eye trouble which the specialist I was sent to said might be the consequence of one of the clouts over the head that I'd had. It cleared up completely but I was forbidden to do any work for six months. Jonathan Cape had read this and I said: "Don't publish it, I want to completely rewrite it." I even had another 30,000 words written and I wanted to rework the whole thing. I had chosen the whole background, the family was different. There's the Dutch background, not my family's background. My family were all

---

3 Denis Norden, from a Jewish family in Hackney, served in the RAF as a wireless operator during the war and later was a renowned comedy writer and broadcaster.

plain, hardworking people — we didn't have an Uncle Moss if you remember that character, a great spiv, although he's probably the most successful character in the book. And I deliberately made this book about observed people, pushed it right outside my own life, but everybody has taken it as my one autobiographical novel. It truly isn't.

It would never have been published, certainly not in that form. But when Jonathan Cape heard that I'd been told not to write for six months — Jonathan Cape got in touch with my American publisher and they said: "We'll publish this as it stands." And they put up an advance, really to keep me for this period. And that's how it got published.

Is the protagonist of *The Lowlife* also an observed Jewish character?

Yes. I wonder where Harryboy Boas came from.

It's actually set in Foulden Road.

Oh yes. Completely! And Foulden Road in its heyday, when the black people who came were so gorgeous and respectable — and the sight of them all going up to the Baptist chapel on Sunday mornings, the wives wearing these big Ascot hats and the Dads were polished from head to foot, the boys wore Eton suits. A marvellous sight.

I've always had a great love for Foulden Road. I've sometimes said to my wife, if I had become a really successful writer, I think I would have bought that house in Foulden Road, my Mum and Dad's house.

First of all there's something of course that hadn't occurred in my family, I don't say that out of respectability, this gambling streak in the Jews. And secondly, I have come across in my time, in the army among other places, some of these chaps — one or two of the old school Jewish gangsters as well. I love the streak of generosity in them, of humour — and very often, a strange kind of feeling for culture, like Harryboy's love of books. Something grew on me until one day — I hadn't written for some months, which often happened to me — and I didn't make notes or anything, I just put a sheet in the typewriter and began writing the first chapter. After that I was plotting the book ahead and working it all out and so on. And that was *The Lowlife*.

One thing. I don't know if you've noticed it in East End life — he has a kind of humour, ironic humorous expression, which is as much native East End as it is Jewish. To me, there was a kind of symbiosis, certainly between the young Jews and the young Anglo-Saxons, whatever you call them. So that sometimes you couldn't tell one from the other. They spoke in the same idiom. East End boys from Christian families that I met in the army used more Yiddish words than I knew. And if they were dark haired at all, you couldn't tell one from the other.

What was the last novel?

I wrote one volume of what was going to be a two-volume epic about Spain. The first volume was set in the end of the Civil War; the second volume is set during the weeks when Franco was dying. I wrote the second volume first.[4] I was foolish enough to show it to my publisher, who grabbed it and said: "This is a great suspense novel." It wasn't meant to be a suspense novel.

To me, Spain is everything that's happened in the earth in our time. I've still got the first volume upstairs half finished — I did an enormous amount of research for it. Sometime I've got to get that off.

How involved were you with Spain?

Well, I — like Ted Willis and several of our friends in the Labour League of Youth — was very much involved with Spain. In the first place, virtually every boy of our crowd volunteered. But the people in charge of recruiting, the communists, sent us all home — partly because we were nearly all under age. At the time we volunteered, I was twenty. They were determined not to be caught under the Foreign Enlistment Act. And so first, they wouldn't take anyone under twenty-one. And second, they said that Ted and myself and one or two others who were running the national committee were far more important to the Popular Front where we were. We were very much on the political inside by then. We were protegees of Nye Bevan and Stafford Cripps and that crowd and met all the communist leaders frequently. Ted ran the food ship to Spain committee and was travelling to Spain all the time. I never got any further than Paris. I used to get to Paris regularly to see people, and met heaps of International Brigade people either on leave, or on the verge of going out, or coming back.

---

4   Alexander Baron's novel *Franco is Dying* was published in 1977. The prequel *The War Baby* is being published for the first time by Five Leaves in 2019.

Anyway — this novel about Spain became a must. I think that even though we had excuses for not going, or we weren't able to go, it burned pretty deep into all of us that we hadn't been there. Lots of ordinary lads from the branches just trickled off — a lot of them were killed. That's why I think World War Two came almost as a relief, if you know what I mean. Now we are in it.

Was Hackney in the Thirties a strong political culture? I'm not sure how much it has been mythologised.

Well, things always get mythologised or given a fictional shape somehow as time passes by — I found this going round former International Brigaders, it very often becomes sentimentalised in their memory.

Looking back on Hackney in the 1930s up to the war, most of the population were respectable. It's modern journalists who have called Hackney in the East End, or perhaps it is the East End now. I've got plenty of respect for the working class in the East End, but the East End was Spitalfields — the boroughs of Stepney and Bethnal Green. If you could just move up to Dalston, my goodness! I bet my parents thought, my Dad thought: "I'm taking her out of it" — just to move a couple of blocks past Dalston Junction.

There weren't thousands of young people in the Labour League or the fascists. There were strong branches — much stronger than they are now. The Labour League of Youth branches had a couple of hundred members each, that kind of thing. And equally large bands — in some areas much larger bands — of quite decent and cheerful boys and girls who joined the fascists. We had a curious relationship with them because on duty it was all boots and knuckledusters and off-duty we used to fraternise. It was like British and German troops in 1914. We all knew each other by name. In fact, one of our fellows started going out with a fascist girl. We had long political discussions with them and asked them, wonderingly, how they could believe — and they would ask us, how can you believe in all this bloody Bolshie stuff.

I would say that the working class was old-fashioned Labour in Hackney, passive, non-political, highly respectable. The amazing thing, it may have been humanitarian but I remember how moved I was — at the beginning of the Spanish Civil War, we at the Labour League of Youth started this food ship, a ship load of food that later became many ships and railway wagons. All the branches of the League of Youth hired

52

lorries and went round the streets. And everybody had the same tale to tell. There wasn't a doorstep, there wasn't the poorest room where a woman didn't say: "Wait a minute duckie" — and she would go in, she would fiddle around the shelves and come out with a tin of corned beef or a tin of cocoa or something. Because they read either the [*Daily*] *Herald* or the *News Chronicle* or the [*Daily*] *Mirror* and these had pictures of the rows of dead kids in Barcelona and all that kind of thing. And then we held a meeting in Finsbury Town Hall and it was so wonderful. Branch after branch was turning up with railway porters' trolleys and wheeling these piles of boxes of grub. And these really came from every single door that anybody knocked at in any borough in north and east London. That is the one moment of mass politics that I can think of.

In the East End proper, the only real mass politics was fascist. It became a real movement of people for a period — until it all melted away in the great rent strikes and things like that.[5] Thank heavens. The worst thing the left could have done would be to try to mobilise the Jews against their neighbours. They didn't, but in the rent strikes, I never thought it would happen, they just all joined together.

---

5 Rent strikes erupted across London's East End in 1938–9, supported by the Stepney Tenants' Defence League in which Communist Party members were prominent.

Chapter 2
"Very Heaven it was to be a Young Communist"

Andrew Whitehead

When Alec Bernstein was in his late teens and early twenties, allegiance to the Communist Party was the defining aspect of his life. He was shy and socially awkward and at the same time clever and ambitious. The Party gave him purpose. As a teenager, he was taken under the wing of John Gollan, then in charge of the Young Communist League and later the Party's general secretary. He was tasked first of all to work quietly within the Labour Party's youth organisation and then to edit the Communists' youth paper and help with party organisation. Alexander Baron — as he later became known (and, for consistency, that's what he will be called here) — was good at this. He abandoned the prospect of university to serve the Party. And he enjoyed it all — the secrecy, the subterfuge and the access he was given to the national headquarters.

After Baron's enlistment in the armed forces, his engagement with the Communist Party became less intense, but his post-war work with Unity Theatre again brought him within the Communist penumbra. It was only in 1948 — just as his writing career was taking off — that he made a clean break with the Party. In his novels, he wrote powerfully from his own experience and observation about the human aspect of fighting across Europe (*From the City, From the Plough*; *There's No Home*) and about the pains and stresses of post-war Jewish life in London (*The Lowlife*; *With Hope, Farewell*). His literary endeavours to address the Communist Party and the conflicts engendered by the loyalty it demanded — attempted in *Rosie Hogarth* and in *Seeing Life* — were nothing like as successful. He didn't let the subject rest. Indeed, in his later years, communism became an almost obsessive interest — because it harked back to the glory days of his youth, and also because of a remorse made more intense by the excitement his Party avatar continued to evoke in him.

The nature and extent of Baron's communism can only really be retrieved from his own writing. There's little trace of him in what's available of the CP archive, and not much more in the communist press. It is possible that Baron exaggerated his importance to the Party — not so much out of deliberate self-aggrandisement, which was not one of his vices, but out of a desire to invest his youth with political valour. It certainly offered material for his writing which he was keen to use.

Towards the end of his writing career, he produced two novels which are largely about communism: *The In-Between Time* (1971), an account of youthful political activity in 1930s London and the most autobiographical of his novels; and *Franco is Dying* (1977) — his last published novel — which concerns a British Communist of Baron's generation who has moved away from the Party but by chance gets caught up again with the movement. Perhaps because he knew he hadn't written a commanding novel about the Communist Party — it's difficult to think of any British author who has — he kept on trying. At his death, he left three unpublished works largely or entirely about communism: a novel, *The War Baby* (to be published in 2019 for the first time); a memoir, *Chapters of Accidents*, on which this chapter draws heavily; and a work of political science, *The Party*, to which he variously appended the sub-title "the life and death of a legend" or "a study in presumption". There was something he wanted to say — and he was never quite sure that he managed it.

The purpose of this chapter is to explore Baron's role in and work for the Communist Party and the manner in which this was manifested in his writing.

*

Alexander Baron's immersion in left-wing youth politics in north London has been addressed by Ken Worpole's contribution to this book. He devoured books on Russia and socialism precociously: "I think I read Volume 1 of [Karl Marx's] *Capital*, and roughly understood it, when I was about sixteen", he declared without any apparent swagger.[1] He made common cause in the Labour Party's League of Youth with a group of like-minded youngsters, notably Ted Willis, who became an enduring friend and confidant. Very quickly this small group came to the attention of — and was quietly recruited by — the Communist Party. The hallmark of Baron's early years as an active Communist was deception. While presenting himself as a loyal member of the Labour Party's youth wing, his focus was on identifying potential Communists and promoting the CP's interests and policies. "We formed a kind of Militant Tendency," he told Worpole looking back across almost half-a-century.[2] He was, in modern parlance, an entryist.

---

1   Transcript of Margot Kettle's interview with Baron, January 1984 — People's History Museum, Manchester.

2   An abridged transcript of Ken Worpole's interview with Baron in June 1983 is included in this volume.

By the time Baron became active in politics, the international communist movement was beginning to emerge from its intensely sectarian "Class against Class" period and embrace the politics of the Popular Front, working with — and within — other progressive parties and movements. Baron was no doubt convinced that the communists were those most dedicated to preserving democracy in Spain, resisting the wider rise of fascism and championing the interests of the marginalised and disadvantaged. Part of the new political turn was a move away from simply seeking to organise the working class to an emphasis on winning over groups such as students, intellectuals and the young. In Baron's first three years associated with the Communist Party, its membership doubled to 16,000. There was a vitality and energy about communism, in the late 1930s in particular, which Baron and many others found compelling. That was also cover and excuse for a style of operating of which Baron was later ashamed.

The means by which Baron was brought within the CP's orbit are recounted in his unpublished memoir. At a local Labour Party meeting, and much against character, Baron — then sixteen — made a brief but enthusiastic intervention in support of women strikers at a Tottenham clothing factory. That brought him to the attention of a young woman present at the meeting, who — when Baron mentioned that he wanted to be a writer — suggested that he come home to meet her husband. "This was a momentous invitation. As far as I can recollect she was the first grown-up with whom I had ever had a conversation outside of the family and school. ... Her flat was not in Bloomsbury but Stamford Hill would do." He got on well with the couple. They were communists, and indeed had spent time in Moscow, and they introduced him to a friend:

> He was John Gollan, a Scot. Gollan was an engaging fellow. He was slight and bony with hollow cheeks and bad teeth which he often showed in an open-mouthed grin. The skin of his face was waxen and faintly tawny. His characteristic expression was patient and slightly smiling. He spoke all the time in a mild, reasonable voice and I was flattered by the air of intent consideration with which he listened to everything I said.
> (*Chapters of Accidents*)

Baron was aware that Gollan was national secretary of the Young Communist League and was excited by the prospect of "gingering-up" the Labour League of Youth. "Gollan was so helpful in suggesting to me what steps I could take, that I began to stand up at branch meetings of the LLY to put forward ideas, his ideas, for more militant activities."

> It must have been very soon after this that I recognised that I was now a communist, one of Gollan's entourage. I was not formally recruited. In the fourteen years of work for the Young Communist League and the Communist Party that followed I never officially joined either organization or paid a week's dues, although I became a leader of the YCL and an apparatchik... of some standing in the Party. (*Chapters of Accidents*)

Among others quietly won over to the CP was Baron's friend and political associate, Ted Willis. They had been talent spotted and Gollan was right in recognising their potential. "Ted and I became great friends of [Gollan's], respected him enormously" — Baron told Margot Kettle — "and were really ready to go wherever he led after that."

It's quite possible that Gollan had a role in his recruits' most remarkable venture, a new political monthly aimed at a young readership, and he must have been delighted by its success. The first issue of *Advance* appeared as a duplicated sheet in December 1935, the month of Baron's eighteenth birthday. By the following summer it had developed into a printed monthly, still produced from Ted Willis's living room in Harringay. This was a breathlessly exciting and challenging time for the left with the almost simultaneous election victories of the Popular Front in France and Spain and then the agony of Franco's right-wing rebellion and Spain's descent into civil war. At the core of the League group which brought out the monthly were, alongside Willis and Baron, Oscar Lewenstein, already a member of the YCL, and Frank Brown, whom Baron described as his "first secret recruit" to communism.

The Labour Party has a long history of youth movements more left-wing and less biddable than the party establishment would like. But it could not ignore the success of *Advance* nor the need to serve an increasingly radical and politically restless constituency in their late teens and early twenties. *Advance* had flair and energy and was much livelier than the Labour League of Youth's official publication, *New Nation*, which died a natural death in July 1936. By the close of that year, the new publication was able to declare that it was the League's monthly magazine. The success of the paper (one special issue had a print run of 100,000) and growth of the League of Youth was such that it attracted the attention of other far left groups. In March 1937, Ted Willis wrote in *Advance* about the Soviet trials of alleged Trotskyists, linking this to

Advance, the left-wing monthly which Baron established along with
Ted Willis, August 1936

Trotsky's sympathisers within the League: "We have our Wreckers too!
Expose them as splitters, and creators only of dissension! Turn them
lock, stock and barrel out of the Labour Movement."[3] Baron wrote a by-

---

3   Ted Willis, "The Soviet Trials: Trotskyists in the League of Youth", *Advance*,
    March 1937.

lined article for *Advance* a couple of months later on the same theme, complaining of disruption by a group called Young Militant: "There's room in the League for all who are willing to work for Socialism," he declared, "but not for the enemies of our fight, whatever the guise."[4] In the following issue, he was even more direct, listing five Young Militant leaders and appealing to the local branches of the League to weed them out: "How about it Stoke, East Islington, Peckham and Golders Green? The League looks to you to clear out the wreckers!"[5] It was an audacious demand — one group of left-wing entryists insisting on the expulsion of another — and suggested not only dedication but a streak of ruthlessness.

It was quite a coup for John Gollan to engineer a group with loyalties to the Communist Party in charge of the paper of Labour's youth wing. The continuing success of *Advance* required the group responsible to keep quiet about their primary political allegiance. "It was made plain to me that, so far from trying to win me away from the Labour League of Youth, my mentors wanted me to stay in it," Baron recalled. "I had, of course, to keep my membership of the YCL a secret." Communism made other demands on its adherents which Baron was pleased to meet.

> As I became used to the YCL and Party ways, I learned nothing that repelled me. On the contrary, I was thrilled and proud. The Party was not fettered by a "bourgeois" democracy. Its command system was militant. Excellent: my dreams were militant. I wanted to become a good soldier. (*Chapters of Accidents*)

According to Baron, the Young Communist League gained complete control of the Labour Party's youth wing. "The national committee of the LLY consisted of eleven elected members and a paid organizer provided by the Labour Party," he recalled. "Ten of the eleven were secret YCL-ers."

There was glamour attached to being one of Gollan's gilded youth. While still at school, he was sent by the CP to France, a country he loved at first sight. He was to speak on behalf of the Labour League of Youth — pledging support for a United Front, which was not Labour policy — at a conference of French youth organisations. Baron was

4   Alec Bernstein, "See How They Run!", *Advance*, May 1937.
5   Alec Bernstein, "Enemies of Socialism", *Advance*, June 1937.

awestruck to find himself sitting next to one of his heroes, the left-wing novelist André Malraux, who translated his fraternal greetings into French. The following year he attended an international youth conference in Toulouse, again ostensibly on behalf of the League of Youth but to promote the CP line. No wonder that Baron found his political life giddyingly exciting. "As for me, bliss was it then, indeed. And very heaven it was, to be a Young Communist at this time," he wrote in his memoir, paraphrasing Wordsworth's lines about the French Revolution.

The battle in which Baron was engaged required discipline and focus. He was offered a place at University College, London, but turned it down. "Gollan had lit a fuse in my mind. ... From now on I took it for granted that I would one day become a professional revolutionary, employed full-time by the Party" (*Chapters of Accidents*). In the meantime, Gollan suggested factory work — a step too far for Baron who instead took a clerical job at County Hall. Baron's political vocation took another toll:

> Gollan despised the arts and I believed that he must be utterly right about everything. For the next six years, until I joined the army in war-time, I did not read a line of poetry and I read little more than half-a-dozen novels (I am sure of this) and these only books of which the Party approved

> Ted [Willis], who was more mature by four years and much experience, kept a mind of his own and never put aside his interest in such things. ... Our partnership soon took the shape that it was to retain. He, bold, full of initiative and new ideas and a compelling platform speaker... I, limited by my shyness, tried to keep in the background, speaking only at internal meetings and doing the office work. (*Chapters of Accidents*)

By the beginning of 1938, Baron was acknowledged as the editor of *Advance* and Willis was the star contributor, his articles often accompanied by his photograph. "I used to work all day then spent every evening editing *Advance* till two or three in the morning (kept going by a saveloy sandwich at the all-night coffee stall round the corner from Grays Inn Road and going home to Stoke Newington on the all-night 43 tram) or biking round London to meetings."

Baron was at one time simultaneously a member of the executive committee of the London Labour Party and the national council of the Young Communist League and was sometimes asked to attend meetings of the Communist Party's district executive. "I no longer had time to go to my local branch except when I wanted them to pass a resolution for me. The friendships I had made there faded away. The happy days were over." Ted Willis was by this time working full-time for Aid for Spain, a campaign to support the Republicans and help refugees from areas overrun by Franco's falangists. Baron followed his friend into full-time political work. A party nominee had been appointed as editor of *Tribune*, a newly established fortnightly linked to Labour's left-wing. Baron was told to apply for the post of assistant editor and got it.

Spain was the burning issue for the left. Ted Willis visited on behalf of Aid for Spain and wrote about his mission in *Advance*. Baron wanted to get to the Republican-held areas of Spain but never managed to make the trip out. He regarded the left's willingness to stand up against fascism — whether against Mosley's homegrown blackshirts in London's East End or Franco's rebels in Spain — as one of its nobler attributes. In his novel *Rosie Hogarth*, he describes the keen support for the Spanish Republican cause in a distinctly poor district of inner London as "one of those blind and beautiful upsurges of human solidarity that sweep their class from time to time." Many of those who enrolled to fight in the International Brigades were Communist Party or YCL members; about 2,500 Britons went to Spain, and more than 500 died. Baron was still under twenty-one, the minimum age for enrolment, and would not in any event have been allowed by the CP to sign-up. "Ted Willis and I were reaping a harvest of success in the Labour Party and were certainly not to be spared," Baron recalled in his memoir.

Both Alexander Baron and Ted Willis were asked by Gollan to find volunteers to fight in Spain from within the Labour League of Youth. According to his own account, Baron tried and failed to persuade one colleague to enrol but didn't persist in the effort. He was aware of the malign influence of the Soviet Union in deploying agents and informers to police political loyalty among the Brigaders. He knew of people who served in the secret police, and many years later in published materials from the Soviet archives came across evidence of a British volunteer detained, and then killed, because of what he wrote in his letters home. "From the words of the page came a whiff of the sulphur and brimstone of Stalin's Great Terror which was at its height in 1938 and which raged across Republican Spain." And in an aside which conveys something of the lasting personal and political impact of such injustice, he declared in his memoir:

> I am an old man now but I am ridden by the memory of these distant events, of [Bill Featherstone] and of Monty, the one murdered by the secret police, the other in their ranks, both brave, honourable in intent and so alike; and I am all the more fervently relieved that I did not send Bill Featherstone or anyone else to fight where I did not go myself.

He rehearsed many of these issues — the bravery and suffering of the volunteers, the hopelessness of their task and acts of betrayal within their own ranks — in his compelling but until this year unpublished novel *The War Baby*, set amid the Ebro offensive of the summer and autumn of 1938, the failure of which signalled the collapse of the Republican war effort. Another event from those times, which Baron discovered only many years later, also troubled him. Ted Willis — apparently acting at Gollan's behest — arranged to divert money given for food to Republican Spain to fund Communist Party activities. "If I had known of the episode at the time it took place I would not have been troubled. If I had been in Ted's shoes I would have obeyed Gollan with a light heart. I knew that everything we did was for the highest good" (*Chapters of Accidents*). The dishonest deeds of good people for a cause which demanded unquestioning loyalty — that's what shamed Baron most about his time in the CP.

"Early in 1939," Baron recorded in his memoir, "all our enterprises crashed in an abrupt defeat." An awkward political truce between the Labour Party and its more radical youth wing broke down and the Labour Party establishment lost patience with the cuckoo in its nest. The League of Youth's national committee was disbanded and its annual conference was cancelled. The April issue of *Advance* had the customary article by Willis on its front page, but with a plaintive headline: "Call off this Attack on the League of Youth — says Ted Willis". The YCL imagined that if there was a parting of the ways with the Labour mainstream, they would be able to bring over to them many of those energised and engaged by *Advance*. In preparation for that, Baron made clear to all where his own political loyalties lay. In May (indeed on May Day, perhaps no coincidence), Baron wrote to the most prominent figure in the Labour left, Sir Stafford Cripps. "Dear Comrade" he began — and courteously he explained that he was resigning from the staff of *Tribune* to join the Young Communist League's

1st May
1939

To Sir Stafford Cripps-

Dear Comrade,

I wish to resign from my position with
the TRIBUNE, as I have decided to accept a
job offered me by the youth paper, "Challenge".

As you know, we are working very urgently
to strengthen the united youth movement at this
critical period, and in view of the introduction
of conscription it was considered that an immediately
necessary step was to broaden "Challenge" into a
weekly that would serve the whole united youth
movement, instead of just one section of it.

In order to carry through this development
without delay, various people, including myself,
in the different youth organisations have been
invited to collaborate in the paper, starting as
soon as possible. Since I agree with the necessity
of this step, I have accepted the job and have
promised to start as soon as can be managed without
causing inconvenience to the TRIBUNE.

I have been very happy to work for the
TRIBUNE during the last six months, and very much
regret having to leave. However, I feel that I
ought to be in the youth movement, where my work
is most directly useful.

Yours sincerely,

Baron's letter to Sir Stafford Cripps resigning from the staff of *Tribune*,
May 1939

fortnightly paper, *Challenge*, with the aim of broadening the publication
into one "that would serve the whole united youth movement, instead of
just one section of it".[6] Baron became its editor. A well-choreographed

---

6 Alec Bernstein to Stafford Cripps, 1 May 1939, Alexander Baron papers,
University of Reading.

plan was drawn up to accept the inevitable, and make a public break with the Labour Party. Ted Willis was to write an article declaring his allegiance to the Communist youth organisation. Alex Massie, a British Communist, reported to Moscow that:

> This open letter will be the basis for a drive to get the best of the LLY, and even its majority, into the YCL. We aim to bring over openly into the League not only our present fraction members, but all who agree with our manifesto.[7]

In July, *Challenge* duly devoted a full page to an article by Willis, who still described himself as national chairman of the Labour League of Youth, explaining his decision to come over to the Communists: "'I've decided that the best way I can help defeat Chamberlain is by joining the YCL,'" ran the headline. But the strategy didn't deliver. Baron recalled that about 400 Communists already in the League of Youth came over to the YCL. "Few others followed them. Gollan became grim and impatient." Baron was sent to Bristol to try to win over League members there. "Not one agreed to join. When it came to the point they were obdurately Labour like their parents. It was all very well being militant but they were militant Labour" (*Chapters of Accidents*). Two years later, Ted Willis recalled, the Young Communist League had fewer members than before the breach with the League of Youth.[8]

Baron now became a full-time CP worker with a modest weekly salary. *Challenge* was put together in what he described as a small attic in Hoxton. He and Willis were put on the four-man executive of the YCL along with another activist, Mick Bennett, and Gollan. He was also given other party responsibilities — looking after a group of YCL members at an engineering factory in South London and overseeing the activities of a sizeable branch in Shoreditch. In *Chapters of Accidents* he commented that the League's members were generally "young people of an excellent sort, often capable of great initiative and devotion. ... Of course they were dupes and I was a dupe." Baron's standing in the party was greatly enhanced by his status as a full-timer, one of the youngest in the Party, and his closeness to the leadership. He reminisced that he was "totally unknown to the Party membership but that did not weaken

---

7   Alex Massie in London to Lewis Povey in Moscow, 4 July 1939, Communist Party of Great Britain archives, People's History Museum, Manchester.
8   Morgan, 1989, p.316.

my authority. The local leaders and the rank-and-file welcomed and obeyed anyone who came to them in the guise of 'a comrade from the Centre.'" But his growing prominence brought with it scrutiny which was not always welcome. Towards the end of 1938, as Baron recalled, Comintern — the powerful international Communist network based in Moscow — expressed misgivings about him. Whatever these were, Gollan — who Baron found "utterly lacking in the prevailing servility towards the Comintern and Stalin" — was apparently "unconcerned by it, even amused." In November 1939, Baron's political suitability again came into question. An American Communist based in Moscow, Max Weiss, came to London and put together a private report for Comintern, which survives in archives which were opened up after the collapse of Soviet Communism.

> [Baron] is a good journalist rather than a well-developed political leader. Thanks to his insufficient political development, and also his working methods acquired in the Labour League of Youth, he has absolutely no sense of political vigilance. ... His good qualifications as a journalist could be useful if he worked alongside a politically developed comrade, who would be the senior editor; on no account should he serve as the sole editor of the newspaper.[9]

For a report on a Communist Party full-timer, this was a deeply damaging assessment. It's not clear how much of this judgment trickled down to Baron himself — but almost sixty years later, he tried hard to find out more about what Weiss had been up to, even approaching his old comrade Mick Bennett, whose refusal to talk deepened Baron's suspicions.

Whatever the cloud looming over Baron, it was made insignificant by the cataclysm into which Europe was stumbling. The Communist Party, determined opponents of appeasement, were completely wrong-footed by the Nazi-Soviet pact concluded just days before Hitler invaded Poland so triggering the Second World War. The Party did an abrupt about-turn: a "People's War Against Fascism" became an "Imperialist War". Members were unaware of the furious row that erupted in the Central Committee, the only public sign of which was Harry Pollitt's decision to stand aside as general secretary (a post he resumed when the line changed once more two years later when Hitler attacked the

---

9 Document dated 15 November 1939 in the personal file of Alec Bernstein, Russian State Archive of Social-Political History.

Soviet Union). Baron later described this episode as "the most disgraceful and the most ludicrous" of the "infamies" committed by the Party. But it didn't shake his loyalty and indeed few left at this time. "Only one YCL member rang up on August 23 [the day the Nazi-Soviet pact was announced], audibly in tears, to tell me that he had torn up his membership card. I said, 'Good riddance,' and put down the receiver" (*Chapters of Accidents*).

Communists now opposed the war while — once Churchill replaced Chamberlain as prime minister in May 1940 — Labour took its place in a national government determined to prosecute the war effort. It was a Labour Home Secretary, Herbert Morrison, who banned publication of the Communists' newspaper, the *Daily Worker*, in January 1941. The CP expected this to herald a wider crackdown. "For all our self-imposed restraint, we waited in the first days of 1941 for the police raids that would announce a government attack upon the Party and the YCL," Baron wrote in his memoir. Those raids never came. A cabinet committee gave active consideration to suppressing the Communist Party and a Labour minister was among those advocating the internment of its leaders, but no action was taken, apparently because of the fear of provoking industrial unrest.[10]

Although the Communist Party itself was never outlawed, its leaders went to some trouble to prepare for illegality. This was, by its nature, a secret activity and the plans were never acted upon — but it constitutes one of the most remarkable, and hidden, aspects of the CP's history. Baron mentions in passing in his memoir how "a small class of picked people was formed to be trained for possible underground work in the future; I taught the class, which met in Hackney." Whether this was simply about how to make posters in your back room, or whether it displayed a more considered approach to sustaining an underground political movement, is not at all clear. He was certainly, by his own account, a frequent visitor to the Party's headquarters on King Street, close to the Covent Garden fruit and vegetable market.

As part of the counter-measures put in place in the event of a ban, Baron and Willis were among those expected to go underground.

> A cache of money was to be put away for me and a hideout was
> found. It was in a big psychiatric hospital in South London.

---

10 Morgan, 1989, p.240.

> When the Party gave me the word I was at once to go into the hospital as the private patient of a senior consultant who was an undercover Party member. I would have a room to myself, with a telephone. I would be able to go out and to receive visitors. In any case, a courier would keep me in touch with the outside world. A girl was to do this job. I met her in the evenings in Regent's Park to train her for her duties while we walked round the lake like a courting couple. (*Chapters of Accidents*)

It's hardly surprising that this remarkable subterfuge provided material for his novels. A similar arrangement is used by underground Spanish Communists in *Franco is Dying* while a network of undercover London Communists in the civil service and the professions, with a woman providing the link between them and Party HQ, features in *Rosie Hogarth*.

The Communist Party placed one of its most experienced officials, Jimmy Shields, in charge of preparations for clandestine work. "He was in fact a member of the Control Commission of the Comintern, its police and security section," Baron recorded in his memoir. "He was thin and grey, with a skull-like face which was frequently softened by a ghost of humour." Everyone at the top ranks of the CP was well aware they were under close surveillance. "Opposite our building was the showroom of a funeral mason, with his range of tombstones on display. Scotland Yard detectives took over the showroom and crouched behind the tombstones watching our front entrance. Sometimes we stood in the street and contemplated this comic sight. Others followed us when we went to and fro." Arrangements were made to keep *Challenge* going, in miniature format, using a small printing press installed in the home of an undercover CP member, a scientist, in a commuter village in Hertfordshire. A stack of printing paper was stored away (not well enough, it was ruined by damp). A printer in Lincoln was approached to produce "some harmless-looking catalogue covers which could one day be used to conceal political pamphlets".

Baron relished the excitement. "So far from feeling a furtive, potential outlaw, I was filled with confidence and pride with these activities. I trusted the Party, which always knew what to do and seemed to have its eyes and ears everywhere." But alongside the pride, there was a hollowness. "My life at this time ran in two streams, for beneath my fanatical belief which was beyond question and despite the elation, happiness and optimism that I felt, all deepened by the pride in the responsibilities which the Party had entrusted to me, another stream ran underground as it were, one of depression which I refused to acknowledge...." His Party colleagues were all older, many much older; he felt at times patronised, "in some way excluded from full comradeship" (*Chapters of Accidents*). His immersion in the CP and its activities had upset his mother and tarnished his links with his parents. His acute loneliness was eventually abated by love — again a Party affair. Nelly (he never mentioned her surname) was an activist at a big electrical factory in north London. How long the romance lasted is unclear, but it seems to have survived for quite a while after his call-up and her move to Lancashire.

Scotland Yard sought to disrupt the running of the Young Communist League by the simple stratagem of enlisting their leaders in the army. Alec Baron, Ted Willis and Mick Bennett were called up at the same time, in July 1940. Baron was happy to go. On the evening before his departure, he and Bennett went round saying their goodbyes. The new general secretary, Rajani Palme Dutt, was at his Party arranged "hide-out", a flat above a butcher's shop in Bloomsbury. "He sat in the kitchen looking glum and gave us as cheerful a send-off as a professional mourner shaking hands with the relatives after a funeral" (*Chapters of Accidents*). At HQ, Harry Pollitt wished them luck while another senior figure, Robbie Robson — who had fought at Passchendaele — proffered some advice: forget about politics for six months and concentrate on becoming good soldiers.

It was five years or more before Baron was demobbed. In his memoir he recounted how "the army gradually replaced the Party as the object of loyalty" and that with time he "came to feel less and less like a Communist among soldiers, more and more like a soldier among all the rest." But that was a gradual process. He felt a sense of "duty" to the CP, which encompassed enlisting fellow recruits to sell *Challenge* and attending an informal meeting of Communists in the army. He wrote occasionally for *Challenge* and a short story he posted to Nelly was published in the *Daily Worker*.[11] In Sicily in 1943, during lulls in the fighting, he read Stalin's landmark Soviet Constitution of 1936 and was still at that time "solidly... one of the faithful." When in London, he kept in contact with some comrades. "I felt a stranger at the YCL office but I liked going to 16 King Street, to chat with Robson." Shortly before his army discharge Baron suffered a head injury — well away from any

---

11 "Toy Shop" by Corporal A.J. Bernstein, *Daily Worker*, 19 October 1943.

A Unity Theatre outing to Box Hill in 1948 — Baron, with glasses, is in the front row towards the left; Muriel Walker, who worked with him on *New Theatre* and kindly shared this photograph, is three from left on the front row

battle line — which clouded his return to civilian life. According to his memoir, he was not looking forward to slipping back into his old London routine: "the thought of an end to the war depressed me almost as much as its continuance. Then I would have to go back to the life of a Party professional, the life I had escaped from. I thought of it as drudgery."

Back in London after the war, Baron was — by his own account — "in a poor mental and bodily state." Ted Willis and his wife provided both emotional and practical support. Willis had shortly after his wartime call-up addressed a Communist-organised People's Convention in London while in uniform. It was, Willis declared in his autobiography, "almost the only political decision in my life which I regret."[12] He had broken King's Regulations and two months later he was drummed out of the army. He went back to working for the YCL and served as its national secretary — but not for long. In 1943, Willis decided to bow out of full-time politics and to prioritise a career as a writer. That was

---

12 Willis, 1970, p.192.

an example to Baron, who wanted above all to write. After the war, Willis became artistic director at the left-leaning Unity Theatre and developed plans — which proved damagingly over-ambitious — for a move towards a professional company and a linked film enterprise. Willis asked Baron to work with him on a newly-launched monthly, *New Theatre*. Although not a theatre enthusiast, Baron "was glad of a chance to get my hand in at journalism again" (*Chapters of Accidents*). He spent two years there, and while the journal was not deeply partisan, he was back in an intensely political environment. Oscar Lewenstein, who was to become a considerable figure in theatre and film, also came on board — the triumvirate that had made such a success of *Advance* more than a decade earlier was re-united in another political venture. "Unity was… run by a strong nucleus of Communists," Baron recalled in his memoir. "I was a trained Party worker, a valuable catch, and six weeks after I joined I was installed as Chairman of the theatre." Muriel Walker worked closely with Baron on *New Theatre*, which developed into a prestigious and well-regarded monthly — at that time her life revolved around Unity Theatre and the friendships she made there. She recalled joining the CP for a year or so, not out of deep conviction but "only because everybody else did" at Unity. Baron was modest and meticulous and not all gregarious — as she remembers him — and gave no indication that he wanted to be a writer.

Baron's old mentor, John Gollan, was based in his native Scotland at the close of the war, looking after one of the Party's largest contingents. In 1947, he returned to London as assistant general secretary. He invited Baron to lunch and asked his guest to work at Party HQ as his assistant with the task of rebuilding the youth movement. Baron replied that he didn't want to go back to Party work and added that he was writing a novel:

"A novel?"

"That's what I want to do. I want to write."

[Gollan] said, in a sickened tone, "Oh, Christ!" Then in his old persuasive way, "That's not a job for you. What does a writer do, even a good writer, even one of ours? He describes the world. You are one of the people who have to change it. And one day to run it."

I said nothing.

71

> He leaned across the table and went on, "Look at me. An Edinburgh slummie. I am one of the five hundred men who matter most in the world." (*Chapters of Accidents*)

Baron made use of that striking remark about being one of a global top five hundred in one of his novels, *The War Baby*.

There was one practical outcome of this awkward encounter: Gollan persuaded Baron to see a CP doctor — a psychiatrist as it turned out. "She told Gollan that I was disturbed and should be left alone for a year or two." When they next met a year or so later, they had a row and Baron recalled that he was "for once as fierce and eloquent as [Gollan] was."

> I remember that he employed a familiar argument, that the Party had made me, that I owed to it whatever qualities I had, and that I had no right to make away with them for my own purposes. I recall, too, that when I presented him with some facts about Stalin's misdeeds he cried, "Don't tell me! Don't tell me what I know. I could tell you a thousand times worse! I'm saying this to you, but outside this room they could tear my nails out one by one and I wouldn't open my mouth." (*Chapters of Accidents*)

The final act in Baron's slow, painful divorce from the CP was a sour exchange of letters in July 1948 with Bill Rust, editor of the *Daily Worker*. Baron complained that an article in the paper about Berlin written by Claud Cockburn (under the name Frank Pitcairn) was "flippant" and had a "sneering tone". Rust replied robustly that Baron's real objections were "based on your political disagreement with his line of argument" — in other words, that Baron was deviating from the Party line.[13]

By this time, Baron — encouraged by Ted Willis, who was again a key guide and influence — had sent the typescript of his first novel, completed in the spring of 1947 and then consigned to a drawer, to several publishers. Jonathan Cape accepted it and *From the City, From the Plough* was published in the spring of 1948. His regular work and income also allowed him to reflect more deeply about the legacy of war and about his own Jewish identity — part of what he described as his "rendering of accounts" with the CP. Jewish Communists thought that they were becoming part of "a fellowship in which race was forgotten and in which all were simply comrades," Baron wrote in his memoir —

---

13 Alec Bernstein to Bill Rust, 11 July 1948; Bill Rust to Alec Bernstein, 16 July 1948 — Alexander Baron papers.

but that was an illusion. He started reading widely about the Holocaust, and the horror of it prompted a reassessment of the ideology to which he subscribed. "The fact is that being a Communist had inoculated me with indifference. Even the most humane of Communists took into themselves the brutal indifference of the Party towards human suffering." The literary expression of Baron's interest in the Holocaust and in anti-Semitism is discussed in this book by Susie Thomas. His growing unease with Communist morality also surfaced in a discussion with Ted Willis towards the close of 1948. Willis had accused Baron of being a poor Marxist. That same evening, Baron typed out a four-page response, complete with that essential of Marxist education, a reading list. "I doubt whether I've been a Marxist for the last three years," he asserted. The only morality that Communists practised was expediency. Their opponents were no more principled, but — he concluded — in what reads a little like a political last testament: "Communism and humanism... are, in fact, incompatibles."[14]

Baron's first novel brought with it a new identity. Jonathan Cape encouraged their new author to adopt a pen name sufficiently short to fit across a book's spine. "The book came out in the year that I severed my last tie with the Party and I seized the chance to shed my Communist identity and start life again with the new name" (*Chapters of Accidents*). Alec Bernstein the Communist was the past; Alexander Baron the writer was the future. The sizable cheque from his publishers allowed Baron to open his first bank account. He gave up his job with *New Theatre* and a few months later stood down as chairman of Unity. "Since then," Baron declared in the closing words of his memoir, "I have given all my time to writing."

This was not quite such an impermeable line in his life as he suggests. For many Communists, the loss not simply of the status and purpose that the Party provided, but of the friendships and social networks often abruptly closed to "renegades", was a powerful incentive to remain loyal. Baron was fortunate that he was not peremptorily abandoned by his Party associates. "Leading Party members spared me that treatment and continued to be friendly." Alison Macleod in particular, later film and TV critic for the *Daily Worker*, remained close. She recalls defending Baron from accusations that his debut novel was insufficiently political.

14 Alec Bernstein to Ted Willis, undated (November 1948), Alexander Baron papers.

When Macleod came to write about her own rupture with the CP in 1956, the year both of Khrushchev's "secret" speech denouncing Stalin's cult of personality and of the Soviet-led invasion of Hungary, she expressed her gratitude to Baron for trying "to shake my illusions before I was willing to give them up."[15]

Baron's time with the Communist Party stayed with him in another, much less welcome, way. MI5 kept tabs not simply on activists but on some who had long left the Party — in part to try to reconstruct networks of members and sympathisers to seek to identify possible "sleeper" agents for the Soviet Union. The defections of Guy Burgess and Donald Maclean in 1951 and of Kim Philby in 1963 — all active members of the Party as students at Cambridge — alerted the Security Service to how much it didn't know about the youthful political allegiances of those who had risen to prominence and influence. Olive Shapley, a CP member at Oxford in the early 1930s who made her career in the BBC, recalled in her autobiography how decades later she was still "visited regularly by a gentleman from MI5 who quizzed me about my activities over a cup of tea. ... I always looked forward to his visits. It was one of the few occasions that I ever got news of my old friends."[16] Baron seems to have escaped such intense scrutiny, but in 1967 he became convinced that he was under intrusive surveillance and that his mail was being opened. "I have always assumed that, having worked prominently in a subversive organisation, I would remain under official scrutiny; and properly so," he wrote to Ted Willis. But the recent level of surveillance was something new. "It is an ugly thing to be openly haunted, and has affected my health and work."[17] Willis, by then a Labour member of the House of Lords, took up the matter and was able to offer some reassurance: "There should be no more trouble for you, Alec, at all in the future," he wrote, and if several years hence "some new madman" decided to do further checks, it would simply be a matter of routine and take no more than a couple of weeks.[18]

Once Baron was established as an author, he wrote quickly — four years after *From the City, From the Plough* appeared, he had four published novels to his credit. Two were about war, and are discussed

15 Alison Macleod, *The Death of Uncle Joe*, 1997, p.ii.

16 Olive Shapley, *Broadcasting a Life*, 1996, pp.28-29.

17 Alec Baron to Ted Willis, 28 February 1967, Alexander Baron papers.

18 Ted Willis to Alec Baron, 26 June 1967, Alexander Baron papers.

in this volume by Sean Longden; the other two were about the pains of post-war London. The novel which eventually appeared in 1952 as *With Hope, Farewell* was the first to be written, but *Rosie Hogarth* (1951) was the first in print. It's a tender, sympathetic account of an inward-looking, respectable and entirely gentile working-class community in Central London and its response to the changes brought about by war and its aftermath. Lamb Street, the setting, was invented, but it is precisely located — indeed, the dust jacket of the original edition which at first glance seems to be an abstract design is in fact a street map — just off Chapel Market in South Islington.

It's the story of Jack Agass, an orphan of the First World War, who returns home after serving in the Second World War and several years working abroad. He's a shopfitter, and finds lodgings on the street he was raised and begins a romance with his landlord's daughter. But he is haunted by the flying bomb which fell on the street, demolishing his childhood home and killing Kate Hogarth, the woman he regarded as his mother. Rosie is Kate's daughter and Jack's childhood friend. She's moved up and out, to Russell Square, barely a mile away but a much more fashionable area. Jack hears that she's either being kept as a mistress or is a high class courtesan. Towards the end of the novel, they meet. Jack aggressively insists on sex. That leads to a revelation which provides an awkward close to what is otherwise a successful novel. Rosie explains that her secretive lifestyle is because of her allegiance to the Communist Party:

> "Many of our people work for the Government. Scientists. Senior Civil Servants. If they're found out they lose their jobs. They have to remain undercover members. They can't belong to Party branches, where we know that police agents are active. ... So I keep in touch with each of them, separately. I meet them, discuss their problems with them, put them in touch with others where it's essential, help them to plan their work, and above all — since they're mostly well off — I collect all the money I can from them for the Party funds."

It's an unconvincing twist to the plot. The CP certainly had sympathisers who were either reluctant to declare their Party loyalty or under instruction not to. The advent of the Cold War added to the suspicion of and hostility to Communists in positions of influence. Baron would have been well aware of the young woman at Unity Theatre who was forced out of her clerical role in the civil service, in which she saw details of sensitive defence contracts, because she was suspected of being close to the CP. There seems, however, to have been no precise model for Rosie and her surreptitious CP role.

Baron used the character of Rosie Hogarth to say something about the arrogance of Party loyalists and their sometimes strained relationship with the working class they championed. Rosie had come to regard Lamb Street as a "dreadful little street — oh, I know it's not a slum but it's a slum of the spirit." The Communist Party had provided her with a way out and — much as with Baron a decade or more earlier — it gave her a purpose in life. "'I could go down on my knees and thank the Party for what it's done for me,'" she declares. In a cathartic, Shavian-style dialogue in the pub in Lamb Street, she asserts: "'We're the first people on earth to discover the laws of history.'" Her father responds by lamenting her "'bloody cold, hard arrogance.'" In words which perhaps echo Baron's own view, Rosie's father tells her: "'you're just a self-appointed saviour... you really think yourself better than those you want to lead.'"

> "D'you know what beats me about you, Rosie? What absolutely defeats me? It's that granite certainty. You're right. You're always right. Your newspaper is doing good. You've no doubt of that. There's no glimmer of fear in your mind that it might be doing harm. The truth is whatever you happen to tell other people. Anything they say to you is just a noise in your ears while you're deciding what to say next. ..."

Jack Agass, who is present at this denouement, is unmoved by communism — and in that he represents his class. By the time *Rosie Hogarth* was published, the Communist Party had lost some of its sheen. Its membership was down from a wartime peak of approaching 60,000 to under 40,000 and the two Communist MPs elected in 1945 had lost their seats.

A few years later, Baron was drawn back to writing about the Communist Party in *Seeing Life* (1958), a novel set in the tumultuous year of 1956, and concerned primarily with the rise of a celebrity culture on TV and in pop music and which also touches on the concealed gay scene at a time when the Wolfenden report was ushering in changes in the law on gay sex. Baron ignored the advice of a publisher's reader to drop the political sub-plot, which as with *Rosie Hogarth* is at an awkward tangent to the main storyline. Hagerty, "a member of the political bureau of the Communist Party", is based in part on John Gollan; Fisher, a photographer and former member, has a bit of Baron about him. Fisher confides in a friend about the hold Hagerty once had over him:

> "He recruited me. He trained me. I did a good deal of work for him when I was abroad. We were friends for sixteen years. When I told him one night I was leaving them, and the last argument had failed, he opened the door and told me to get out. I should say he forgot me then… But you know I have never forgotten him."

Seeing Life also touches on the repression of the Hungarian uprising by Soviet tanks and the divisions this created within the ranks of British Communists, thousands of whom left the Party over the issue.

The In-Between Time (1971) is set mainly in the 1930s, and returns to the political milieu where its author was happiest — left-wing youth politics in north London. It's not a fictionalised autobiography, but Vic Mason, the central character, has a great deal of Baron in him. He's in the Labour Party, close to the Communist Party, and is in that time in-between school and university. Alongside the accounts of meetings, rallies and collecting money for Spain, Mason tries to volunteer to fight in Spain but is told he's too young (echoing Baron's own experience). At one point, he calls at the Communist Party's headquarters to press his case to enlist and finds himself in Harry Pollitt's office:

> He had not expected to encounter the top communist in the country. He saw a heavy oval face, scanty hair brushed down in the remains of a quiff, and large clear eyes that rested on him humorously but with great intentness.

At the heart of the novel is a romance. Olwen is a young Communist from South Wales and Vic is keen to impress her. She ends up having an affair with an unpleasant local Communist — a head teacher, Tom Arbalest (a name that feels as if it's an anagram) — by whom she becomes pregnant, though Vic gets the blame. At the book's close, Victor Mason is a middle-aged advertising executive in the Home Counties looking back "with a smile of mild enjoyment and despair" on the pains endured and lessons learnt from his youthful dalliance into politics and love.

A few years later, Baron wrote a more accomplished novel drawing on his youthful engagement with revolutionary politics. In *Franco is Dying* (1977), Frank Brendan — who as a young Communist had briefly served in Spain during the Civil War — returns to Spain for the first time in thirty-seven years, just as the dictator is on his death bed. He had been a "fifteen-year-old recruit to communism… clever, passionate and ambitious enough to become the professional functionary of 1938." Four decades later, he's a TV scriptwriter — the craft which Baron pursued. In Barcelona in 1975, Brendan chances across a prominent Spanish Communist he had known during the civil war. Terres had then commanded a section of the secret police: "He had done terrible deeds in a terrible time." He is now back in the country clandestinely to help to prepare the Communist Party for a post-Franco existence. The novel is a political thriller, and the skills Baron had honed as a screenwriter are deployed to excellent effect. Brendan's musings about his youthful political allegiance appear to reflect Baron's own perspective. "Whatever had led him to the party in his boyhood — young rebellion, young play-acting, a young man's hopes that were after all decent and generous — his years in it had been among the most enjoyed in his life." Much like Baron, Brendan "had not so much broken with communism as become detached from it. … He had recovered his nerve in the big war, but not his old faith." Towards the close of *Franco is Dying*, Jose Terres, the Spanish Communist on the run, says to Brendan: "'Frank, we shall not see each other again. Tell the truth. You cannot stop arguing about communism. It attracts you.'" Frank responds: "'My youth attracts me.'" That perhaps is at the root of Baron's repeated return to communism for material for his novels — it's not simply the Party but the moment in his life it represented.

Baron wrote what would now be called a prequel to *Franco is Dying* to which he gave the title *The War Baby* — although completed and revised, he couldn't find a publisher, but the typescript is among his papers, and it will finally be published this year. This is his most sustained criticism of Communism. Brendan, though too young to fight, goes out to Barcelona on behalf of the CP — much as Baron aspired to do — where he revels in the excitement and indeed the opulence of the Communist-aligned elite in the nerve centre of the Spanish Republic. As the anti-Franco forces embark on their last major offensive, Brendan is sent to the front as a political commissar to the British battalion and, when they are pushed on the defensive, he willingly picks up a rifle and fights. It's a desperately unequal contest, made more so by the lack of organisation and munitions on the anti-Franco side. As morale slips, the secret police on the look-out for spies and malcontents step up their activity. At one stage, Brendan is informally enrolled in this task. He comes across a Welsh soldier, a loud-mouth but not worse, who is incarcerated — and the reader supposes killed — as politically disloyal. A left-leaning American war correspondent is shot dead because he had witnessed some of Stalin's show trials in Moscow and was intending to write about them. All this is concealed behind a wall of deception and counter-information — "fake news", you might say. Few of the British volunteers make it out alive; none are unscathed. It is a blistering account of the moment and the movement, deeply critical of Communism but generous towards those who chose to enrol under that flag.

In the mid-1980s, Baron was asked by Margot Kettle — herself a onetime Communist activist — whether he had regrets about his youthful political loyalties and activities, "No, I don't regret it at all," he insisted.

> First of all I think it's foolish to regret anything that one went into unless it was for base reasons, for mean or selfish reasons. … I also don't regret the way in which those years formed me, or the residue of it that's with me still and the way in which it formed my modes of thought.[19]

It's a revealing remark. He remained moulded by Marxism. It was "a narrow, mean and fallacious theology" but "behind it there are many things which are part of my mode of thinking still, and a way of looking at all human activity which I think enlarged me, and which I regard as valuably formative in my life." Yet he had forsaken the call to action which was also part of the socialism of his youth. In part this was because of his "despair" of politics and pessimism about the prospects for the human race but also because he had chosen to become a writer rather than a political activist. Baron told Kettle, "I believe now that the writer has to be the spectator who sees a bit more of the game than the players, and has to stay on the sidelines."

Baron's memoir, *Chapters of Accidents*, is a more rigorous attempt to explore and explain his association with the Communist Party. It is one of the most rewarding accounts of CP activity — at both local and national level — at a time when its influence was relatively high, and has hitherto not been used as a source for Communist Party histories. While Baron was working on this memoir, he was also embarking on another substantial work of non-fiction. "The Party" combines pan-European history, political science and social psychology. Baron said it was

---

19 Transcript of Margot Kettle's interview with Baron, January 1984 — People's History Museum, Manchester.

intended as "an examination of the mystique, the legend of the Party" — and the manner in which adherents across nations often displayed noble qualities and at the same time a willingness "to perpetrate any necessary atrocity". He was spurred on by the demise of Soviet-style Communism and the tearing of the veil which had in part concealed the increasingly feeble moral and intellectual case for the Leninist political organisation.

> What has disappeared, as swiftly as a puff of smoke, is the aura, the legend, in which for so many years the communists were able to present themselves. Never again can communism exist as a creed of messianic hope. ("The Party")

The urgency with which Baron took to the task of writing "The Party" points to a personal imperative. His son Nick suggests that this unpublished work was intended "to serve as a catharsis, if not an atonement." Baron's wife, Delores, took on the typing of "The Party"; her husband was — she once told me — "getting it off his chest."

Forty years after Alexander Baron broke with the Communist Party, he had still not completed his "rendering of accounts". He never did.

Acknowledgements

This article has been informed by conversations about Baron and his politics with three women who knew him well: Delores Baron, Alison Macleod and Muriel Walker. Colin Holmes kindly alerted me to Margot Kettle's interview with Baron and shared with me a transcript. I am grateful to Nick Baron for sending me a copy of the slender file on his father in the Moscow archives and for providing a translation from the Russian. He also read and commented on a draft of this chapter, as did Geoff Andrews, a historian of British Communism — my warm thanks to them both.

Sources and Further Reading

Baron, Alexander. 1951. *Rosie Hogarth*, Jonathan Cape: London.

Baron, Alexander. 1958. *Seeing Life*, Collins: London.

Baron, Alexander. 1971. *The In-Between Time*, Macmillan: London.

Baron, Alexander. 1977. *Franco is Dying*, Macmillan: London.

Baron, Alexander. 1990. *The Party*, unpublished typescript included in the author's papers at the University of Reading.

Baron, Alexander. 1997. *Chapters of Accidents*, as yet unpublished typescript held at the University of Reading.

Morgan, Kevin. 1989. *Against Fascism and War: ruptures and continuities in British Communist politics, 1935-41*, Manchester University Press: Manchester.

Willis, Ted. 1970. *Whatever Happened to Tom Mix? the story of one of my lives*, Cassell: London.

What, you're not doing all this so we can return to you?

...ATHER THE REVERSE

This story is by CORPORAL A. J. BERNSTEIN, Pioneer Corps, and comes from Italy. It is an authentic reflection of the feelings of our fighting men, expressed through soldiers who stopped to explore a

TOY SHOP

WE had broken into the town the night before, attacking from the landward side, and now, almost none, we were scrambling down the cobbled streets towards the harbour.

From the hills on which we had stood the previous day, the little Sicilian port had looked like a picture-postcard scene, gleaming white and tantalising.

Now the beauty had vanished like a mirage. Shelling and air bombardment had left gaping houses, cobblestones heaved up as if by an earthquake, great mounds of rubble and splintered timber were everywhere.

Behind us there were still streets ablaze. Smoke and dust blinded us and befouled the air.

But it was quiet at last in the town. There was no more cracking of snipers' rifles, or the disjointed chatter of machine-guns; only the crackle of flames, the occasional roar of an exploding mine and the slither and crunch of our boots as we picked our way through the debris.

WE saw few people. Most of the inhabitants had fled. Some, I suppose, were still cowering in their cellars. Only a few very old men and women stood in the gutters and watched us uncomprehendingly.

One old woman, with a dark, wrinkled face and wispy white hair, clasped her hands in an attitude of prayer and, opening her toothless mouth, pointed to it to show us she was hungry. She did not speak, but whimpered like an animal.

We halted for a moment and each of us gave her a couple of biscuits, though we were running short ourselves. When we marched away, the old woman was sitting on a doorstep gnawing painfully at a biscuit with her pallid gums.

The sun was right up in the sky now. We were plastered with sweat and white dust, hungry and exhausted.

I led the section into a deserted street and, after making sure we were safe, gave them permission to fall out.

Before they broke ranks I said a few words to them. I told them: "Don't wander off. Keep in the shade. Be careful of these houses—they're still with booby-traps. If you find any wine you can have a drink, so long as you don't overdo it. And remember—no looting. We're not Germans."

AFTER that we looked into some of the houses.

The outside of Italian buildings are always a hundred per cent Fascist. There are big slogans boldly painted—

"Believe, Obey, Fight."

"To Have Many Enemies is To Have Much Honour."

"The Valorously For The Fascist Empire."

Pompous, sickening, typical slogans.

But inside these houses there was no Fascism. Each front door led to a living-room, and they were all the same; the big double bed, the religious pictures on the walls, the photographs of sons away fighting, the heaps and heaps of letters spilled everywhere.

The Italians must be great letter-writers. We found three letters and cards all over the place.

I left my men and went down the street to fill some water-bottles. "Remember," I warned them again, "no looting."

When I got back the street was deserted. I was surprised. I had learned to trust my men, and they had never let me down. I put the water-bottles down by a wall and went in search of them.

A COUPLE of blocks up the street there were some shops, the same kind of humble little shops you would find in an English slum—a tobacconist's, a grocer's, a dressmaker's. The window-frames had been jerked awry by blast, with jagged teeth of glass still clinging round the edges. It was in one of these that I found my section.

To picture the scene that they made, you would have to know my men. They are men moulded by three years of battle training, hardened by their first weeks of real warfare, grim, sunburned men from the docks of Liverpool, the coalfields of Fife and Durham, the streets of East London.

And here they were, in—of all places—a toyshop.

It wasn't the kind of toyshop our youngsters have become used to, full of glamorous dolls and model aircraft and all sorts of miniature mechanical wonders. It was more the kind of place you could imagine in a story-book, with a little old man behind the counter and Pinocchio peeping his nose against the window; a tiny, dusty den with only a few simple toys of wood and tin and coloured paper on its shelves.

A couple of the lads had found packets of scissors, streamers and were flinging them at each other, the flimsy coils of pink and blue and yellow writhing through the gloom of the shop and settling on heads and shoulders. It was like the Christmas parties we used to have for the kiddies in our street used to have every year.

Another was delightedly winding-up a clockwork toy he had found, a little acrobat on a horizontal bar. The artful clot with a cricket cap, a striped jersey and tights. There was a fierce black moustache painted on his florid face. When he was wound up he swung stiffly over and over the bar until the spring ran down.

But the greatest attraction was a musical box.

It worked with a weight, and it seemed to play for ever, tinkling over and over again the same jolly, silly, childish little tune—the kind of tune you hear children singing when you pass a school. It played clear, soft, fragile notes like fine glass or a tiny dulcimer.

THE musical-box was an playing on the floor when we left the shop. We could hear it when we marched out of the town.

Its tune was still with us in the days that followed as we fought our way up the coast road. We remembered it when we saw Etruscans in the seemed lemon groves and crouched in our slit trenches in the hills.

The recollection of it clung to us, incongruously, when Messerschmitts howled over our heads at zero feet, when the ground quaked with bombardment, when we fought it out with the Goering Division in front of Catania.

...TEN: TWENTY THOUSAND BRITISH CLASS TEACHERS

meals for the children, saving and salvage. No wonder the Board of Education said in one of its latest circulars:

"In present circumstances the services of such women as uncertificated teachers are particularly valuable."

★

WHAT price is paid for these "particularly valuable" services? It seems almost incredible, but it is a fact that they start at 50s. per week, and after

by——

LEWIS DAVISON

a long life of valuable service they are still getting only 55s. per week. And this includes their war bonus.

All workers who know the facts about these village teachers must feel indignant that their years of toil to educate the village child should be so shabbily rewarded.

These teachers have to explain to their children that this is a noble war for liberty. But what liberty is there on such a wage?

Surely, you will say, they are paid for the extra work they are doing? Have they no overtime rates? No! Teachers' extra work is nearly always strictly voluntary.

One County Council known to the writer does actually pay its teachers the princely sum of 6d. per meal served, but it knocks off the tanner if there are less than 12 children sitting down. To such perfunctory employers the feeding of 11 children is not worth one farthing. There are some surprising things still going on in the lower-paid rural areas.

WHAT must be done? All teachers, all trade unionists, all Daily Worker readers, in fact, all decent British people should help to put this matter right.

Remember that many of these teachers are very isolated from their fellows, they are in small schools, with small staffs, far off the beaten track. Indeed, much further off the map than they were in peace time.

The facts about uncertificated teachers' pay must be made known far and wide.

Training courses must be arranged for the younger ones so that they can qualify for a certificate. The long service of the older ones should qualify them immediately.

There must be an immediate increase in the war bonus of these teachers.

LETTERS TO THE EDITOR

Russia's Old Age Pensioners

I SHOULD like you to write us an article on how old age pensioners are treated in Russia. We get 22s. a week to live, clothe ourselves, and keep clean, and have to live in common lodging houses.

I am a daily reader of the Worker, and helped to build up its circulation.—Jack Davies, Doncaster, Yorks.

The principles on which old age pensions and social insurance are administered in the Soviet Union through the trade unions are laid down in Article 120 of the Stalin Constitution of 1936, which reads:

"Citizens of the U.S.S.R. have the right to maintenance in old

age, and also in case of sickness or loss of capacity to work."

Male workers reaching the age of 60 with employment records of 25 years or over, and female workers reaching the age of 55 with 20 years' employment to their credit are entitled to a superannuation payment amounting to 50 per cent. to 80 per cent. of their average earnings.

People on pensions may continue work while receiving their pension. In addition, in December, 1938, it was decreed that, when the average is computed, the higher rates of pay obtained in recent years should be the determining factor.

CRADDOCK CASE

If I were a member of the Women's Citizens' Association, Mrs. Bentley Taylor would soon get short notice.

As for Mrs. Ainslie, member of the League of Mercy and the R.S.P.C.A., does she apply mercy to animals only and not to human beings?

Mr. Barton, chairman of the Hereford Lads' Club—well, what do the lads think?

Mr. Morrison has said he could not intervene, but in future he must, otherwise the women of this country will make him or clear him out. There must be a nation-wide investigation into Juvenile Courts to make certain that there is no charge are, in fact, human.— Mrs. M. Williams (a mother), 25, Wellesley Road, Ilford, Essex.

Notebook

assistance to us, and the final result of the loan.

"Please accept my thanks for the part which you played. I should be glad if you would convey my appreciation and thanks to the members of your Party.—Yours sincerely,"

J. B. Chifley, "Treasurer."

The "new Tribune is published under the slogan "Unity for Victory," and here is evidence that the Australian Communists work on the principle of deeds before words.

Land Army Injustice

SOME months ago I drew

inform you that we have received instructions to withdraw our lottery for the Benevolent Fund. After receiving this letter, therefore, you must not sell any more tickets and must return your book to me . . .

"It is very annoying that this should have happened, but some lady in West Kent drew the attention of the police to the lottery and so it has been stopped."

And so you have this position. The Land Army is put included in State provisions for welfare as some members are not only dependent on charity but are also at the mercy of any cantankerous old nut who likes to play the copper's nark.

Land Army women might to be

The *Daily Worker*, Tuesday 19 October 1943

This story is by Corporal A.J. Bernstein, Pioneer Corps, and comes from Italy. It is an authentic reflection of the feelings of our fighting men, expressed through soldiers who stopped to explore a

Toy Shop

We had broken into the town the night before, attacking from the landward side, and now, almost noon, we were scrambling down the cobbled streets towards the harbour.

From the hills on which we had stood the previous day, the little Sicilian port had looked like a picture-postcard scene, gleaming white and tantalising.

Now the beauty had vanished like a mirage. Shelling and air bombardment had left gaping houses, cobblestones heaved up as if by an earthquake, great mounds of rubble and splintered timber were everywhere.

Behind us there were still streets ablaze. Smoke and dust blinded us and befouled the air.

But it was quiet at last in the town. There was no more cracking of snipers' rifles, or the disjointed chatter of machine-guns; only the crackle of flames, the occasional roar of an exploding mine and the slither and crunch of our boots as we picked our way through the debris.

In Eighth Army uniform, 1943

We saw few people. Most of the inhabitants had fled. Some, I suppose, were still cowering in their cellars. Only a few very old men and women stood in the gutters and watched us uncomprehendingly.

One old woman with a dark, wrinkled face and wispy white hair, clasped her hands in an attitude of prayer and, opening her toothless mouth, pointed to it to show us she was hungry. She did not speak, but whimpered like an animal.

We halted for a moment and each of us gave her a couple of biscuits, though we were running short ourselves. When we marched away the old woman was sitting on a doorstep gnawing painfully at a biscuit with her pallid gums.

The sun was right up in the sky now. We were plastered with sweat and white dust, hungry and exhausted.

I led the section into a deserted street and, after making sure we were safe, gave them permission to fall out.

Before they broke ranks I said a few words to them: "Don't wander off. Keep in the shade. Be careful of these houses — they're stiff with booby-traps. If you find any wine you can have a drink, so long as you don't overdo it. And remember — no looting. We're not Germans."

After that we looked into some of the houses.

The outsides of Italian buildings are always a hundred per cent Fascist. There are big slogans boldly painted:

"Believe, Obey, Fight."

"To Have Many Enemies Is To Have Much Honour."

"Die Valorously For The Fascist Empire."

Pompous, sickening, typical slogans.

But inside these houses there was no Fascism. Each front door led to a living-room, and they were all the same: the big double bed, the religious pictures on the walls, the photographs of sons away fighting, the heaps and heaps of letters spilled everywhere.

The Italians must be great letter-writers. We found these letters and cards all over the place.

I left my men and went down the street to fill some water-bottles. "Remember," I warned them again, "no looting."

When I got back the street was deserted. I was surprised. I had learned to trust my men and they had never let me down. I put the water-bottles down by a wall and went in search of them.

A couple of blocks up the street there were some shops, the same kind of humble little shops you would find in an English slum — a tobacconists, a grocers, a dressmakers. The window-frames had been jerked awry by blast, with jagged teeth of glass still clinging round the edges. It was in one of these that I found my section.

To picture the scene that they made, you would have to know my men. They are men moulded by three years of battle training, hardened by their first weeks of real warfare, grim, sunburned men from the docks of Liverpool, the coalfields of Fife and Durham, the streets of East London.

And here they were, in — of all places – a toyshop.

It wasn't the kind of toyshop our youngsters have become used to, full of glamorous dolls and model aircraft and all sorts of miniature mechanical wonders. It was more the kind of place you could imagine in a storybook, with a little old man behind the counter and Pinocchio pressing his nose against the window: a tiny, dusty den with only a few simple toys of wood and tin and coloured paper on its shelves.

A couple of the lads had found a packet of coloured streamers and were flinging them at each other, the flimsy coils of pink and blue and yellow writhing through the gloom of the shop and settling on heads and shoulders. It was like the Christmas parties the kiddies in our street used to have every year.

Another was delightedly winding-up a clockwork toy he had found, a little acrobat on a horizontal bar. The acrobat wore a cricket cap, a striped jersey and tights. There was a fierce black moustache painted on his florid face. When he was wound up he swung stiffly over and over the bar until the spring ran down.

But the greatest attraction was a musical box.

It worked with a weight, and it seemed to play for ever, tinkling over and over again the same jolly, silly, childish little tune — the kind of tune you hear children singing shrilly when you pass a school. It played clear, soft, fragile notes like fine glass or a tiny dulcimer.

The musical box was still playing on the floor when we left the shop. We could hear it when we marched out of the town.

Its tune was still with us in the days that followed as we fought our way up the coast road. We remembered it when we bivouacked in the scented lemon groves and crouched in our slit trenches in the hills.

The recognition of it clung to us, incongruously, when Messerschmitts howled over our heads at zero feet, when the ground quaked with bombardment, when we fought it out with the Goering Division in front of Catania.

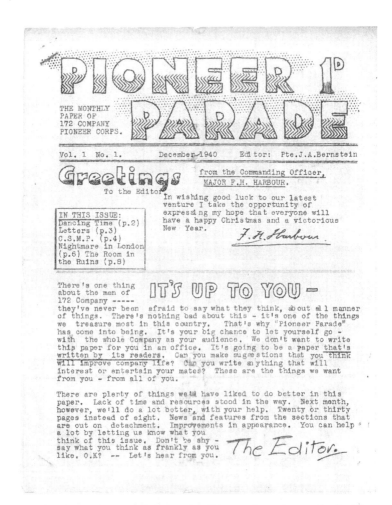

The first issue of *Pioneer Parade*, a monthly newsletter Baron edited while a member of the Pioneer Corps

Chapter 3
Men, Women & War

Sean Longden

The struggle in my soul: a Communist goes to war

When the literary legacy of the Second World War is examined, the memory is always of tales of escape and evasion — of spies, secret agents and commandos. Like the Great War — remembered for its poets and valiant breed of officers who had swapped the red coat of the fox hunter for the khaki tunics of the army — the public perception of the literature of this war is almost entirely from a middle-class perspective.

This is in keeping with the simplistic retelling of British literary history in which working-class literature explodes in the 1950s with a new school of writers, the so-called "angry young men". But these were not the first authentic voices of a literate British working class. Throughout the 1920s and 1930s there existed a stream of left-wing writers, many from the factories and mines of industrial Britain. Many of these were active in the Communist Party, the trade unions, or the left wing of the Labour Party. Yet few of these writers ignited the literary world. Instead they are largely forgotten, in favour of their more successful literary descendants from the 1950s.

If there is one writer who bridges the gap between the militant, socialist realism of the 1930s writers and the new breed of "angry young men" with their kitchen sink dramas, then that writer would be Alexander Baron. Baron's historic position is secured due to his being a man of both the old and new worlds and, more importantly, being a writer who chronicled the pivotal events that forged the new world: the experiences of the ordinary British soldier in the Second World War.

In three novels, *From the City, From the Plough, There's No Home* and *The Human Kind*, Baron gave his readers a vivid and intense introduction to the realities of war. And, for those readers who needed no introduction to the horrors of modern warfare, he became widely recognised as providing the authentic voice of the British infantryman. Baron himself referred to these books as a trilogy and it was his lifelong ambition to see them published in a single edition under the title *Men, Women & War*. Baron wrote "My three war books constitute a single body of work in which the broadening exploration of the theme can be seen." He called it a "cycle of experience". In this trilogy, *From the City, From the Plough* is the book about "men", *There's No Home* is about "women" and *The Human Kind* is about "war" as it impacts upon everyone.

It is no exaggeration to say that Baron's life was shaped by war. His pre-war experience as a Communist Party activist had limited his outlook on life, following the Party line and reading mandatory "tedious texts" of political thought, as Andrew Whitehead's chapter shows. Though at first opposing the war, Baron soon found his opinion changing as the course of the war began to change his understanding of politics. When he saw the men returning from Dunkirk he found himself with new thoughts, later writing that he had been "obscurely stirred, with a touch of distress. I am sure that this was the other self in me awakened again… There was something going on around me that I did not want to be left out of anymore." When he was eventually called up for military service he felt what he described as a "drench of pleasure" and the start of what he called a "struggle in my soul" as his experience of life expanded beyond his formative years. This was the beginning of a change in Baron's life, one that led him through the battlefields of Europe to the bestseller lists of the post-war world.

His early experiences in the army were a disappointment. He wanted to be an infantryman yet was rejected as a result of his poor eyesight, instead being sent to the Pioneer Corps, serving in 243 Company. He seemed to have the correct skills to become an officer but was rejected as a result of his political beliefs and activities, being interviewed by the security services clearly aware of his past. And so, instead of being sent for officer training, he remained a labourer in the Pioneer Corps, whose myriad tasks included digging defensive positions, tunnelling, road building, clearing enemy defences, laying mines and generally carrying out "pick and shovel" duties. Effectively, they were the "muscle" of the army, who shed sweat and blood without sharing any of the glory.

During his initial period in the army, Baron continued to act on behalf of the Communist Party. He wrote for *Challenge*, the newspaper of the Young Communist League and even recruited fellow soldiers to sell the newspaper around the company. Such were the strict division lines between the various elements of the British left that his activities forced him apart from a fellow veteran of the Labour League of Youth serving in 243 Company. Harry Ratner, who first read *From the City, From the Plough* in 2010 aged 91, later recalled: "I have no real memories of Joe Bernstein

(Baron) because he was a Communist Party member. I had been in contact with him in the Labour League of Youth. But I was a Trotskyist. Relationships between Stalinists and Trotskyists were very fraught. Their official line was that all Trotskyists were fascist agents."

Ratner recalled the violent division between the two groups: "We used to run street corner meetings opposite Whitechapel Hospital. One evening we would be attacked by the fascists who told us 'Go back to Moscow', the next day we would be attacked by the Communist Party who said we were bloody fascists!" He remembered there was no wartime reconciliation: "When I found out that there was a Joe Bernstein in my company, who had been in the Labour League of Youth in the East End of London, I didn't really want to get into an argument with him — and I don't think he wanted to get into an argument with me. So we kept a distance from each other. Now, looking back on it, I'm very sorry I didn't try to get into discussion with him because we might have found out we agreed more than we disagreed."

Yet, removed from the familiar streets of East London, Baron was soon struck by a new understanding of life. Taken out of the East End he began to realise the world was not one-dimensional. He was shocked to discover that there were men prepared to exploit a young homosexual soldier for sexual favours — and doubly shocked when he discovered the men were former miners, a breed that Baron, as a dedicated Communist, had idealised as models for the perfect proletarian.

Baron's active role in the war began in Sicily where as a Pioneer he took part in the Allied landings in 1943. Many of his experiences made their way into his later works. However some of the most dramatic were carefully excluded. One of these was an incident that occurred whilst bathing in the sea. As Baron and his comrades swam, some soldiers from a Highland Regiment began throwing Italian hand grenades into the water, forcing them further out. When the Jocks finally got bored and went away, Baron and his mates swam to shore. It was then they discovered one of their mates had drowned in the deep waters.

Throughout this period Baron was struck by the way soldiers build close, almost familial, relationships among their pals. Baron and his comrades in 243 Company built these relationships as they filled in bomb craters to allow roads to be used, cleared minefields and dismantled enemy defences — usually under enemy fire. And at the end of battle, it was Baron and his comrades who dug the graves for the dead. As he later admitted, he found that the "womblike warmth of comradeship" began to replace his allegiance to the Communist Party.

From Sicily they moved onto Italy before returning to England to take part in the Normandy landings. Despite the dramatic nature of events in Normandy, Baron later admitted he was hardly able to remember them. Instead the words of his post-war novels had supplanted his memories, his fiction taking the place of his reality. As his son Nick Baron later noted, his father seldom spoke of Normandy, preferring to allow his published work to tell the story.

On the morning of D-Day Baron was part of a "Beach Group" whose job was to help clear the area in order that supplies could be landed and dumps established for the immediate build-up of stores for the campaign ahead. What is clear is that Baron landed among the earliest groups on D-Day. One fragment of his memory was seeing soldiers of the Hampshire Regiment cut down by machine-gun fire as they crossed the beach. Other memories included his landing craft being hit by incoming fire and the distinct sound of mortar rounds landing in sand. His later experiences included having a trench blown in on top of him, but more importantly he unconsciously began the process of recording memories of the sights and sounds of the Normandy campaign that would form the basis of *From the City, From the Plough*.

The war continued, with Baron and his comrades remaining for some time in Normandy, continuing to unload supplies and send them on to the front, then following the advance into Belgium. Eventually he ended up in Antwerp, unloading ships in the docks — often working nineteen hours a day. All the time the area was under attack by V1 and V2 flying bombs. After surviving Normandy, the effects of this bombing took a toll on his nerves. As he later described it: "I felt that innumerable fine wires inside me were being tightened on violin pegs."

With the army desperate for reinforcements, Baron was finally offered the opportunity to go to the front as an infantryman. The problem was that by this time his enthusiasm for war had waned. He was physically exhausted by the long weeks of toil in the docks, and mentally exhausted by the almost constant bombing. Although he did not express it in his memoirs, it was whilst in an infantry training depot near Bruges that he appeared to suffer a breakdown. As he wrote home in early 1945, he was: "a bit humiliated about not being able to stand the pace."

Concerned by his health, Baron's superior officers arranged for a medical examination. The result was that he was pronounced fit, but that

Lance-Corporal Baron demonstrating how to dismantle and clean an army issue rifle

he was "getting wound up". As a result he was sent back to the UK, ending up in a camp in Northern Ireland. Whilst in Northern Ireland he was disappointed to be missing the final stages of the war. With the war over, Baron reached a mental and physical low that was aggravated by an accident in which he was hit by a lorry, from which it took some time to recover. As it stated on his army discharge papers, he had a "Psychoneurosis... aggravated by war service, but not attributable thereto."

From the City, From the Plough: the solemn little corporal

After the war he began writing theatre reviews and started work on the novel that would bring him worldwide fame. The text was written at night, bashed out on a typewriter he had received as a gratuity when he was demobbed from the army. When Jonathan Cape Publishers wrote to him in August 1947 he was still Alec Bernstein and *From the City, From the Plough* was still entitled *The Fifth Battalion*. The letter was brief but exciting and he was offered £50 advance on signature and £50 on publication. The first thing they did was to request he changed his name — quite simply, Bernstein didn't fit onto the spine. They told him to find a five-letter name, thus Alexander Baron was born. Then they changed the title, telling Baron that booksellers were facing a reaction against war books, as had happened following the First World War. It was only when *All Quiet on the Western Front* had been published to great acclaim that a change occurred. Thus, the publishers wanted a grand, slightly mysterious title that helped to raise it above the action books swamping the market. On the suggestion of his publisher's wife it was called *From the City, From the Plough*.

It was published in May 1948 to immediate acclaim and commercial success. The first imprint of 3000 sold out even before publication — something his publishers did not expect for a war book. In its first year it sold over 20,000 copies in the UK and even sold 6,300 copies in first American edition. Ten years later Baron was told by Pan Books that they had sold over 200,000 copies of the paperback edition. Even as late as the 1970s a new edition of *From the City, From the Plough* sold 7,500 copies, and is back in print today once again.

The book tells the story of an ordinary infantry battalion — the fictitious 5th Wessex Battalion — following them through the final months of training, then into the battles through Normandy until it is all but decimated in a single action to capture a single hill. There is little military action in the book. Instead the focus is on the soldiers and their relationships — both among themselves and with outsiders — and their emotions. In particular it focuses on what happens between battles. It is a story of the slit trenches, train journeys and mess halls rather than of victorious bayonet charges and heroic deeds. He deliberately does not make them one of the first wave battalions on D-Day — that would have been too dramatic and, more importantly, too easy. It was a bold choice for Baron, who had landed in Normandy in the early stages of the battle, to give his characters a less exciting introduction to the battle than his own.

When a man expresses the desire to kill his wife, Baron makes no effort to criticise. This lack of censure helps to draw a dividing line between Baron and the pre-war Communist writers — at no point does he lecture his readers. He treats his readership intelligently — allowing the reader to find out about the lives of men in wartime just as he had learned, purely by observation. To create this realism, Baron drew on his own memories. Some points are just minor details — like the soldiers picking flowers to wear in their helmets or eating fluffy fragments of biscuits pulled from their pockets. Others reflect the waste of war, like seeing how many lives it costs to cross a narrow river. But importantly he plunders his memories for his characters. Not all the characters are based on individuals, but they are amalgams of men whom he knew. He faithfully records the story of a soldier who went missing, with all his comrades believing him dead. Instead he has merely strayed into enemy territory, laid low, and then returned as soon as convenient. There are also two disreputable soldiers who specialise in theft. These men are direct portraits of two pioneers serving in Baron's unit in Normandy. They were responsible for the constant theft of supplies from trucks heading between base dumps and the front lines. Although Baron shows the criminal activities in a less than favourable light in the early stages of the novel, he does allow one man to redeem himself on the battlefield. This reflects Baron's real life experience, in which, although critical of the behaviour of the two men in his unit, he was prepared to eat the extra food they stole.

There are also real glimpses of the sexual behaviour of the wartime years. In conversation in the book, he makes reference to a story of an incident between fifteen Polish soldiers and a single British girl. This was based on an earlier incident in which Baron had witnessed an RAF woman having sex with a procession of men in the back of an army truck.

Another character with his roots in reality is "The Mad Major". His character shows a barely concealed homosexuality. He is a vicious, frustrated man who believes that everybody should share his desperate desire for action. He takes risks at the expense of his own men, costing lives, until he meets his match when one of the sergeants in his company murders him on the battlefield, after the major strays forward and gets their jeep blown up. This is a direct reference to an officer Baron served under in Sicily who had put his men in danger by parading them in open locations. Once in Normandy the major was killed whilst taking a group out to fix barbed wire in no man's land. The given reason was that they had been hit by shells. However Baron knew that it had been the work of one of his comrades, frustrated by the constant danger caused by serving alongside the "Mad Major". As he later wrote: "he got us in the shit and some bugger done him."

In direct contrast is another man directly based on a real person, Corporal Gonigle. With his horn-rimmed spectacles, this "solemn little corporal" as Baron puts it, is in many ways a self-portrait. Gonigle is the battalion's poet, writing verse for his comrades. This reflects Baron's own experiences from the early war years when he wrote a magazine for his unit (see p. 86 above). This character is fitting for this book — Baron does not make himself into a hero, rather he is a small, quiet man who makes a brief appearance and then disappears again.

The battalion's internal democracy is shown by the fact that there are just two incidents of overt heroism in the novel. One of these is by Scannock — earlier revealed as a thief — who is a violent man from the most impoverished sector of society. The second revelation of heroism is when the commanding officer loses his life in the final stages of the battle. By focusing on two incidents — one featuring the most senior man and one featuring the lowliest — Baron depicts the war as a social leveller, one that subverted his pre-war notions of the class struggle. Looking back at his time in Normandy — surrounded by a pile of dead Germans — Baron found he was struck by the struggle between his belief in communism and his feelings about war. He was still a Communist at that time, but later he looked back at the fate of the dead Germans and saw them as doomed youth who had been, he said: "misled like me by blind faith and poisoned by wicked lies." By the time *From the City, From the Plough* was published Baron had relieved himself of the struggle within his soul for his political beliefs.

What is interesting is that the novel's scenes of the final days before D-Day are less dramatic than Baron's later account of his own experiences. In the book the final preparation of their kit is glossed over, whilst Baron had sat around with his comrades burning spare kit in a stark gesture of finality. There are two possible explanations of why this should be so. The first is that he may have considered such a dramatic account to appear unbelievable. Alternatively he retained a sense of connection with those events that he still felt unable to put on paper. At this point in the novel Baron makes a brief dramatic change in the text. Suddenly he switches into the first person saying of the last night before D-Day: "It was a strange, sad, beautiful feeling to know this was your last evening in Blighty. It was like being very much in love, and very young, the evening before your wedding." This abrupt change of tone jolts the reader, it is as if it is a mistake that should have been re-worded by the book's editor, yet it immediately lets us know that the author is speaking directly from experience.

The war book that tells it all

When the former Secretary of State for War, Sir James Grigg, reviewed it for the *Sunday Times* he was so impressed by the book's depiction of the fighting in Normandy, he passed it on to Field Marshal Montgomery, surely an accolade in itself. Grigg was just the first in a long line of reviewers who heaped praise on Baron: "every reader who fought in Europe will acclaim his story as the real thing" (*The Star*); "I have found the war book that tells it all…We have waited a long time for this war's *All Quiet on the Western Front. Here it is*" (*The People*); "deeply stirring" (*Illustrated London News*); "the first really impressive, perhaps great, novel in English to come out of the Second World War" (BBC Radio European Service); "Conveys, unabated, a sense of quiet reality more remarkable than any American World War Two novel has yet achieved" (*Time Magazine*); "The only war book that has conveyed any sense of reality to me" (V.S. Pritchett writing in *The Bookman*); "Get this book and read it. Pester your library until they stock it" (*Tribune*); "The most moving war book that has yet appeared in this country" (*Clarion*); "There is no attempt at sensationalism, no hysteria, no indulgence in horrors or heroics … the finest presentation of infantry in modern warfare that I have ever read" (*Montreal Daily Star*).

One publisher — himself a veteran of the front lines — wrote to Baron's publisher and openly admitted envy that he had not published the book. His praise was of the highest order: "What a book! What writing! What depth and tenderness of insight into the common soldier, with all his vices and virtues. How perfectly he maintains the balance which expresses the truth about them — that for all their drinking, whoring, going absent, and filthy habits, they were brave and intensely lovable."

The big question was why were they all so impressed? The answer was that this book reflected the real war, one that was missing in all the POW camp escapist literature or tales of the exploits of spies and commandos. The previous year an article had appeared in *Soldier Magazine* stressing that what was needed was a novel by someone who had seen the war from the front and yet held a rank no higher than corporal. With hindsight, these words appear almost a challenge to

Baron. The reviewer in *Tribune* also summed this up perfectly when he wrote: "How is one to convey something of its splendid quality to readers saturated with slightly bogus glamour tales of the RAF and the Commandos and the Parachutists and the rest? Mr Baron's story is heroic only by implication. His people are not conscious of heroism." This sentiment was echoed by the reviewer who noted that Baron's characters "never quite become soldiers. This free, persistent, ineradicable civilian quality is the very soul of their achievement and their moral greatness."[1]

Within the novel Baron himself alluded to the ridiculously dramatic accounts in most war novels when he describes the men's last letters home as being: "brief, guarded and sentimental letters for the most part, not at all like the last letters of story-book soldiers going into battle." He later reiterates this point when he describes the journey across the Channel, telling the reader: "there was no sentimental talk, no soft singing or playing of harmonicas, no writing of farewell letters, no men sadly gazing at the distant shore." It struck a chord with the men who had sat in silence in slit trenches whilst mortar fire rained down upon them. He shows the infantryman's world as being little more than his view of the sky from the floor of a deep slit trench. It allowed veterans to say "Read that. That was my experience."

This sense of reality was at the heart of the book. One reviewer, who admitted to being acquainted with the events in Normandy, chose to title his review simply "What the Infantry Endured".[2] In Baron's private correspondence there is a letter sent to his publishers just weeks after publication. The reader had fought as an anti-tank gunner attached to the British 43rd Division and was convinced Baron was writing of the 5th Battalion of the Wiltshire Regiment, part of the 43rd Division, and of their role in the battle for Mont Pinçon. It was an obvious fit: the '5th Wessex' and 5th Wiltshires were immediately recognisable as similar names. Furthermore, the 43rd Division was known as "the Wessex", being formed from regiments raised in the south and south west of England. But the similarities did not stop there. In Baron's book, the battalion comprised of soldiers from both the West Country and from London: as he referred to them "The Bumpkins" and "The Doggy Boys" — so-called because of their love of greyhound racing. These were men

---

1   *Illustrated London News*, Saturday 5 June 1948.
2   *Yorkshire Post and Leeds Intelligencer*, Friday 28 May 1948.

"from the city" and "from the plough". This was exactly how the 5th Wiltshires was itself comprised, having originally been raised from Wiltshire and the surrounding counties. As the war progressed, men were drafted in from London and Birmingham, giving the battalion its distinct identity. As one South London-born 5th Wilts veteran recalled: "We got on alright with the 'Swedebashers'."

Bitter, bloody and deadly

In the novel, there is a climactic battle, in which the "5th Wessex" have to cross a river then capture a hilltop position, achieving the objective only after a combination of bloody slaughter and genuine heroism, costing the life of Lieutenant Colonel Pothecary and so many of his men. During the Normandy campaign, the British Army fought for two vital hills: Hill 112 and Mont Pinçon. Both battles were fought by the 43rd Wessex Division, both battles were fought by the 5th Wiltshires and both were costly encounters. But only one involved the crossing of a small river under fire, leading to the death of a battalion commander: the assault on Mont Pinçon on the 6th and 7th July 1944.

These battles were among the most intense fought by the British Army during the entire war. In the words of one 5th Wilts veteran: "Once action started, everything was very chaotic. It is impossible to describe what it was like. There was a tremendous amount of noise and smoke. Most of the time all you knew was that you were going forward." As Vic Coombs (who was at the heart of the action dramatised by Baron) later recalled, his memories of Normandy were of hand-to-hand fighting to capture German trenches. It was bitter, bloody and deadly: "It was them or me."

The sufferings endured by the 5th Wiltshires in Normandy is revealed by its casualty figures. One figure is starkly revealing: The 5th Wiltshires landed in France in the last week of June 1944 with a complement of 36 officers. By May 1945 just two of them remained with the battalion, the rest had been killed or wounded. Indeed, at the height of the fighting in Normandy, many reinforcement officers were dead within days. Of the unlucky thirteen officers who became casualties in the week of the battle for Mont Pinçon, six had been with the battalion for less than two weeks. One junior officer joined the Wiltshires at Mont Pinçon and was dead within three days.

One dramatic departure between the novel and the reality is that after capturing Mont Pinçon the 5th Wessex are given one final job and then promised: "A rest ... a long one." For the 5th Wilts there was no such respite. Just two weeks after the battle described in *From the City, From the Plough* they led an assault crossing of the River Seine at Vernon. It was a bitter battle with many men lost during the crossing and many more in the long, hard fight up the wooden hillsides that dominated the river. Five officers became casualties, four of whom were replacements for those lost in the previous battle. By the time Vernon was secured one company had been reduced to platoon strength, with around thirty men left out of the 120 that started the battle. All the platoons in the assault companies were commanded by sergeants who had to replace their wounded or dead officers, or platoon commanders who had been promoted to command companies. One of the latter was Lieutenant Holly, who had only joined the battalion as a platoon commander after Mont Pinçon and for whom it was his first major engagement. As Vic Coombs, who was taken prisoner during the battle, later recalled, casualties had been so high in the 5th Wilts that by the time of the battle at Vernon he didn't know the names of any of the men in his section: they were all reinforcements who had arrived after Mont Pinçon.

This high turnaround in personnel is shown in the novel through Baron's use of an interesting dramatic device: At the close of the novel the reader doesn't learn which of the characters has survived the battle. The men that Baron has introduced to us are lost in the fog of battle and in the final scenes the soldiers are anonymous. Each man is no more than a uniform, rifle and helmet. This reflects both the idea of the "5th Wessex" as a single family unit, but also the terrible toll that war inflicted upon its participants, tearing friends apart in the most dramatic circumstances imaginable. The impact of these battles, as shared by Baron, was recounted by one of the veterans who had recognised his unit's experiences in *From the City, From the Plough*: "Years after I used to disturb my wife with nightmares. I would wake up shouting. I saw a lot of things in battle that I will never tell anyone."

There's No Home: the friendship of the body

Baron's follow-up was *There's No Home*, based on his personal experiences in the Sicilian town of Catania. As noted by the reviewer in *The Scotsman*, it was "that rare event, a worthy sequel to an outstanding first novel."[3]

---

3 *The Scotsman*, Thursday 2 February 1950.

Published in 1950, it tells the story of an infantry battalion resting in a Sicilian town. Such was the publisher's faith in Baron's name following the success of *From the City, From the Plough* that there is no mention of war on the front cover of the first edition, although this changed for later editions. Instead the dust jacket simply showed rooftops. Indeed, the very first sentence of this novel is: "This is not a story of war." In many ways, the town itself is as much a central character as any of the soldiers — and the people living there seem indistinguishable from their surroundings. It was a bold move by both Baron and his publisher to follow a "war novel" with such a peaceful book.

Despite this initial claim, the book opens with an almost journalistic description of the arrival of the troops in Catania — both in terms of the visual depiction of the troops and the scenes of poverty in the streets around them — suggesting Baron's own recollections of his arrival in the town. Yet soon the reader sees the other side of these dirty, dusty men as one among them is revealed to be treating it like a tourist trip, revelling in the town's history and architecture.

Just as in *From the City, From the Plough*, Baron follows human themes from the perspective of the "ordinary soldier". His officers aren't caricatures of the public school types typified in many representations of the army. Instead, they blend in with their men, and one is revealed to be a former insurance salesman with the same sexual appetite as the men under his command. Similar to the blinding of one character in *From the City, From the Plough*, Baron takes the opportunity to kill off one of his most sympathetic characters in the early pages as the youth senselessly falls to his death from a balcony. Once again the reader enters the real world of soldiers. Their first interactions with civilians are to give them food, the next is sex. There is no room for romance in their world and Baron is uncritical of the loose morality of the soldiers and the women they meet, referring to sex as a "friendship of the body". He offers no criticism of the soldiers who have sex with a fifteen-year-old girl, instead allowing the reader to make their mind up and judge the men according to their own appreciation and understanding of the circumstances.

Beyond that, they settle down to have the women launder their clothes. The theme of laundry is central to the book. Baron even compares British army uniforms drying on washing lines to the flags of armies: for Baron the soldier's flag is not the one they march under, but the ones that flutters clean on a washing line, with the blood and sweat of combat washed away.

The soldiers are shown "warts and all". They are coarse and blunt towards Italian children, but still give them chocolate. They moan about the population but happily pay for the funeral of a child killed by a booby trap. These inter-relationships are real and vivid with Baron capturing the nature of the troops. When he tells the story of soldiers stealing watches he does not offer judgement, and does not even need to finish the story with the act of theft itself. Instead that is left to the reader's imagination. Similarly he steers clear of criticising the Italian civilians, instead presenting their behaviour as a recollection of inevitable events.

At the heart of the story is the character of Graziella Drucci, a young war widow, and her relationship with a British soldier. Graziella was very real, to the extent that Baron's own photographs of his time in Catania show a young woman believed to be the basis of the character. In his following novel, *The Human Kind*, he even revealed the true story of what he had fictionalised. As well as being very real, Graziella is also a device by which Baron introduces the reader to the world of Sicilian women. He contrasts their lack of freedom with the freedom enjoyed by British women. He uses Graziella's surprise at the relative freedom of British women to condemn the closed life afforded to Sicilian women and yet, at the same time, he celebrates the sense of community it creates.

In this book we once again see a version of Baron realised in the soldier who learns enough Italian to converse with the locals. Small details ring true, as the soldiers continue their lives as if unaware of the horror of what is around them. They chat as ambulances disgorge injured men and sunbathe on beaches littered with the detritus of war. The coils of barbed wire and graves remind us of the very real beaches where Baron's comrade had been drowned in an accident.

The Human Kind: born to put the world right by worrying

There's No Home was a critical success, with the *Illustrated London News* describing Baron as "the most persuasive of war novelists"[4] and one reviewer noting it left the reader "clamouring for more".[5] It also proved to be a commercial success and by the late 1950s Pan Books reported they had sold 95,000 copies in paperback. The success of this book —

---

4 *Illustrated London News*, Saturday 22 April 1950.
5 *Aberdeen Evening Express*, Thursday 24 April 1952.

though nowhere near as resounding as that of *From the City, From the Plough* — meant it was inevitable that Baron would write another war novel. This was *The Human Kind*, a selection of short stories that again saw Baron exploring the themes of men and women adapting to life in wartime. Though the memories are transposed to new locations, they have a personal touch, being told in the first person. *The Human Kind* is effectively a series of vignettes: part novel (in that the stories follow an identified, historical path), part memoir (in that it follows Baron's own experiences) and part collection of short stories (in that most of the stories can stand alone). The book does not identify its narrator except towards the end when he is referred to as "Alex". However, as Baron later wrote: "I have written three books about the lives of men and women in the war. I made use in these books of my own experiences as well as of scenes that I witnessed and stories that others told me."

Despite the use of the name "Alex", the narrator is not Baron, but a composite, an "everyman" who reflects the good-natured, positive-thinking men that helped make Baron's wartime service such a defining experience. These were the men whose comradeship helped divert Baron's politics away from the hard line espoused by the Communist Party. As a communist he had idealised "the working man", yet as a soldier he grew to love the ordinary men that he met, seeing them as fully rounded individuals rather than romanticised, proletarian ideal types. These are ordinary men who surprise Baron by their love of Dickens, Burns and Beethoven.

It is probably one of his bleakest works. There is little excitement, little action or drama. Instead we see slices of life in wartime. We see drunks who hate the world, passionately brief love affairs between men and women unable to speak each other's languages, boastful cowards and quiet heroes. As readers we visit smoky railway carriages, bleak Nissen Huts, the vineyards of Sicily and the brothels of Antwerp.

In *The Human Kind* Baron paints a variety of literary portraits depicting the men he had served alongside. These characters were good and bad, sometimes both. More than anything, as advertised by the title, they were human. In effect, they were men who carried on with their own lives, in their own way, against a backdrop of war. As Harry Ratner later noted: "They didn't really have any opinion about the war. It was just something that happened. And they happened to be in it. And they had to make the best of it. Any loyalty they had was an immediate loyalty to their mates."

The book begins with a seemingly unconnected tale, the story of a youth during the 1930s, taking part in a cycle trip into the countryside as part of a large group of local teenagers. This opening sequence reflects the freedom of youth at an age when "death is an impossibility" — a concept that was soon to be torn from the grasp of Baron's generation. In this introduction Baron constantly hints at the impending war: swimming in a river, the youths feel "the tug of the current against our own strength" as it pulls them towards a weir that surely presages war. When the rains come, they appear as if from the gathering storm clouds of war. It is obvious but realistic, reflecting the world that Baron had inhabited — where youthful political activity had also provided an environment to meet girls (a theme developed in his 1971 novel *The In-Between Time*). When the narrator falls from his bike and is injured, a cigarette is placed between his lips and he is handed a cup of hot, sweet tea. As Baron had witnessed so many times, this was exactly the initial treatment given to wounded men in wartime. In these opening pages Baron gives the reader a synopsis of his early life: bespectacled youth enjoys freedom, is dragged into the "storm of war" and is injured. But at the end he is ready to carry on with life.

The short stories reveal so many elements of war: the futility of kindness, the dislocation of society, the collision of cultures and the cheapness of life. More than anything, Baron reveals the careful psychological balancing act between the callous disregard for humanity developed by soldiers and their — at times — overwhelming appreciation of beauty, however small and insignificant. In Baron's world, good men grow hard and sullen, their manners and values changed, whilst quiet, seemingly inoffensive men, grow embittered - however well they are treated.

In "The Hunchback Woman" Baron shows the sexual ignorance of many of those of his generation, contrasting it with the antics of the older, more worldly-wise, men he served with. The story is loosely based on his own experiences and the tale of the relationship between a comrade and a local woman known as "Black Bess". In "Old Beethoven" he describes what one might call "the comradeship of shit": the often-ignored element of depersonalisation that takes place in every army as men learn to live together without embarrassment. In Baron's case it is the story of soldiers sharing a slit-trench, under gun fire, when one is suffering from dysentery. In one of the most important chapters, "The Pillbox", Baron makes reference to the Pioneer Corps and reveals how he and his comrades had so often been in the heart of the action. More importantly, he admits to the degree to which war changed him as — in another aside — he reveals how for years after the war he told a tragic story as if it were a comedy, forgetting that the punch line revolved around pointless deaths.

"Victory Night" is perhaps the most personal of all the vignettes within the book. The narrator recounts the story of Frank Chase, although Chase is clearly Baron himself. Whilst his unpublished memoirs and personal letters give snippets of his experiences in the final months of war, it is this chapter that brings them all together to starkly reveal the true effect of all he had experienced. In a glaring admission, Baron notes: "Frank imagined himself born to put the world right by worrying." It also admits to how "political theories" had "gripped him with the force of religious mania" but that he could no longer reconcile the dogma of his politics with the real world he saw around him.

It is ironic that *The Human Kind* took Baron in a new direction as a writer. For the first time, one of his books was adapted for the cinema. However, Baron — whose mission was to portray the realities of the British Army at war — would not see his memories on screen. Instead the film-makers did not believe the British soldiers were marketable enough for a worldwide audience. And so they became Americans. He had striven for so long to see the realities of war presented, it was a blow to have the British role subverted. When the film, now known as *The Victors*, was released he requested that publishers bring out a new edition of his book as well as the paperback of the film script. He wanted the serious reader, identifying them as the buyers of the *Observer* and *Sunday Times*, to have the choice as to whether they read his truth or Hollywood's version of the truth.

The shadow of war: rootless, drifting men

Despite the fact that Baron himself drew a line under his "war novels", neatly identifying them as a trilogy, some of his other novels found him unable to let go of his past. The London novels, *With Hope, Farewell*, *Rosie Hogarth* and *The Lowlife*, offer a view of post-war Britain which forms the literary equivalent of how British cinema was sometimes stronger when examining the aftermath of war and its impact upon individuals, than portraying the war itself. The power of British cinema to look intelligently at the aftermath of war, in films like Ealing Studios'

As for me, I have never worked so hard in all my life. I had hardly finished one novel and put it into the press when — while I was resting and wondering which part of the Continent to grace with my presence — I went mad about yet another, and started on it. It will take me at least till November, and as it is a very long, complex and delicately-woven story the labour is quite heartbreaking. I write and write, round the clock, tear up, revise, polish passages again and again, go to bed at one in the morning and — after lying awake for an hour — return to the typewriter at two o'clock and work on till daylight. It is all quite insane. I haven't gone out, even for the simplest form of relaxation or human company, for months, and am in fact merely a sort of human (if human is the right word) extension to my typewriter. In June I went to Devon, swearing that I'd take a month's rest. I lay in a stupor for a week, having a wonderful time in lovely weather, then I went mad again and stormed off back to London and the novel. I suppose the gruesome end of it will be that the book will turn out to be no good.

An extract from a letter to Muriel Walker (then Muriel Dobkin) in August 1949 — the novel Baron was working on was probably *With Hope, Farewell*

Frieda, *Cage of Gold*, or *The Divided Heart*, is as effective in portraying the genuine impact of war as most of the action movies of the period.

In particular, these novels offer men with two separate and fully defined lives: that of their pre-war and post-war selves. Just as, before the war, there is Joe Bernstein and after the war there is Alexander Baron — from pre-war Communist to post-war non-aligned left-wing humanist. And in between the two men there is the conflict that acts as a pivot in the lives of Baron and his characters. As Baron wrote in *Rosie Hogarth*: "It was the war — the war — that was when his life had been sheared in two".

One only has to look at the characters of Mark Strong in *With Hope, Farewell*, Harry Boas in *The Lowlife* and Jack Agass in *Rosie Hogarth*, to make the connection between Baron and his characters and the transformational role of the war. Strong, Agass and Boas are characters born around 1917 or 1918 — Baron himself was born in December 1917 — all of whom exist in the shadow of war, with their thoughts regularly returning to their experiences of combat and conflict. For Agass this comes in the form of bouts of drug-like memory that leave him mentally and physically depressed, appearing ill to those who see him walking along with his eyes shut, his legs trembling, his body shivering despite the warm weather. Strong experiences similar symptoms, feeling lost "in the street, and in time, and in life." Analysis of these symptoms might suggest a diagnosis of Post-Traumatic Stress Disorder (PTSD), something that might also be found in Baron's own discharge from the army with "psychoneurosis aggravated by war service" and his later admission that he was in an "unsettled state".

The sense that Baron himself cannot step out of the shadow of war, even when he is writing a book that is about so much more than war, is also revealed in a passage from *The Lowlife*. Boas, as the narrator, offers us thoughts that might as well come straight from Baron's mouth: "Who realized, when we were fighting for our own lives, what was happening? Who realized, till years after, when all those books started coming out? Believe me, I've read plenty of those books. I've had plenty of nightmares from them." This passage shows a sense of psychological conflict in the life of the infantryman, a difficulty in coming to terms with the experience of constantly struggling just to stay alive.

In *The Lowlife* Harry Boas is a veteran of the wartime infantry and a man devoted to the world of greyhound racing. He is the literary continuation of the so-called "doggy boys" — a group of characters in *From the City, From the Plough* who are dedicated to gambling and all of whom display the "wide" attitude of smart clothing and dodgy deals. Thus, in *The Lowlife* we are seeing a glimpse of the post-war lives of those who came "from the city". As for those who came "from the plough", Baron's published work does not reflect their lives. However, in his unpublished novel *Bugler Sound Reveille* one of the characters is a farmer, a veteran of the Wiltshire regiment which had been the model for the 5th Wessex.

Yet Boas is more than just an avid gambler, he is also an avid reader, just like some of the characters portrayed in the war novels. Baron shows what might have been the fate of some of the men whose worlds were portrayed in the war novels. Boas is a continuation of these men: some might have achieved all they searched for in bettering themselves through education. Baron, himself one of those khaki-clad enthusiastic readers, is one of the lucky ones. Others, like Harry Boas, are rootless. It reads like Baron's confessional account of how his own post-war world could easily have slipped into rootlessness. There, one might argue, but for the grace of God.

In Strong, Agass and Boas, we see an entire generation of servicemen who, despite their differences, have lives in parallel. Baron, whose own parents left London in both World Wars to avoid bombing, looks at how different his own life could have been had his parents not made that move. Jack Agass is an orphan of two wars, his father most-likely killed in action in the First World War, his adoptive mother killed in the Blitz in the Second World War. Upon his return, he struggles to cope with this new reality of life without the one person who had given him hope and a family. He tries to reintegrate into his home streets but always feels like an outsider, realising that he is yearning for an "irrecoverable past". Harry Boas's post-war life also pivots on the death of his mother in the blast of a flying bomb, leaving him without a clear connection to the streets of East London where he'd grown up, streets to which he keeps returning as if to find a trace of a world that has moved on.

These are drifting, rootless men: Strong has his souvenirs and his memories but has lost his hope for a better future. He spends his time wandering the streets of London "lonely and despairing". As his wife describes him, it's like being married to a ghost. She is right, as Strong admits he wishes he had died in the war. His wanderings reflect those of Baron in the immediate post-war period when he later admitted haunting the streets hardly conscious of where he was going.

The description of Strong's arrival in London following discharge from the military, arriving at Waterloo Station and feeling a sense of terror for a world that waits outside the station gates, is also a direct reflection of Baron's experience. In 1946 Baron had arrived in Waterloo and admitted to being "reluctant and frightened" as he left the station. A more extreme reaction to the situation was reported by a man Baron later met and whose feelings might have influenced the character of Strong. As the man told Baron: "It was lucky they'd taken my pistol off me, or I'd have shot myself sooner than walk out under that arch at Waterloo."

The sense of a need to escape from this life is reflected in *Rosie Hogarth*. Jack Agass returns from working overseas, something he needed to do to escape the loss of both his real family and the "family" that life in the army had offered him and to which he is tempted to return in order to avoid his loneliness. The theme of finding one's place within the world is central to Baron's work: he recognises the family atmosphere created within the wartime army, showing how it is the essential humanity of that "family" that allows men to survive in

Delores and Alexander Baron with the actor George Hamilton at the
opening night of *The Victors* in 1963

wartime — both physically through the protection and support that
comrades offer in the heart of battle, and mentally through the network
of support from men who understand the emotional chaos they feel in
the aftermath of battle. For Mark Strong, wartime service in the RAF is
the first time he develops truly deep friendships and finds himself
accepted as a whole person. Like Jack Agass, he considers, then
dismisses, a return to military service. His wartime friends are
considered "his brothers" who had, in their own way, replaced his real
brother who had been killed in action. This underpins the arc of the
story: in wartime he is an RAF pilot and recognised as that. In his pre-
war and post-war life he feels that he is an outsider, his Jewishness
hanging over his understanding of his place in the country he considers
to be his home and for which he has fought.

The theme of war as a pivot is less obvious in *With Hope, Farewell*.
Mark Strong gains confidence, both in himself and in his place in the
world, through his service as an RAF pilot. In the words of that
generation, it "makes a man of him". Yet this is torn away from him with

his crash and long slow recovery from his wounds. War has, quite literally, lifted him "into the air" and sent him crashing to the ground. It has lifted him psychologically by helping him realise his dreams, but then drops him again once he is discharged from service, returning him to the uncertainty of his pre-war life. His simple desire to live among good people, and to be accepted by them, is brought into focus by his realisation that he "had met so many of them in his lifetime and he had failed to truly see them." This realisation that he has a future within British society brings his mind into focus and he feels a sense of release from his own psychological burdens.

Where the theme of the pivot within *With Hope, Farewell* becomes interesting is in the choice of the date for the post-war section. The novel was published in 1952 and yet Baron sets this section of the book in 1948. Thus the date for Strong lifting himself out of his post-war malaise is the same year that *From the City, From the Plough* was published, replicating the date when Baron began his new life as a successful and respected author.

The clearest evidence of Baron's theme of war as a pivot in both his own life and that of his characters comes in the form of the title character in *Rosie Hogarth*. She is a Communist, an activist with a confidential role which reflects Baron's own past as a Communist Party member who, at the start of the war, had been expected to "go underground" if the British state had clamped down on the Party. Rosie is Baron's own past, his pre-war life, and the longing for her felt by Jack Agass reflects Baron's own struggle to move on from the pre-war certainty of his political convictions. It is the war that gave Baron a broader understanding of the world and which caused his split from the Communist Party, just as it is the war that takes Jack Agass away from Rosie Hogarth, and only once he has finally come to an understanding of her that he is able to settle down and move forward with his life. The certainty of Baron's decision to abandon communism is illustrated by the disdain that Rosie holds for the streets she has grown up in and the negativity she feels about the people of those streets. Comparing this to Baron's warm descriptions of these people, their homes and their lives, of the warmness of the relations among them, it is clear where Baron's sympathies lie. It is not that he is critical of her thinking, but simply he has moved on from how he had seen the world during the 1930s. It is in the words of Rosie's father that Baron reveals the impact of the war years upon his own worldview:

> "You're still young. Not enough has happened to you yet. When
> you've been bashed around a bit by the years, you'll know you

can't change the world, because the world's made of people and people aren't only made of flesh and bone and hope, but of savagery and envy and fear. All your lot'll be able to do, even if you win, is to pummel and pound the world around you till you've changed the shape of it, but it'll be the same world, with the same human beings in it, and the same yeast of good and evil breeding and bubbling among them."

The statement is a close reflection of Baron's own feelings in that period towards some of the Communist Party members living in his mother's street, whom he described as "earnest and good hearted" but "innocents".

The recognition that the real world is composed of people who are less than perfect, a process of realisation that Baron went through as a result of his war experiences, is perhaps best highlighted in a passage from *With Hope, Farewell*. In the latter stages of the book Mark Strong volunteers to defend his local synagogue from resurgent anti-Semites. It is at this point that Baron gives us a powerful insight into the British psyche. As Strong waits for an attack, he sees two suspicious men approach, one of them carrying a jack handle. They laugh at the synagogue, thinking it's not much of a building and that the Jews "with all their money" could build something more impressive. They laugh at the Hebrew inscription on the "Jews' church", comparing it to the imprint of bird's feet. It is the typical language of the anti-Semite, but only in the world of easy, stereotypical literary presentation. As Mark awaits their attack the men instead reveal themselves as railway workers sent by their trades union to defend the synagogue. They don't love the Jews but have got nothing against them. They simply don't want to see anybody under attack, or as they put it "Fair's fair." Then, in a typically British moment, they take guard of the synagogue and send him inside to make them a cup of tea. Those two railwaymen are the perfect encapsulation of Baron's world, one which reflects that human nature is more interesting and more complex than presented in political theories.

In later years Baron continued to explore many of the same themes, feeling that the lot of the average infantryman had still not been fully explored in the mainstream media in the post-war period. He was of the opinion that the films made during the 1950s and 1960s failed to reflect war as he remembered it. And, in particular, he felt that the film *The Victors*, which swapped his characters for Americans, had cheated his generation out of a film that was rightfully theirs. In his role as a writer for film, television and radio, Baron endeavoured to get onto screen an authentic version of the infantryman's experience. He wrote the script for a film that never reached the screen — *The Poor Bloody Infantry*. Set in Normandy, although based on events that had actually taken place in Belgium, the proposed film looked at a single attack by a single platoon. In his proposal he explained what was missing from other war films: "It is a lack of realism in detail which has spoiled British war films so far." Baron concentrated on the way soldiers move on the battlefield, crouching and hiding, walking with a stoop — the movements he had witnessed from men who expected incoming fire to hit them at every moment. He wanted to show wounded and dead in a realistic manner.

He also thought the actors should be taught battle drill to ensure they move correctly, "not just run fiercely about." This is something later film-makers have striven to do. A good example would be films like *Saving Private Ryan* or TV's *Band of Brothers* for which the actors were actually sent to a "Boot Camp" to prepare for their roles. In the proposal Baron pointed out explosions should be realistic, not just puffs of smoke. *The Poor Bloody Infantry* explored violent and controversial themes like a soldier wanting to shoot a surrendering soldier. As Baron remarked: "the keynote of this – I've never seen any film before that portrayed this – is suspense, not knowing, and waiting. Waiting, waiting, waiting, that is the real strain of war."

In order to fully grasp Baron's personal understanding of the terrible impact of war, the reader needs to look back to the finale of *From the City, From the Plough*. There is no dramatic conclusion, nor is the reader given a breakdown of who has survived the final battle. Instead it is inconclusive, with the reader left wondering who, if any, of the characters has survived. This harsh treatment of the reader reflects an earlier passage in which Baron refers to the way men come and go in the front lines and yet are hardly missed by their comrades, who are too engrossed in their own lives to have time to worry about the passing of others.

Perhaps the final words should come from Baron's wartime comrade Harry Ratner, who first discovered *From the City, From the Plough* in 2010 and was pleasantly surprised to find so much of his wartime world had been immortalised: "Reading this book, and now reviewing it brings back many memories for me. Fare well comrade corporal Joe Bernstein!"

Chapter 4
Jew-boys, Gamblers and Whores:
Commemorating the Holocaust in Hackney

Susie Thomas

As Ken Worpole points out in the first chapter, Baron grew up in a secular Jewish family and considered himself to be an English writer above all. Baron's youthful involvement in the Communist Party, the subject of Andrew Whitehead's chapter, had little to do with being born a Jew. On the contrary, as Baron recalled in his memoir, Jewish Communists thought they were becoming part of "a fellowship in which race was forgotten and in which all were simply comrades". As Whitehead shows, this turned out to be an illusion. In Chapter Three, Sean Longden demonstrates that Baron's first novel, *From the City, From the Plough*, was primarily about the consciousness of the common British soldier. This chapter begins with Baron's first novel to focus on a Jewish theme, *With Hope, Farewell* (1952), in which the protagonist, Mark, is torn between his fury at anti-Semitism and his hatred of the vulgar, East End Jewish community from which he longs to escape. Drawing on articles and interviews in the *Jewish Quarterly* from 1953 to 1963, this chapter will go on to explore how "Jewish preoccupations, obsessions, and symbols" gradually took possession of him. Although Baron said that this "wound" was at the heart of his writing, he struggled to find a "way of coping with it in literary form" ("On Being English and Jewish"). Baron continued to work through this traumatic history in his essay, "The Anniversary" (1953), which recounts his attendance at a commemoration for the mass deportation of the Jews from Paris in 1942. Finally, the chapter analyses *The Lowlife*, both the aborted film project, and the novel: a fast-paced thriller and gambler's tale, told in a voice both humorous and haunted; the only novel in which Baron used a distinctively Jewish voice and which convincingly connects English racism with the Nazis: "these haters of life. They can even murder babies".

It couldn't happen here

How would it feel to come back to Britain, after six years fighting the Nazis, only to find them on your doorstep? Baron had been present at the Battle of Cable Street in 1936, but it must have been a blow to find the Blackshirts staging a post-war comeback in Dalston. For over two years Mosley's supporters set up platforms in Ridley Road, spewing anti-Semitic venom with almost complete impunity, while anti-fascists of various stripes, including the Communists and the Association of Jewish Ex-Servicemen, attempted to drive them out. In two pieces for *The New Yorker* in August 1948, Rebecca West vividly evoked the hate-filled hysteria of the fascist rallies. On one occasion she witnessed:

> about a hundred young men and women, marching two by two and singing as they marched:
>
> > Two — four — six — eight.
> > Who do we appreciate?
> > M – O – S – L – E – Y
>
> It was as frightening as if the London earth had opened and there had risen out of it singing barbarians bedizened for some ritual slaughter of the innocents.

Baron's first London novel, *The Reign of Fear*, attempted to tell this story in 1949; his editor at Jonathan Cape, Daniel George, persuaded Baron to revise the manuscript, which was published in 1952 as *With Hope, Farewell*. When Baron broke from Cape in 1955, he expressed his gratitude to Daniel George for making him hold back and rewrite the novel. Nonetheless, in the correspondence between Baron and George in 1951, after Baron had made the revisions, it is clear that the two interpreted the novel very differently. George came up with the new title, which was borrowed from Milton's *Paradise Lost*, because he considered *The Reign of Fear* was "too portentous, solemn, intimidating. It suggests Hitler, the Blitz, and other things which people are tired of reading about".[1] George also seemed to agree with the readers at Cape who charged the novel with being a "tract against anti-Semitism" and "melodramatic".[2] In 1948, Cape had published Baron's Second World War novel, *From the City, From the Plough*, which became a bestseller. It is possible that three years later the public was glutted with Hitler and All That and just wanted to forget. Or, it may be that a novel about fighting the Nazis abroad was a much easier sell than having to recognise that fascism was alive and kicking in England.

With Hope, Farewell is set in the turbulent years of 1928–1948. It narrates key moments in Mark Strong's life, from his upbringing in

---

1   Daniel George to Alexander Baron, 7 June 1951.

2   Alexander Baron to Daniel George, 26 April 1951.

The onetime fascist leader Oswald Mosley addressing a street meeting on Ridley Road in Dalston, 1950 (Getty Images)

Hackney to his glorious career as a fighter pilot in the Second World War. After the war, unable to find a decent job, Mark and his wife Ruth struggle to make a home together. The climax of the novel occurs at a fascist rally in Dalston during which Ruth suffers a miscarriage. In the original version, Ruth dies, which Baron conceded could be considered melodramatic. In the revised version she suffers a miscarriage, a re-writing that is both more plausible and more symbolically resonant as we'll see. Baron was clearly stung by his publisher's critique, particularly because he had a profound aversion to any kind of "special pleading". He acknowledged that there was no point in complaining that he hadn't intended to write a tract, if that was how it came across, but in his correspondence with Cape he emphasised that he had gone to considerable trouble not to represent the Jews "in an unreally virtuous light" or to suggest that they had a monopoly on suffering: he had tried to show "everyone in the same boat, one human group turned against the other by the same pressures."

Baron certainly nails the pervasive anti-Semitism of British society. In the opening chapters (set in 1928) the Strong family cut short their summer holiday in Margate after they are frozen out of the boarding house by the polite taunts of their fellow guests: "Always, as far back as [Mark] could remember, he had wanted to be the same as other boys; he had no other ambition; always the word 'Jew' sprang up like barbed wire between himself and the world." Back in the East End (in 1935), a family wedding party is attacked by a pack of ragged youths hurling insults: "It was not the words that they uttered that made him flinch — he was used to such things — but the note he detected in their voices; a pitiful ferocity, born of misery and envy." Mark wants to explain to his attackers that many of the men in the hall are unemployed too, and had "pawned, sold, borrowed" to pay for these few hours of ostentation, but tribal loyalty compels him to beat up the leader of the pack. His first job is in a respectable firm in the city, where he thinks he is accepted by the other young men in the office, until one of them turns on him: "'It's always one of you! Whenever there's one of your lot.'" Overwhelmed, Mark waits for his friends to speak up for him but they huddle in embarrassed silence: "in his inflamed imagination they were all united against him."

The outbreak of war comes as a relief for Mark, who has always dreamt of becoming a pilot; he can barely wait to join the RAF. His wartime experience is a revelation: "He had come to mingle with young men of a kind he had never before known, cheerful, courageous and superbly poised. They accepted him without question, just as they accepted the Australians and Canadians who had come to fight, the Indians, the coloured Jamaicans, the beaming Czechs and the suicidally-daring Poles." He forms two profound friendships, with Bones and Davy, both upper-class Englishmen, and for the duration of the war he is able to say to himself: "*I belong*" (Baron's italics). By 1944, Davy has been hospitalised with severe burns, Bones has been killed; and Mark is badly injured when his plane is shot down.

Baron emphasises that on his return to civilian life Mark's struggle to find a job is "one he shared with millions of ex-Servicemen". Nonetheless, "the disillusionment he felt as a Jew who had come home thinking that the war had made possible a new relationship with his fellow men" is a double blow. It is one he also shares with Ricky, the hero of E.R. Braithwaite's autobiographical novel *To Sir, with Love* (1959). In his years as a pilot in the RAF Ricky had never encountered racial prejudice, but after the war he is turned down for a job for which he is eminently qualified simply because he is black. Despite having risked his life for the "ideal of the British Way of Life" he is seen as an alien. After his interview he steps out of a grand, imposing building in Mayfair: "disappointment and resentment were a solid bitter rising lump inside me: I hurried into the nearest public lavatory and was violently sick." Remembering the joyous celebrations on each Royal visit to British Guiana, he concludes: "Yes, it is wonderful to be British — until one comes to Britain."

Baron's representation of the effects of anti-Semitism on Mark's character is too psychologically acute to be dismissed as a "tract". Instead, this judgement reflects a reluctance to acknowledge the reality of English prejudice; a reluctance that was widespread. Betty Miller's exposé of the anti-Semitism in upper-class Gentile society, *Farewell Leicester Square*, suffered a similar fate to *With Hope, Farewell*. It was turned down flat by Victor Gollancz in 1935, even though he was Jewish himself and had published her first three books (on other themes). Miller, who considered it her finest novel, was devastated by the rejection. Although it was published by Robert Hale in 1941, it was soon out of print and remained in obscurity until Persephone Books reissued it in 2000. *With Hope, Farewell* is not Baron's finest novel, but as John Betjeman said in his review for the *Telegraph*: "it tear[s] the heartstrings" without ever indulging in self-pity. Betjeman likens it to Alan Paton's *Cry the Beloved Country*, which put the "case of the coloured people of South Africa" and concludes: "[*With Hope, Farewell*] is not propaganda. It is a human document which everyone should read. And everyone with a heart, whatever his creed, will be moved and encouraged by it."

The most striking aspect of Baron's first attempt to write about Jewish themes is not his indictment of anti-Semitism, but the way he bends over backwards to present the Jewish community in an unflattering light. Localities and characters that are recognisable from Baron's unpublished autobiography, *Chapters of Accidents*, and from his later novel, *The Lowlife*, are rendered here without any of his characteristic warmth and affection. Mark's family home in Khartoum Road, "is a noisy child-infested thoroughfare" of "decaying houses with gloomy basements": "each house is filled with the squawling [sic] and brawling of several families". It is a negative version of Foulden Road in Hackney, which Baron recalls fondly in his autobiography, and mythologises as "a proper little United Nations" in *The Lowlife*'s Ingram's Terrace. The "golden parents" of *The Lowlife* are merely an embarrassment in *With Hope, Farewell*. Mark's Uncle Moss, who has made a pile as a bookmaker, is a crass vulgarian — "his voice sounded like simmering fat; thick, prosperous, with a bubble at the back of his throat" — and a black-market profiteer to boot. He is a far cry from the genial bookie in *The Lowlife*, who bails out Harryboy repeatedly because Gus is "a good fellow". Gus has a library and appreciates fine wines: "You think a bookmaker has to be a fat ignoramus?" The old Jewish East End, which is evoked nostalgically in *The Lowlife* — "Hessel Street... the last ghetto market... I love it, the stink of home, of all that is good" — is anathema to Mark: "The voices of the stallholders sounded thick and raucous to him, their faces mocking and ugly. His own people! He hated them, clamouring to him with outstretched hands like Oriental beggars, screaming and supplicating for custom." Mark wants to escape his own people; "to live gloriously". Uncle Moss offers him a job in the lucrative family firm, telling him, "'You're safer among your own'", but Mark's only thought is "how could he escape?" The war is, above all, a way out from his family.

Baron's determination not to indulge in special pleading results in a portrayal of the East End Jewish community that is not so much "warts and all" as all warts. Although it draws on aspects of his life that also appear in *Chapters of Accidents* — the seaside holiday, the first ecstatic flight as a child, his own desire to join the RAF — it is the least autobiographical of his novels. It is also his only book to carry a dedication: "For My Parents". Philip Roth, an American Jew whose grandparents were Hungarian immigrants, has a scene in *The Ghost Writer* in which the father reads his son's story and is appalled: "'This story isn't us, and what is worse, it isn't even you. You are a loving boy.... You are not somebody who writes this kind of story and then pretends it's the truth.'" It is hard to imagine what Baron's bookish and gentle parents would have made of *With Hope, Farewell*, but perhaps the dedication was intended as reassurance: as if to say, "I am a loving son". In *Chapters of Accidents* Baron recounts how he had always recoiled from his paternal grandmother's anxious love and had written a story about her "as an act of repentance". "My Grandmother's Hands" is a touching remembrance of his *booba*, and a bitter recrimination of his childish callousness towards her, before he had learned "the lesson of love". It was published alongside Philip Roth's story of childhood rebellion, "The Conversion of The Jews", in Gerda Charles's collection, *Modern Jewish Stories* (Faber, 1963).

In the correspondence with Cape, Baron responds to the criticism that Ruth's miscarriage is "too loud" by suggesting that the real stumbling block is the evocation of the political meeting: "I find that most people who don't know what the atmosphere was like in north-east London in those first couple of years after the war... discount it as 'the kind of thing that doesn't happen in this country.'" Baron contrasts this English refusal to face reality with Americans who take the truth of his version for granted, and he cites the reception of Rebecca West's articles for *The New Yorker* as corroboration. In the novel, Ruth and Mark are attempting to avoid the trouble in the streets by taking a bus when it is overrun by an angry, panic-stricken crowd and Ruth is crushed. It is a dramatic scene, but Baron's letter insists that it is not melodrama:

> The number of people injured in this period must in fact have run into a couple of hundred, and a lot of them were not people who had gone out to riot, but ordinary passers-by. It was difficult... to make your way through any of the main thoroughfares without coming up against some roving gang of hooligans (on one side or another), or without suddenly finding a fleeing crowd bearing down on you with mounted police in pursuit. Several times, buses trying to get through Kingsland High Street were boarded by crowds of people running away from the police, who were themselves pretty maddened at the whole business (I know several of them), and would follow them on to the vehicle and lash out pretty indiscriminately'.[3]

After Mark's return from the war, Ruth is confused and frightened by his behaviour. The RAF hero she had married seems to have been replaced by a depressed and alienated man who barely speaks. She places all her faith in the baby: "her child was the clue to the future. ... Life must become better — nothing else would bear thinking of." The miscarriage symbolises a loss of faith in England.

But the novel does not end in despair. While Ruth is in the hospital, Mark prowls the streets looking for revenge: "Now, at last, he understood the men of whose deeds he had read about in the past two years, during the Palestine struggles, with loathing and repudiation, the tailors and the pedlars and the mild Talmudic students who, tormented into terrorism, had prowled like beasts among the dark alleys of Jerusalem." Later that night he finds himself at the Willoughby Row Synagogue, which he had previously avoided. Earlier in the novel he had refused to act as volunteer guard when local representatives had canvassed for his

---

3   Alexander Baron to Daniel George, 26 April 1951.

117

support against the fascist attacks. Now he is itching for a rendezvous with his enemies. Some cockney railwaymen arrive looking for "'the Jews' church'" but they are not the enemy; they have come to protect the synagogue because "'the world's getting more like a bloody madhouse every day'". The novel ends with a hard-won sense of solidarity and faith in human decency. Mark vows to himself to be a better husband to Ruth: "helping her would give him strength", and to try for another baby.

Although Betjeman praised *With Hope, Farewell*, most reviewers agreed with Daniel George at Cape that the novel was too bleak to be successful. It is ironic that Baron's first fiction about Jewish themes met with such resistance, since it was not a subject of his own choosing but one that was forced on him by historical pressures: it was anti-Semitism that initially made him a Jewish writer.

On Being Jewish and English

What do I know of Jewish life? Nothing. Is there such a thing as "Anglo-Jewish" writing? I change my mind every day. ("The Jew Inside Me")

In a series of articles and interviews for the *Jewish Quarterly* from 1953 to 1963, Baron grappled with the question of what it means to be an Englishman and a Jew. Unlike his father, Baron did not speak Yiddish and lamented the fact that he was "cut off" from the work of writers such as Peretz and Sholem Aleichman because so little of their work was translated into English ("As an Englishman and as a Jew"). At the same time, he said he had no more interest in keeping Yiddish alive than he did in "the preservation of Morris dancing. It is not that I am against it. I feel too remote from it for that." Although Baron begins by asserting he is only interested in Peretz and Sholem Aleichman for the same reason that he cares about Anatole France, or Mark Twain or Gorky, he later concedes that "it *does* matter to me that these writers were my fellow-Jews" (Baron's italics). For Baron, being Jewish and English gave him what Salman Rushdie, in his essay *Imaginary Homelands*, would later call the "stereoscopic vision" of being both an insider and an outsider: "I work as a writer in English. My upbringing is English. As far as I know my outlook, my prejudices, my feelings, are very much like those... of my fellow citizens. But, as an individual, I bring to my job a complicated mixture of perceptions, impulses, peculiarities of temperament, reflexes, ideas, ethics, that determine the kind of writer I am; and many of these things are determined, in turn, by the fact that I am Jewish."

Although Baron was averse to what he called special pleading, he acknowledged that "a Jew has grown up as a member of an insulted — even in this country — minority" ("On Being Jewish and English"). There are aspects of his childhood that would be instantly recognisable to the Windrush generation and their children growing up in England. In *Chapters of Accidents* he refers to the "To Let" advertisements in *The Hackney and Kingsland Gazette*, which ended with the words "no dogs or Jews"; and he describes how his family "flinched at Jews in the variety halls". Above all, Baron was dismayed by his Polish immigrant father's timidity:

> I was depressed when my father told me always to step out of the way on the pavement. It did not fit with my heroic dreams; nor did the implication of not being English. Some Jews respond to all challenges, of whatever sort, by pushing back, or anticipate them by pushing first. I have always stepped out of the way.[4]

As the son of an immigrant, who had lost a whole world only to end up a factory worker, Baron had to succeed: "Certainly [my father] saw me as the one who might realise his own dreams. That was in part the story of my life; not only my early life."

---

4 In an email to me Nicolas Tredell observes that this recalls a passage in Freud's *Interpretation of Dreams* where he is explaining his admiration for Hannibal: "I may have been ten or twelve years old, when my father began to take me with him on his walks and reveal to me in his talk his views upon things in the world we live in. Thus it was, on one occasion, he told me a story to show me how much better things were now than they had been in his day. 'When I was a young man,' he said, 'I went for a walk one Saturday in the streets of your birthplace; I was well dressed, and had a new fur cap on my head. A Christian came up to me and with a single blow knocked off my cap into the mud and shouted: 'Jew! get off the pavement!'' 'And what did you do?' I asked. 'I went into the roadway and picked up my cap,' was his quiet reply. This struck me as unheroic conduct on the part of the big, strong man who was holding the little boy by the hand. I contrasted this situation with another which fitted my feelings better: the scene in which Hannibal's father, Hamilcar Barca, made his boy swear to take vengeance on the Romans. Ever since that time Hannibal had had a place in my fantasies." (*Interpretation of Dreams*, Penguin 1977, p. 286).

Like Hanif Kureishi, whose father migrated to England from India, and whose protagonist Karim in *The Buddha of Suburbia* is the product of "two old histories", Baron was aware that "only part of [his] consciousness was shaped in [his] own lifetime. Much of it is the product of centuries of experience" ("As an Englishman and as a Jew"). Moreover, Baron knew that this dual heritage would bring with it a burden of responsibility, which he refused:

> I do not believe that Jewish writers have any special responsibility to write about Jews, or to create some specific genre of "Anglo-Jewish literature." At some time in his career, almost every Jewish writer is driven by his feelings to write about Jews. For the rest of the time, like every other writer, he looks rather at the whole wide world. Let that be enough. Do not tell him he has a duty to choose Jewish subjects. I am not a "Jewish writer." I am a writer, who freely acknowledges that he is a Jew. There is a big difference. ("As an Englishman and as a Jew")

The war baby

If the Battles of Ridley Road drove Baron to write *With Hope, Farewell*, it seems to have been a personal incident that led to his novel about the Holocaust. Mark's story never refers to the death camps; it is fascism on the home front which preoccupies him. And strangely, there is scarcely a whiff of anti-Semitism in *The Lowlife*: Harryboy has all kinds of problems, but being called a "Jew-boy", as Mark is in *With Hope, Farewell*, is not one of them. It is as if Baron had to work through these traumatic histories one at a time. He first broached the subject of the Holocaust in an essay for the *Jewish Quarterly* in 1953. "The Anniversary" recounts his attendance at a commemoration for the mass deportation of the Jews from Paris in 1942. He describes the groups of people standing about in the Velodrome d'Hiver, no more than a thousand: "there was no tension in the air, no atmosphere of sorrow, of reverence, no memory-laden silence." The well-dressed crowd chatter as if they are at a wedding while the dignitaries on the stage bob up down, scarcely heeded. A woman arrives in a taxi and stands near him: "she was too well dressed. … Her expression cruel and haughty, her carriage erect, her hands folded upon the top of her umbrella as if she were at a race meeting". When a small, middle-aged woman on the platform begins to speak nervously of how the mothers were separated from their children, the crowd hushes. She describes the bewildered and crying children and how the women "threw themselves like wild beasts at the guards," who beat them back, while the older girls soothed the younger children, who toddled away to the trains carrying "their little suitcases so solemnly." Suddenly a shriek pierces the quiet as the too well–dressed woman flings her head back and howls; the women in the crowd rock themselves "uttering that low, ululation of grief" that is the "distilled essence of women's sorrow, of Jewish sorrow." Everything is changed: the women with their proud carriage and fine clothes, symbol of their fight back to life, become a huddled mass of grief. Baron recalls that the woman's shriek "rings again in the memory, the dreadful, driven shriek of human loss, of loss that can never be made good." The fact that Baron tells this story in the present tense is chilling.

In an interview for the *Jewish Quarterly* in 1963, after he had just finished *The Lowlife*, Baron said:

> Perhaps it would be more useful for me to discuss [the Holocaust] with a psycho-analyst than with an interviewer. For many years after the war the whole business of the *Churban* [the Yiddish word for the Holocaust] had no profound effect on me. I knew about it, I thought it was a terrible thing, I drew conclusions from it, and so on, but *it had done nothing to change me* [Baron's italics].

> About ten years ago a personal incident — I am not concerned to describe it now — broke through whatever membrane of resistance had formed in my mind, and I was completely invaded by the knowledge of what had happened, by horror at it, and also at horror at my own superficial reaction to it all. Since then it has been the master obsession of my life. ("On Being English and Jewish")

Although a psychoanalyst would have been very interested in what Baron is "not concerned to describe," he was, in his own estimation, "pretty buttoned-up"; and he does not seem to have left a description of the event that triggered his obsession anywhere.[5] In his late teens Baron spent a lot of time in Paris as a political organiser during the Popular Front and it is possible that the "personal incident" is an allusion to the real life counterpart of the character of Nicole in *The Lowlife*: the Jewish girl that Harryboy abandons in Paris just before the war and who he

---

5   Alexander Baron to Adele Stone, 12 January 1992.

finds out too late was pregnant. He is haunted by the probable fate of mother and child at the hands of the Nazis: "I cannot forget like others do. You can forget a million children. You cannot forget one child." Baron's son recounts that in 1957 his father paid a lot of money for a charcoal drawing by John Bratby of a naked two-year-old boy, which he hung in the house: a portrait of sleeping innocence. In the sequel to *The Lowlife*, *Strip Jack Naked* (1966), which otherwise bears no resemblance to the earlier novel in theme or tone, Harryboy is still harping on a version of Nicole: "The longest I ever lived with a woman was a year. This was a French girl. She got too fond of me, and since then I never let an arrangement go on too long."

It would probably be pointless to speculate about autobiographical influences on *The Lowlife*; as a covert Communist, Baron was adept at covering his tracks. Nonetheless, he referred repeatedly to his identification with Harryboy, and as late as 1981 he was planning a television series based on him. As he wrote to his agent, Stephen Durbridge, he is "a character I have long lived with imaginatively."[6] Baron believed in Edmund Wilson's theory in *The Wound and the Bow*, "that inside every writer, making him write, is the irritation of a wound that can't be healed" ("On Being English and Jewish"). And certainly from Ruth's miscarriage, through Harryboy's son, to his last unpublished novel, *The War Baby* (1987), the lost child becomes Baron's most potent image of man's inhumanity to man.

It is highly unlikely that Baron had ever been an *habitué* of the dog tracks, although he may have drawn on memories of his Uncle Hymie, the black sheep of the family, who used to mysteriously appear and disappear throughout Baron's childhood. In *Chapters of Accidents* Baron recalls that later he found out the mystery: "He was a gambler". Hymie had enlisted in the Great War at the age of seventeen after losing all his money: "he had gambled then came back in khaki uniform". The pattern of his life remained the same: he returned home when he was broke, worked in the cabinet trade, and then left again. Baron's memories of Hymie are uncannily vivid:

> For long periods he was not to be seen. The grown-ups did not mention him. Then one day there he was, sitting on the end of the old black sofa.... As I see the little boy perched on his stool

---

6 Alexander Baron to Stephen Durbridge, 5 August 1981.

> I read in his face a tug of strange feelings. I imagine some
> current of recognition passing to and fro between him and his
> uncle. That cannot have been so. I imagine it because I now
> remember Hymie as *mon semblable* (Baron's italics).

This seems to be an allusion to Baudelaire's poem, "To the Reader":
"*Hypocrite lecteur — mon semblable — mon frère!*" in which "*mon
semblable*" is translated as "my double" in Robert Lowell's version.
According to his son, Baron was influenced by Dostoevsky's *The
Gambler* (a book he hugely admired) and probably by Thomas Mann's
Confessions of Felix Krull, Confidence Man (1955), which he also had on
his bookshelves. The reference to *mon semblable* may allude to the
parallels between the gambler and the artist, living outside respectable
society, driven by a passion that is often self-destructive. If Baron ever
had been tempted by the gambler's life, Hymie's tragic ending would
doubtless have been enough to put him off: "He remained a family
outcast, seldom seen. He died in the nineteen-fifties, untended and in
agony, of a burst ulcer. I saw the room in which he had died, in a slum
as foul as any described by Dickens" (*Chapters of Accidents*).[7] As Nadia
Valman shows in Chapter Five, Baron remained haunted by Hymie's fate
and planned to base a character on him in another novel about Jewish
East End life, which he never completed.

Although Baron acknowledges there was a personal motivation behind
his decision to write about the Holocaust, it took him a long time before
he could do so. Many historians of the Holocaust stress the period of
silence and repression that lasted until the Eichmann trial in 1961. It is
often argued that the trial brought the Nazi genocide of European Jews
into the public sphere for the first time as "a unique episode that has no
equal". From then on the Holocaust began to be remembered as an event
in its own right, not "simply a subdivision of general Nazi barbarism".
The decision to present eyewitness testimony by dozens of survivors of
the Nazi terror at the trial also created a "new public identity: the
Holocaust survivor".[8] It is highly likely that Baron read Hannah Arendt's

---

7   Baron may also have been thinking of his brother-in-law. Nick Baron recalls:
    "My mother's parents both frequented the dog races, and were permanently
    broke, and my mum's brother was a gambler who lost all of his own money,
    and lots of other people's money too. My father refused to have anything to
    do with [him]."

8   Rothberg, 2009, pp.176-177.

reportage of the trial in *The New Yorker* and it is perhaps not coincidental that *The Lowlife* was published in 1963, the same year as Arendt's *Eichmann in Jerusalem: A Report on the Banality of Evil.*[9]

Commemorating the Holocaust in Hackney

Baron would probably have agreed with Betjeman: "Without humour, tragedy loses its full effect". However painful it may have been to write, Baron makes *The Lowlife* a pleasure to read, and in Harryboy he found the perfect mask for material which was too raw to deal with directly. The narrator seduces the reader from the moment he introduces himself: "My name is Harryboy Boas. (Bo-as, two syllables please)." On the first page he contemplates taking a boat to the Canaries and calculates how long he could live there on a thousand pounds: "Four years. A lifetime nowadays. We should have such luck." He is a veteran of the Second World War, but if there is going to be an atomic war all he wants is a way out: "If they drop that big cookie I can always go down to the beach and swim out into the warm sea till I can't swim any more." It is not only the narrative voice that draws us in but Baron's genius for dialogue. Gus, the good-natured bookie, demands to know how Harryboy managed to lose a race when it was fixed and all he had to do was collect the money and go home:

> "You thought you were a genius? The prophet Elijah? You were getting your tips from the Almighty? … From me you got the tip. Not the Almighty. Why should the Almighty care about you? A lowlife like you? Did you ever pay a subscription to a synagogue? At least I've got a seat, you should know what I pay for it. You? An atheist, I suppose. Go on, tell me you're an atheist."

> "I am not an atheist."

> "A discussion now we're having about religion. Thank you. The intellectual. Thank you very much."

The reader is aware that Harryboy will always play to lose: "the gambler is the one who goes on with no peace, no release, till he has annihilated

---

9   Nick Baron notes that his father had a copy of Lord Russell of Liverpool's *The Scourge of the Swastika* in his library too (publ. 1954, and bought sometime around then — it was a very old tattered paperback). Perhaps bought at the time of his first "awakening" to the Holocaust.

himself," but at first we don't understand why. It is only gradually that the novel uncovers his secret guilt, which is confided only to us. To everyone in the novel, he boasts to keep up a front, although "[his] lies come flying back at [him] like bricks."

Harryboy's longing for oblivion, and his repeated failure to retain any material possessions, is connected to the fate of the Jews in post-war Europe, and the need to be exonerated of the guilt of surviving. At one point Harryboy considers becoming a slum landlord in the East End: "I could get a whole tribe of immigrants in here, straight off the boat, paying me a pound a week each to kip on mattresses on the floor. My golden future." But he loses the houses in a crap game: "Empty, the burden of possession lifted from me, I walked away."

The loss of faith experienced by many Jews after the war is evoked in an ironic exchange with the landlord of Harryboy's rundown lodging house, Siskin, who is terrified of being burgled:

> "What have you got for burglars?" I said.
>
> "When you got nothing is worst. With iron bars they hit you."
>
> "You should worry. Say a prayer. Sleep easy."
>
> "Who to, a prayer?"
>
> "You're a Jew?"
>
> "Someone looks after Jews? Since when? Tell me."
>
> "In God you don't believe now?"
>
> "God? Excuse me I don't know this gentleman. He looks after people? If this is his job he must be the biggest messer in creation."

In his interview with Ken Worpole, Baron described London as a site of "accumulated memory". He never experienced the camps, nor was he present during the bombing of London. But he mapped an oblique remembrance of the Holocaust onto the East End where Harryboy's "golden parents" used to live:

> I cannot come to the East End without leaving present time behind me and entering the world of the past. ... I walked down Cable Street — this once respectable street of working people that is now a garbage heap of lost, ferocious schwartzers and the wretchedest of whores — and I stopped at a gap in the decaying shops, and I cried. In the rain I stood and cried.

A flying bomb dropped on the house and his mother "vanished out of life": "I came home from the army and my mother did not exist any more. Not even a body. Not even a gravestone." Harryboy tries to walk away from the pain but "it was waiting for me in Hessel Street where she used to shop, the last ghetto market" and "in the tenement of dark red brick on the other side of Commercial Road where we lived." Harryboy's "mild and affectionate papa" died in agony from gangrene in the London Hospital, his eyes "glazed with bitterness". Harryboy and his sister Debbie left him alone to die: "This is how it ends. This and in a crater full of garbage. In Fieldgate Street round the corner I found the little synagogue he used to go to. ... He was a religious man. He was everybody's friend. Was God his friend when he died?"

The Lowlife not only commemorates the end of the Jewish East End with its markets, synagogues, and sense of community; above all, it evokes the trauma of the Jews who survived the Holocaust through Harryboy's guilt about the dead child who may or may not have existed and may or may not have been killed in the camps. The tenuousness does not diminish Harryboy's anguish but it marks his distance from the horror. Baron believed that only in this novel had he "found a way of creating a link between present-day experience and this obsession," although he worried that he had "introduced the theme in a too small, oblique and unworthy manner" ("On Being English and Jewish"). On the contrary, the indirect evocation of the Holocaust is what gives the novel its extraordinary power.

A major strand in the plot concerns Harryboy's friendship with a six-year-old boy, Gregory, whose parents live in the flat beneath him. Gregory becomes a substitute for Harryboy's lost son. When he sees a pair of Gregory's shoes in the corner, "[he] thinks of the mountains of children's shoes, the shoes of dead children, found in the camps, sixty feet high." He remembers that "they often sent the children away on their own, a cute Teutonic refinement. A baby whose father was not there to help him." It is impossible for Harryboy to marry, settle down and have a family, as at times he longs to do, because whenever he gets close: "in marches this little one, as jealous as any living child, and he won't let others in." When Gregory is injured in a firework accident, Harryboy is desperate to save him by heroically donating his own eye. But at the end of the novel he discovers that his sacrifice is not needed after all and "[his] great gesture [falls] as flat as all [his] other great plans." He is not allowed to atone for the past; the loss can never be made good.

And so Harryboy remains stuck in his room in Hackney. In the London of *The Lowlife*, Hackney is a liminal or in-between space. It is not the old East End of his golden childhood, nor the shiny suburbia of Finchley where his sister Debbie lives with her husband, Gus. They have a mansion and a Spanish couple to look after it; they eat well and drink fine wines. Harryboy loves his sister "with an ache" and she begs him "to be a mensch for a change, a settled man." Harryboy dreams of a home of his own but he cannot make the post-war transition to Finchley. Partly this is because he is still in deep mourning, but it is also a question of class affinity. When he looks at his nieces he sees the respectable future: "Terrible girls. All thin, all snooty, all the sort that flute 'Mummy' and 'Daddy' in high-class accents; they kiss mummy and daddy and feel a little more ashamed of them every year." There is a lot about the lowlife — the dog track, the Soho restaurants, and weekends with Marcia in Brighton — that seems more appealing than middle-class existence in Finchley.

Baron made the transition to respectable north London in 1972, when he bought a house in Temple Fortune with his wife, Delores Salzedo. It could have been the manor of Harryboy's semi-detached dreams: "a nice house in the suburbs. … a shaved lawn in front and a Zodiac in the garage". Baron first met Salzedo at Unity Theatre in the 1950s; they married in 1960 and the following year the couple moved to Brighton, where they had many friends: the thriller writer Vernon Beste and his wife Rosa; the theatrical impresario Oscar Lewenstein (a comrade from the CP days); the academics and historians of the Fabian Society, Norman and Jean McKenzie; and in the 1970s the writer Ivy Litvinov. It must have been in Brighton that Baron wrote *The Lowlife* and perhaps the love and stability of his marriage gave him the confidence to write his masterpiece. After their son Nick was born in 1969, his parents missed having a metropolitan base and they soon moved back to London. In "Bohemian Rhapsody" Nick Baron recalls that they kept the house in Brighton until 1995 for weekends and family holidays. His father would stay alone in Brighton during the week in order to work and after a day's writing he "would go for a route-march on the promenade, regardless of the weather. … He couldn't cook, and on his own would eat at cheap restaurants or bring in fish and chips." Even as a married man, Baron maintained a kind of double life or, at least, never settled into conventional suburbia.

The nostalgia Harryboy feels for the Jewish ghetto differs from some East End literature, which is hostile to modernity and change. Although

Harryboy lives in Hackney in order to be near his childhood home and to remain steeped in the past, he is open to London's transformation into a multicultural city. Baron is one of very few London novelists of this era to represent this change; most white British writers ignored it. He notes with amusement that Ingram's Terrace where he lodges used to be the home of "superior working-class families" like Baron's own parents. The houses have been divided into tenements and are now home to new immigrants:

> The children all play in the street together. I love to watch them. The children are the only real common ground of the grown-ups. The Yiddisher mumma who comes out with a cake for her boy will bring cakes for the kids he's playing with, black, Cypriot, Gentile, the lot.

Harryboy is keenly alert to the possibility of racial tension but says he "never smelt any hatred between one kind and another, not even an ember that might flare up in the future."

Although Harryboy is a loner, who can escape for weeks on end by reading Zola in his room, he is sucked into the life of his neighbours in the boarding house. When Vic and Evelyn move in with their young son, Gregory, Harryboy observes their penny-pinching respectability with distaste but also sympathy, because they are trapped; they have middle-class aspirations but no money. Evelyn's longing for the suburban family idyll is bitterly thwarted by having to live just north of Dalston Junction and when a black family moves in to the building she can hardly bear it. The de Souzas upset everybody in the house apart from the narrator, who says: "the trouble was they had friends"; they were "happy people", who invited their friends home after church. When Joe de Souza asks Harryboy how he can make peace with the other residents, he replies: "'You're living in the house of the dead. I don't know what to advise you.'" It chokes Evelyn when the de Souzas move out to a house of their own in Stoke Newington. At this point Harryboy associates Evelyn with the Nazis. With her snobbery and racism she comes to epitomize the banality of evil: "these haters of life, they can even murder babies."

Baron suggests that there is an affinity between the Jews and the West Indians, which comes out most clearly in descriptions of cooking and eating. After a succulent dinner with the de Souzas, cooked on the communal landing, Harryboy tries to explain to them why Evelyn hates them:

"You see," I said, "the way we eat, the way we live. You and me, Joe, we mop the plate dry. We suck the last gob of marrow. We lick our fingers. From our fathers and our grandfathers we know hunger, and we value food. In our blood we know that an axe can fall on us at any second. So we live. We live."

Michael Rotherberg's fascinating study, *Multidirectional Memory: Remembering the Holocaust in the Age of Decolonization* (2009) explores what happens when different histories confront each other in the public sphere and asks: "When memories of slavery and colonialism bump up against memories of the Holocaust in contemporary multicultural societies, must a competition of victims ensue?" Rothberg argues that although the Holocaust is frequently set against histories of racism and slavery in an ugly contest over recognition, the post-war period of decolonization and the consciousness of the Holocaust are intimately connected and this connection has the possibility to create new forms of solidarity. Nobody knew this better than Baron and his words about *With Hope, Farewell*, ring true today: "everyone in the same boat, one human group turned against the other by the same pressures."[10]

Women and children first

Soon after *The Lowlife* was published it was optioned as a film by Elstree studios, with Baron writing the screenplay. In the correspondence between Baron and Bill Whittaker of the Associated British Picture Corporation, they debated which story line should be most prominent: Harryboy's relationship with Gregory; or Harryboy and Marcia.[11] The significance of Gregory's story is not confined to Harryboy's guilt; it is a wonderfully observed exploration of human nature, and there is nothing sentimental about his portrait of the child. As Harryboy lies in bed he can hear Gregory downstairs, howling to get his own way: "A childhood is one long rearguard action of naked free will against society. Every fit of howling is a Famous Last Stand, an Alamo, a Thermopylae, a heroic little tragedy." Baron's war experience seemed to seep into his descriptions of everyday life and even coloured his description of childhood. One evening, watching a film about a famine in India on the

10 Alexander Baron to Daniel George, 26 April 1951.
11 Alexander Baron to Bill Whittaker, 24 May 1964.

television, Gregory asks anxiously, "'You won't give them any of our food, Daddy?'" Harryboy thinks: "Mankind naked — that is a child." Harryboy observes Gregory cheating ecstatically at snakes and ladders with amused detachment, but he is acutely sympathetic to the child's vulnerability. This emerges early on when Gregory shows him the toy town that he has laid out meticulously on the living room floor: "He pointed everything out to me, then he knelt over his little city and forgot all about me. He had stepped into a world of his own and now he made it function." Gregory stages a crash and an ambulance comes to take the passengers to hospital (trauma and recovery); a policeman stands outside the school so the children can cross the road safely. He is as absorbed in his toy town as Harryboy is when he shuts himself in his room to read Zola: "It was all a perfect, minutely-observed imitation of life." When Evelyn comes in and demands that the child tidy up the mess, Harryboy wonders: "What sort of life could his parents lead, that he was forced to create his own little world of order each day? And this woman, did she know what she was doing when she made him break it up every night?"

Evelyn's anxious mothering and her hankering after gentility make her a type recognisable from the kitchen sink fiction of the era: the woman who is more interested in tablecloths than passion or freedom or creativity. But Baron undermines this stereotype by drawing parallels between Evelyn and Harryboy himself. When the family goes on holiday, Evelyn gives her parents' address in Essex because she is ashamed to admit she lives in Hackney. Vic unintentionally exposes her lie to the other guests and the holiday is spoilt. Harryboy scoffs: "'Who do you get in an eight-pound-a-week boarding-house? The aristocracy?'" But Evelyn's fib is nothing to the yarns that Harryboy spins to Vic: "Oh, yes, I told him how I once lay down on a beach in the South of France, and got a hot tip from the man next to me, who turned out to be Aly Khan." Baron allows Evelyn to voice how life seems to her: she misses her independence; she enjoyed her job, the camaraderie of work, and she was well paid. The baby came too soon and now she is exhausted by poverty and Gregory's demands: "Well, there are two sides to every story, and that was Evelyn's." Although Harryboy disapproves of Evelyn slapping Gregory for playing with the children in the street, later he loses his temper and smacks the child himself: "I'd looked down on his mother for doing it, but I could no more help myself than she could."

The child both fights for life and is completely dependent on adults for security. The climax of the story occurs when Gregory overhears Harryboy squabbling with his parents: "He had heard the things I said about him, and his child's unfailing ears had heard the note of truth, of hatred, in my voice." It is an everyday moment of anger: "'I don't want him... keep him away from me.'" But to Gregory it is a devastating betrayal and the firework accident is another example of how everyday life echoes the war; it is as if Gregory has been injured by a bomb. Harryboy does not let himself off the hook with the "old universal human excuse, 'I never meant any harm.'" Evelyn probably never meant any harm when she complained about blacks moving in. But it isn't good enough. Baron said that he couldn't "summon up any belief in a Supreme Being, certainly not a benevolent" one, but that he loved "a religion which holds us to the idea that we shall be judged inflexibly by our conduct... to our *fellow-humans*" ("On Being English and Jewish"; Baron's italics). The adults' treatment of the child is the most rigorous test of this ethical code: "Perhaps when the species is no more, all the armies of human souls will wail that one excuse in front of the almighty, 'We never meant any harm.'"

Bill Whittaker wanted the film to end with Harryboy trying to donate his eye to Gregory, in a failed attempt to take responsibility. Baron voted for a finale focused on Marcia, "the classiest tramp in the West End." Harryboy tells us she is the "only lady I ever knew. She lives in Half Moon Street near Piccadilly and she charges twenty pounds for a short time." He can only "enjoy the best." When Harryboy is in the money he treats himself to a trip up west. This is when he lets his fantasies run riot. Going up west means browsing the bookshops on Charing Cross Road and lording it in Italian restaurants: "This is the ointment that soothes away all the bruises on my pride, closes the wounds of humiliation, heals my self-respect." On one of his sprees, he takes Vic along:

> He walked through the Soho streets like a kid at a circus. By my life, his mouth was open. The neon lights in the dusk, the smell of cheese from the delicatessens, of French bread from the bakeries, of coffee and gutter refuse, the girls in the clip-joint doorways, the photos outside the nude clubs, the rivers of cars gleaming in the narrow streets, the jostle of many people, the Maltese toughs on the corners, the blackies rolling dice in the side alleys, the restaurants, the boys and girls crowding into the jazz bars and the juke music pouring out — this fellow was Noddy in Toyland tonight.

Harryboy rounds off the evening by taking Vic to Marcia's for a night-cap: "Now he was sick with envy. Now he felt that life, a great mysterious feast — this sleek woman its symbol — was being enjoyed by others, by me." Vic doesn't know that Harryboy is paying for the privilege and Harryboy doesn't know why he is putting on this performance: "A man of forty-five offloading his sickness on to a little schnip fifteen years younger?"

My students tend to think that Marcia is the only female character in the novel with agency: for a start, she makes her own money. Harryboy may tell Vic that he's in property but it's Marcia who owns houses and rakes in the rent. Evelyn is down-trodden and bitter; the kind of mother who will love you as long as you succeed, and who is dependent on her husband to earn the money — which Vic is failing to do. Harryboy's sister is "dumb Debbie": an unconditionally loving mother, who forgives Harryboy however many times he messes up, but whose own children are ashamed of her. Debbie ruled the streets of Hackney as a kid, but as a Finchley housewife she doesn't have a bean. When she wants to bail out Harryboy — again — she has to "steal" from her husband. Neither Evelyn nor Debbie has any money of their own. Baron believed it was the writer's job "to be the spectator who hopes he can see more of the game" ("Seeing Life"). He saw how England was changing and how this was resented by the natives when he tells Joe "You're living in the house of the dead"; he also perceived female strengths which were often invisible to male writers of the time. From the prominence given to the women in the war novels, through Rosie Hogarth, to Marcia, Evelyn and Debbie in *The Lowlife*, his female characters are striking. Baron claimed that his interest in women's role in society was not a conscious theme and certainly did not come from his background in the Labour movement, which was reluctant to take it up. But perhaps his early reading of Shaw and Engels lead him to emphasise the importance of economics in female emancipation. Marcia could be sitting pretty, with her bank manager husband, who gives her a dream mansion in Buckinghamshire with tablecloths galore. But she is bored by monogamy in suburbia and wants financial and emotional freedom. Evelyn craves what Marcia has jettisoned without a backward glance. We know what Evelyn makes of blacks, just imagine what she would say about whores. But Harryboy tells us: "If I was a woman, I'd sell it." He admires and likes Marcia: "she chats to you like a man, relaxed and independent."

There are moments when Marcia could sound hard-hearted. Her devoted husband follows her to London to beg her to come back, but she bats him away with graphic accounts of what she gets up to in the bedroom. Charles is utterly humiliated by the recital and we feel for him but, perhaps especially at this #MeToo moment, the thought occurs that Marcia left him five years before and he is still, repeatedly, pursuing her. Maybe he thinks he is serenading her under a balcony, but she thinks he is a stalker. While the husband begs, Marcia asks him if he would like to come round and watch, but all the time she is gripping Harryboy's hand under the table "like iron". After Charles leaves, Marcia needs a holiday and she invites Harryboy for a weekend in Brighton at her expense. He feels like a duke: "She dressed smartly. She talked well. She could pace me in a fast four-mile walk along the promenade. Like me – and I respect this in a woman — she was not afraid to over-eat." Harryboy wins at Goodwood races and after a "wildcat session in the bedroom" Marcia confides that she will do anything to be independent but she's counting down the days until she is free: in five years' time she'll have an income for life and she can kiss goodbye to her "pitiful" clients. In a rare moment of vulnerability she clings to Harryboy: "'Hold me tighter.'" In the morning Harryboy orders flowers to be sent to the room, but she throws them in the waste-paper basket: "'I don't want that sort of thing. From anyone.'" He doesn't take offence: "thousands of men had seen her body naked, but it was intolerable to her that one man had seen her feelings naked." He doesn't want anyone to see his feelings naked either.

We might wonder why a West End girl would bother with an East End boy at all; she is not looking for love and he doesn't have a lot to offer. But as Baron wrote to Bill Whitaker, Harryboy and Marcia are "two of a kind". In his notes about the screenplay in the Reading archive Baron wrote that they both have a definite idea about how they want to live their lives; they are not drifters and wasters: "they are anarchists".[12] It is not entirely clear what he meant by this since neither of them is overtly political; it seems rather that both are gnawed by the sense that what is conventionally seen as the good life is not for them. Baron here seems to link the conman, gambler, artist with the prostitute as figures who live on their wits, outside the norms of society: it's an unreliable mode of existence but one that makes room for individualism and intensity. The climax of the Marcia and Harryboy story occurs when he steals from her to bail Vic out. There is a bit of dumb Debbie in

12 Alexander Baron notes, 17 April 1964.

Harryboy, but not in Marcia. She tells him coldly: "'I don't like being made a fool of, Mr Boas,'" and she sets her goons on him.

Baron's notes in the Reading archive are adamant the film "cannot carry the overtone that exists in the book: his guilt theme… Auschwitz etc. Is this a Jewish story? No." What? Baron spent years finding a voice with which to tell this story, why would he want to repress it? Perhaps he was worried that a movie would make this theme melodramatic and, remembering the reception of *With Hope, Farewell*, that it would look like special pleading. In the novel Harryboy's guilt is so deftly stitched into the story of the child that it only dawns on the reader gradually how haunted he is. How would a film capture the moment when he walks into the Deaners' living-room and sees a pair of Gregory's shoes and thinks "of the mountain of children's shoes, the shoes of dead children, found in one of the camps, sixty feet high."? Would they use footage from a Pathé news reel? Or send a runner out to Clarke's so they could recreate the shoe mountain in Elstree? Nothing seems appropriate. Baron voted for the Marcia plotline, he said, because it is a "straight human story", without any connection to the Holocaust.

In the end the film was never made, for reasons that remain unclear. Since the studio wanted to cast Harry H. Corbett in the lead role and Baron wanted to keep the Holocaust out of it, perhaps it is just as well. But it has always seemed a shame that the film was never made because, however flawed, it might have given the novel more prominence. The main reason that Braithwaite's *To Sir, with Love* is a Vintage Classic is because of the movie, even though Braithwaite loathed the adaptation. At some point in 2000 Hanif Kureishi expressed an interest in writing the screenplay of *The Lowlife* and it's easy to see why that would work: the ironic voice, the pursuit of pleasure, the sense of being an insulted minority, even in England. Hanif Kureishi also relished the way Aliboy, one of the first Pakistanis in London literature, outplays Harryboy in a game of craps for a slum in the East End (*My Ear at His Heart*). But that adaptation didn't happen either. So all that remains of "The Lowlife: the Movie" are Baron's notes and screenplay. They are a reminder of Marcia's importance to the novel, and the delicate balance it strikes between commemorating the Holocaust in Hackney and the pleasure of going up west. To borrow Harryboy's appreciation of Zola, Baron can "be tougher than Mickey Spillane, and when he gets on to sex he's red hot. But I'm giving you the wrong idea about him. He's a serious writer. Profound. Terrific."

Acknowledgements

I am grateful to Nick Baron for reading this chapter and for his insightful comments on his family history and the contents of his father's bookshelves.

The quoted letters are all in Baron's archive at Reading unless otherwise stated.

Sources and Further Reading

Betjeman, John. 1952. "An English Jew", *Daily Telegraph*, 18 April, 1952.

Baron, Alexander. 1952. *With Hope, Farewell*, Jonathan Cape: London.

Baron, Alexander. 1953. "As an Englishman and as a Jew", *Jewish Quarterly*, vol. 1, no. 2, 1953, pp. 10-12.

Baron, Alexander. 1953. "The Anniversary", *Jewish Quarterly*, vol. 1, no. 4, 1953, pp. 7-10.

Baron, Alexander. 1956. "The Jew Inside Me", *Jewish Quarterly*, vol. 4, no. 2, 1956, pp. 6-7.

Baron, Alexander. 1963. "On Being English and Jewish", *Jewish Quarterly*, vol. 10, no. 1, 1963, pp. 6-10.

Baron, Alexander. 1963. *The Lowlife*, Introduction by Iain Sinclair, Black Spring Press: London, 2010.

Baron, Alexander. 1963. "My Grandmother's Hands", *Modern Jewish Stories*, edited by Gerda Charles, Faber and Faber, 1963, pp. 151-57.

Baron, Alexander. 1966. *Strip Jack Naked*, Collins: London.

Baron, Alexander. 1988. "Seeing Life", Interview with Jeb Nichols, *Words*, December 1988, pp. 2-7.

Baron, Nick. 2016. "Bohemian Rhapsody", *Jewish Renaissance*, April 2016, p. 25.

Braithwaite, ER. 1959. *To Sir, with Love*, Introduction by Caryl Phillips, Vintage Classics: London, 2005.

Kureishi, Hanif. 2004. *My Ear at His Heart*, Faber and Faber: London.

Roth, Philip. 2005. *The Ghost Writer*, Vintage: London.

Rushdie, Salman. 1992. *Imaginary Homelands*, Granta: London.

Rothberg, Michael. 2009. *Multidirectional Memory: Remembering the Holocaust in the Age of Decolonization*, Stanford University Press: Redwood City, California.

West, Rebecca. 1948. "Heil Hamm! — 1", *The New Yorker*, August 7, pp. 24-37.

The Anniversary

(*Jewish Quarterly*, Spring 1954)

The Velodrome d'Hiver is a stadium on the left of the River Seine, in Paris. One day, in July 1952, I went there, to a meeting. On the same day in July ten years before, the Germans had begun their mass deportations of Jews from Paris. Thousands of people had been herded in the stadium, loaded into transports and taken away to the ovens. Today was a commemoration.

The city was radiant with sunshine but there was no sunlight in the street. The walls on each side were high; and the railway bridge across the Seine was overhead, shutting out half the sky. Pillars and girders, shadows, litter underfoot: it was a dank, cold, graveyard street.

Groups of people stood about, beneath the wall of the stadium, in the roadway, among the ugly girders. A wooden platform rose unregarded in their midst. There could not have been more than a thousand present. There was no tension in the air, no atmosphere of sorrow, of reverence, no memory-laden silence, no anger. There were only the groups, and the people wandering from group to group, and the taxis pulling up, and smiles, and shrill greetings, and laughter and handshakes; the same swirl and chatter that one sees outside a synagogue before a wedding. Here and there a lonely face, a woman's with hollow, waxen cheeks, or that of a skullcapped, bearded old man, with distant eyes, bore the marks of grief. No other face was conscious of the occasion. The shabbily dressed, the lonely, were few. There were paunches and rings and gold teeth, and good clothes and loud voices everywhere.

The speeches began. The groups closed in to form a crowd, but within the crowd there was the same hum and chatter as before. Voices rose. Bursts of laughter sounded. On the platform speakers bobbed up and down, scarcely noticed. Rabbi So-and-So. The Secretary of This. The Chairman of That. The Fraternal Delegate from Somewhere. Their bray of oratory was a background to the crowd's chatter, a rise and fall of sound that had no meaning. People grew tired of standing, changed from one foot to another, sighed with impatience. Some pushed their way out of the crowd to rest on the seats under the bridge. The speakers gabbled on. A woman got out of a taxi. She was a tall woman, with the heavy arrogance of cheek and lip and nostril of those who have no foundation for self-respect except money. She came into the crowd. She wore too much make-up. She was too well dressed. She stood near me, her expression cruel and haughty, her carriage erect, her hands folded upon the top of her umbrella as if she were at a race meeting.

The speakers were getting up and down. After each finished, there was a mutter and a conferring beneath the platform. An inner belt of the crowd, those who could hear the speakers, stood with their faces uplifted, staring at the empty structure. At the back of the crowd the shuffling and the strolling and the talking went on. Around me the conversations mingled. "... taking a villa at Antibes..." "... seven hundred thousand francs, she paid for it..." "Cabinet-making? It's a dying trade. Gets worse every season..." "... my oldest boy married their daughter last May..." "... that servant-girl drives me mad. But what can you expect of a *Normande*?..." They were all safely insulated within the present; a blessed, a necessary protection; the past, their own past, become remote beyond remembering, a dream, inconceivable. The story of torment and death was no more than an unheeded rise and fall of voices from the platform.

There was a woman on the platform; small, middle-aged, with large, liquid eyes. She looked around at the crowd. Her voice was low and husky. A man in front of me cocked his head on one side. He was trying to listen. Someone else said, "Shush!" It was her fright that attracted people's attention; her eyes, like those of the child which appeals for a hearing; her voice, nervous and hesitant. People were looking up at her, curious, quiet. A voice behind me: "Who is she?" Another voice: "No one. A survivor." Another voice: "Hush!" I could hear her now.

"... what was the worst thing inside the stadium, was that they separated the children from their mothers. I can remember as if it was yesterday. A fine day. The sky a pale blue. The sun shining. The faded grass in the middle of the stadium. It did not seem real. Everything that happened to us seemed to be happening in the middle of a holiday. On one side, in the stands, there were the mothers. And on the other side, in the stands, there were the children. The mothers cried for the children, and the children cried for their mothers, and the guards kept them apart."

The woman was looking up, as if she could see the past in the sky. The crowd was in a reverie.

"... among the children, it was chaos. There were little ones wandering about, four and five years old. They were lost. They did not know where they were. They did not know what was happening to them. They did not know why they could not go to their mothers, or who the big, rough men were who pushed them back. They could not blow their own noses. They wet themselves. They were hungry. They were thirsty. They cried. They became frightened, and they sat down on the grass and shrieked. They had all come with little bags and bundles and suitcases, and the guards had made them leave these things in heaps, and when they had to go and find their own they were bewildered, so bewildered, poor little things. We women, from the other side of the stadium, could see them wandering among the heaps of baggage, frightened, piteous, not able to find their own bundles.

"And the older ones, the girls of ten and eleven and twelve, began to take charge of them. They took the little ones under their care, so motherly, so proud of themselves, and they soothed them, and they found their bundles for them, and they told them they were going on holiday, to a nice place, and they must behave themselves, and they would soon be with their mothers again.

"And soon we saw them, the twelve-year-olds, leading the little ones away, in their innocent processions, like children going to school. The women wept and shrieked and threw themselves like wild beasts at the guards, and the guards beat them back. And over there, on the side of the stadium we saw our children, our treasures, our hearts' blood toddling away to the trains, to *those places*, and they carried their little suitcases so solemnly, and some of them turned round to wave goodbye to their mummies..."

A shriek pierced the quiet. It did not sound a human cry. No human emotions were articulate in it. It was as intense and piercing as the shriek of an express train's whistle. Hundreds of heads turned. The shriek sounded again and again. It was the woman who was too well dressed. She stood on the edge of the crowd. Her body kept its haughty pose. She still leaned forward upon her umbrella. But her head was flung back, her eyes glared like those of a maddened horse, her mouth was wide open, and the shrieks burst from her, the rapid, deafening, cloud-piercing shrieks, again and again, punctuated by quick, hoarse inhalations.

Two men took her by the elbows and led her to a seat under the bridge. Her shrieking grew weaker, and she interrupted it, from time to time, with a babble of heartbroken words. The woman on the platform was speaking again. But the shrieks had broken the protecting shell of present time. The crowd was stirring like a disturbed herd. I heard men around me muttering brokenly. A woman began to moan, "*Ai, ai, ai!*" in a lost voice, and other women wept, and soon, throughout the crowd, women were rocking themselves with their fists clenched at their breasts, and uttering that low, continuous ululation of grief, that incredulous, despairing, "*Ai, ai, ai, ai!*" which is the distilled essence of woman's sorrow, of Jewish sorrow. The whole appearance of these women was changed. Their proud carriage, their fine clothes, their trinkets, had been the way in which they flaunted their victorious fight back to life. Now they huddled, grotesque, pathetic, rocking themselves, moaning, their expensive hats awry, tears scrawling down through their make-up, the smart lines of their Parisian clothes disarranged, swaying, weeping, nodding to themselves before their Wailing Wall.

The tall woman had calmed down. She was whimpering quietly. They were putting her into a taxi. But her shrieks still lingered in the ears. They were the kind of sound that would always linger, lifelong scars of sound in the memory; that for us who had heard them, would become the difference between us and our neighbours; that would return, whenever we were lifted up by our own happiness, to chill the heart; that would sound in our minds when we saw the sunshine in a blue sky, or when we saw joyous and innocent children at play; a sound which, when the calm voice of the B.B.C. announcer fills the room, "Mr Eden said... M Bidault declared... Doctor Adenauer gave an assurance..." rings again in the memory, the dreadful, driven shriek of human loss, of loss that can never be made good.

On Being English and Jewish
(*Jewish Quarterly*, Spring 1963)

Alexander Baron, interviewed by Jacob Sonntag

Alexander Baron was among the contributors to the very first issue of The Jewish Quarterly, *ten years ago. Since then he was frequently represented in these columns. One of his finest stories,* The Anniversary, *appeared first in this magazine. His full and frank answers to the following series of questions, put to him by the editor, have a bearing on the problems with which all serious Anglo-Jewish writers are faced — and they are not very much different from the problems confronting all of us.*

How long have you been working as a writer?

I have been a writer for sixteen years. I have produced nine novels and eleven television plays in that time, with film scripts and journalism as side activities.

Basically, are you a Jewish writer or an English writer?

I am still trying to find out. The question is so big, and so much at the centre of my life, that I feel as helpless as you might if you were suddenly asked to answer the question, "What are you on earth for?" We have had a lot of writers' symposiums about this, of course, and for the last year or two I have refused to speak at any more of them. All the argument on Anglo-Jewish writing seems to me to be of the cat-chasing-tail kind, and a waste of time. The only way a writer can even grope towards a solution is through his work. What he writes will tell him what he is.

It seems strange to me that after sixteen years I have to answer so evasively. Certainly, at the beginning of my writing career I had no doubts. I was an English writer. I would have gone on to add, as perhaps some of the younger writers today may assert, that there is no contradiction between this and my Jewishness. After all, the work that established me was a trilogy about British soldiers. These three books have become, in a sense, classics. I don't over-estimate myself, or wish to make claims. But after many years they still sell in enormous numbers, they are used in whole or part as school books in this and other countries, and as their author I have come to be regarded as a

Baron's great-grandparents, Chie and Golda Bursztyn,
probably in Poland about 1900

kind of spokesman of the voiceless British soldier of World War II. My later London novels, I think, are as deeply rooted in the people they describe. I am English only in the third generation on one side, the second on the other, but I have the most profound emotional attachment to this country. The novelist's business is with the state of man, but he usually sees mankind through his own neighbours and I feel the same obsessive fascination in the English character, the English mystery if you like, and the same pride in it as — without comparing myself to these great masters — Faulkner did in his neighbours of Yokhapatawpha County, as Silone does in the peasants of Fontamara. People often ask me why, since I have freedom of movement, I don't live abroad. I can't for any long period. I can't even stay away from London for long. As a writer I am under the spell of the English, and particularly of those multitudes who were once known as "the lower classes", of their extraordinary virtues, their patience, moderation, courtesy, deep humour, all the qualities that are embodied in the humane and temperate progress of English society; and also by their vices, their ugliness, pettiness, the great national streak of Saxon stupidity, the Puritan poison in the spirit (there are also Puritan virtues) and the vicious prejudices of race and class which sometimes seem to me a purulence caused by the Puritan wounding of the spirit. I am a worshipper of the incomparable literature of England. I believe I spend more time reading than writing, and for most of it I am shut up in the treasure-house that lies between Chaucer and Thomas Hardy. I barely keep in touch with present-day novels, and don't at all mind not being in the swim. I am appalled when I meet younger writers, people of reputation and genuine talent, who tell me happily that they haven't read, or have hardly read, the classical English novelists. In fact they regard such reading as old hat, fuddy-duddy. The work of a writer, like that of a painter, doesn't only derive from life, but from that of earlier writers. Art is a process of handing down. Writers who derive from no-one earlier or greater than D.H. Lawrence are going to be awfully small people. I also feel an immense responsibility to the English language. I don't speak Hebrew or Yiddish. I think and dream in English. It is my greatest possession. Too many cried-up modern novels degrade the language. I believe that every writer, whatever his style and however limited his talent, must try with all his power to do honour to the language. So? Surely I'm English?

All the same, as time goes on, Jewish preoccupations, obsessions, and symbols have more and more taken possession of me and consequently entered into my work. I have to admit that there is a conflict here, perhaps an insoluble one. Perhaps this conflict is what makes me write. I have always believed in the theory put forward by Edmund Wilson in *The Wound and the Bow* that inside every writer, making him write, is the irritation of a wound that can't be healed.

The Jew — a Born Critic

Why do the Jewish obsessions conflict with the English obsessions? And how do they enter into your work?

Two thousand years of history have made the Jew, however assimilated he may be, into a nationality, into an incurable outsider. Or perhaps I should say that part of him is an outsider — the outsider living inside the insider. I don't want to be sentimental about the Jew. Those two thousand years have made him into a strange animal. Scoop up a handful of Jews and you will find some of the ugliest human characteristics in the most exaggerated form. But you will also find certain virtues in heightened form. For instance, the lack of statehood, of chauvinism, and the continuous experience of suffering, the dispersion of the Jewish people and of thousands of individual Jewish families have made it easier for a Jew to have a more universal outlook than his fellow-countrymen, even if he is no less patriotic. Bitter experience has taught him the need for tolerance. He is less likely to be taken in by propaganda (Mr. Khrushchev is said to have complained that a Jew always asks "Why?") because he has heard it all before. In fact I'd sum it up, rather than continue this catalogue of qualities, by suggesting that whereas people generally have no sense of the past and their minds live in small parishes, Jews are dominated by a long past and by its lessons, and they are forced to encompass the whole world in their view. All this makes the Jew a born critic. In short, an outsider. It may be said in reply that every writer, even the most 'inside' and integrated of men or women, has to be at the same time an outsider in the nature of things. The mere taking up of a position from which to observe other people, the act of lending form to a work, implies judgment, criticism. Well, yes, but then we have to add to this that a Jew has grown up as a member of an insulted — even in this country — minority, as the heir to an appalling history of persecution, as the witness (and surely fellow-victim) of the gas chambers, as the bearer of the knowledge that, even after the gas chambers, the human species, even some of the nations that fought Hitler, can still persecute Jews. And if he is religious, he has been brought up in a faith that, unlike any other I know, imposes on each human being, without the get-outs of after-lives or pardon easily bought by prayers, the responsibility of acting rightly during this lifetime. Is it too much to say that in a Jewish writer you may well find the moral sense and the sensitivity not only to all human suffering but to all human weakness, unbearably intensified?

In my own work — who knows? I don't believe that a novel should contain overt preachment, but my intention is always didactic. It's not my place to say now what that intention is. In the first place, books should speak for themselves. In the second place, a writer often doesn't know what he has really said. This he may learn, perhaps with surprise, from other people. After all, when he writes he doesn't set down thoughts that are already clear in his head. He is beset by a vague conflict of perceptions, moods, ideas, and his work is a combined struggle to make something clear to himself and communicate something to other people.

Certainly I find myself again and again using a Jewish character as a critical spokesman, a chorus to the drama. This is the role of Trifon in my historical novel, *The Golden Princess*. In my television play, *The Harsh World*, the little Jewish furrier speaks what is in effect a moral epilogue. In my new novel, *The Lowlife*, the central character, Harryboy Boas, plays a complex part which no other than a Jew could have fulfilled. He himself has to have sufficient vision, sufficient inherited wisdom — even poetry, in a sense — to comment with sufficient clarity on the action of the story. He embodies in his own person a number of universal problems, above all, that of guilt — and the supreme symbol of guilt in our times, as seen in the book, is the mass murder of Jewish children by the Nazis. He is, though he is scarcely aware of it, a religious Jew, which reinforces his critical position. And in his relation to the English family, the Deaners, he is able to view from the outside the whole complex of character and *mores* that they represent.

"A Symbol of the State of Man"

Do you think the present upsurge of Jewish writing is significant?

Yes, because it is not only an upsurge of writing by Jews. It's extraordinary how many non-Jewish novelists today are using Jewish experience and Jewish characters. Perhaps I've already made the reason clear. The word "Jew" has become a sort of shorthand symbol for the whole present state of man. It was for some decades a weakness of the English novel, and it still is to some extent, that only a minority of the best writers concerned themselves with the state of man (which, whether on the world scale or seen in the proverbial grain of sand, is the real business of a novel). They were content with the comedy of manners, the particular observation of small actions and minor emotions. Nowadays more English writers are probing more deeply, or if you like, reaching out farther. I don't think it's merely the war-time massacre of the Jews that has awakened them. Being human, they (or most of them) might have forgotten that easily enough. It's the fact that hundred-megaton bombs are now standing ready to go off. The hydrogen bomb has been a powerful awakener of the literary conscience. An example of this use of the Jew? Well, to me the most formidable English writer is not an Englishman but an Australian, Patrick White, and I commend his novel *Riders in the Chariot* to anyone who is interested in this question.

Obsession with the Past

What has been the impact on your work of the wartime destruction of the Jews in Europe?

Perhaps it would be more useful to discuss this question with a psycho-analyst than with an interviewer. For many years after the war the whole business of the *Churban* [The Destruction] had no profound effect on me. I knew about it, I thought it was a terrible thing, I drew conclusions from it, and so on, but *it had done nothing to change me.*

About ten years ago a personal incident — I am not concerned to describe it now — broke through whatever membrane of resistance had formed in my mind, and I was completely invaded by the knowledge of what had happened, by horror at it, and also by horror at my own previous superficial reaction to it all. Since then it has been the master obsession of my life. It is a literal truth that at the present time not a single day passes without some thought or picture of the *Churban* assailing me. It is usually a picture. Sometimes I go off into a train of generalised thought about it, but mostly one small sharp film or photograph appears in my mind — for instance, I see again and again the children of the Warsaw Jewish Orphanage marching through the streets on their way to the death train; or I see myself in a room with my own family waiting for the S.S. to come, and trying to imagine (to hear, rather) what I am saying to my parents and my wife. It penetrates and darkens every moment of pleasure, a wedding dinner, say, or an afternoon on a Mediterranean beach. At such moments of course there is a complex reaction. I feel that the moment of anguish is itself a

146

hypocrisy, for it passes and I go on enjoying myself. I go on living. One accuses one's self at such times of using even pain as a form of self-indulgence, of easy absolution.

At one level it seems to me that the effect on my work is negative. I can see no way of coping with it in literary form. I try to find a way of doing so, often, if only in the hope of freeing myself a little from the obsession. No, what happens to me is that I can't write about it, but it stops me writing about anything at all for quite long periods. There are times when I can do nothing but walk about in the streets brooding about it and looking at the films inside my head.

It does keep on invading my work. You know, when mentally disturbed people are invited to write or draw, they introduce into whatever they do symbols — words or pictures, always the same — deriving from their own state. In the same way, whatever I write, on any subject, I find myself in the first draft introducing some reference-back to the Nazi holocaust. When I revise I recognise that it is quite out of place in this particular piece of work, and delete it.

Only in my new novel, *The Lowlife*, have I found a way of creating a link between present-day experience and this obsession. Even then, one perceptive critic (I am speaking before publication day and this was in a discussion on the manuscript) told me that this element was an intrusion into the book; and while I do not agree, I wonder myself if I have introduced the theme in a too small, oblique and unworthy manner.

Yet this tendency of mine, this neurotic tendency if you like, has a seed of rightness in it. The *Churban* was not a private Jewish experience. It was not one of many comparable and terrible historical episodes. It is different in kind from anything else we have seen. It calls into question most of our previous assumptions about civilization, about how far man has got in the twentieth century, about the very nature of man. And what is the fundamental job of writers? Whatever area of reality we explore, in whatever genre or mood we write, we are all (if we are of serious intention) research workers adding our small findings, our personal illuminations, to the great self-exploration of man, the attempt to learn what the real nature and destiny of the species is. And this being the case, how can we, who have lived in the time of the *Churban*, sidestep it? How can we fail to take it into account when we are making *any* statement about the human kind? Even if we don't write a word about it, we must give some evidence that it is present in our consciousness.

So that, after all, I come to wonder why *all* writers aren't obsessed as I am. Perhaps it's a good thing that they're not. However I look for it, and I think I have a right to look for it, in other people's work, and especially in the work of those talented young Jewish writers who were only children or even babies when all this happened. I don't expect them necessarily to deal with it. I do hope for some clue, however obscure and indirect, to awareness, not only because they are Jews but because they are writers — spokesmen.

In this connection it is again interesting to look at the work of Gentile writers. A Pole told me that in his country the great obsession of the younger writers is with the Jew, the Jewish suffering. "The years go by," he said, "but they can't break out of it. They can't get away from it." I understand that the same is true of Czech and Yugoslav writers and film-makers, although in all three countries the writers are criticised and even attacked by the authorities for their "obsession with the past". Of course they are — because it isn't the past, it's still the present. The questions posed by the *Churban* are still not answered. The behaviour of man in that time may be a clue to how he will behave in the future, with H-bombs in his hands. A Pole cannot work out an attitude to his own countrymen without thinking about the Jews. How can he create characters without wondering if they were indifferent, if they were among the heroic few who helped, or if they were like those Poles who jeered from the pavements at the marching column of Jewish infants (I'm thinking again of that terrible day when they took the children from the orphanage) and shouted to them that they were going to the ovens? This thing has become a kind of chemical test for human character.

I spoke of Patrick White. I'd like to refer to another British writer — at his best, one of the greatest, Evelyn Waugh. As a man he is an extreme conservative, in political jargon a "reactionary". As an artist he can confront the truth fearlessly, as he did in his merciless self-analysis, *The Ordeal of Gilbert Pinfold*. But I'm concerned now with his magnificent war-time trilogy, a work in which he illuminates a whole complex of human problems and exposes his personal vision of the present state of man. The final climax to the last volume is provided by the encounter, at the very end of the war, of his hero Guy Crouchback with a group of doomed Jews. This is the final test to which Crouchback is subjected, and Guy, whom the author has portrayed as the ordinary sinning man *who is trying to be a good man*, takes their side, in vain as it happens. The last summing-up of the trilogy is a sad antiphony between

Crouchback and a Jewish woman. This is what I'm getting at — when Waugh came to seek the ultimate symbol, he couldn't choose any other than this one.

Religion as a Code of Living

You have mentioned the Jewish religion. Is your Jewishness as a writer based merely on the awareness of the Jewish experience or on Judaism?

On Judaism. My attitude to the Jewish religion is highly personal and perhaps not acceptable to the Orthodox. I don't practise, though I sometimes think I ought to, and respect those who do. After all, if you accept a religion it is impossible to practise it on the family or community scale without its framework of observance and ritual; and above all, there must be disciplines.

I can't summon up any belief in a Supreme Being, certainly not in a benevolent Supreme Being. All the theological explanations of why He looked the other way while children were being herded into Auschwitz do not impress me.

But I am impressed by that aspect of Judaism which represents the most advanced ethical point yet reached by a primitive species. I now believe that multitudes of people can only take hold of a code for living in the form of religion, never a philosophy. Where an attempt is made, as with Marxism, to imbue them with a philosophy, the philosophy turns into a primitive, cruel religion. A monotheistic religion which teaches that perfection exists, that Justice exists, that Law is above man, and which embodies these concepts in the name of God, is (or could be) a profound instrument for human enlightenment. Man, even if he remains for ever imperfect, can only save himself from the pit by aspiring to a perfection that is beyond his reach. Something of this has survived in Judaism, and helped to form Jews for two thousand years. Jewish prayer, unlike Christian prayer, is not an incessant plea for favours, but is always in one form or another a pledge of submission, to the Divinity, that is to the *Ideal*. I love a religion which holds us to the idea that we shall be judged inflexibly by our conduct on earth — that is by *our conduct to our fellow-humans*, which does not degrade itself with the claptrap of death-bed absolutions and similar methods by which the wicked can buy the illusion of pardon, and which holds that

149

the salvation we earn is not in the form of an after-life but in the future of all humanity (for this, in spite of popular accretions, is the essence of the highest Jewish thinking). This is surely a good code for people to live by. Maybe, too (critics are always bemoaning the fact that modern writers, unlike the Victorians, have no firm framework of belief within which to work) — maybe it's a good code for writers to write by.

The Short Story for a Large Audience

You have twice mentioned television plays as part of your serious work. Do you regard them as such?

Yes. To me, basically, the television play is a short story (for which a dramatic form has been found). The television people, who like film people are always preaching the uniqueness of the medium, regarded this as a heresy when I first used to say it. But I was glad to note recently that two fine dramatists, John Mortimer and Alun Owen, both defined the T.V. play as a short story.

The short story as a prose form is almost dead. If I write one, there are only a couple of magazines which might print it. (I am thinking of stories from ten to thirty thousand words long, not of the short piece, for which the superior weeklies still occasionally find room.) Thus, a writer would be lucky to get one story published in a year. Besides this, he can publish his stories in volume form. This is purely a prestige thing, for the benefit of critics and other writers. If he sells five thousand of a volume of short stories he is lucky. I did, in fact, publish one such volume, *The Human Kind*, which became a best-seller and is being filmed, but as it consisted mostly of war stories it was a special case. To me, a large audience, or at least, the potentiality of a large audience, is essential. Since I am a didactic writer, I want to be heard. I turned to television as a means of presenting stories (those suitable to this form) to a large audience. The industry has been very good to me, and has allowed me to write absolutely without censorship or interference, and my plays have gained huge audiences. Plans are at present being made for their publication, in two or three volumes. I shall regard these as books of short stories, and I hope my readers will look on them in the same way.

What is the impact of Israel on your work?

None. I am myself deeply interested in Israel. I have painful hopes for it and, I may add, no small fears. But I've tried to show that a writer lives in a world, a vision, that is not of his conscious creating, and so far — I can't say what will happen in the future — the fact of Israel hasn't entered into my writer's imaginative world.

Baron's maternal grandparents, Isaac and Jane Levinson

Chapter 5
Whose Law Runs Here?
Alexander Baron and the Mysteries of Bethnal Green
Nadia Valman

At the time of its publication in 1969, Alexander Baron's *King Dido* was boldly original. Historical fiction was relatively unusual and portraits of the metropolitan working class of yesteryear even more rare. But even today, when the genre is so familiar, the book stands out for its detailed evocation of the physical environment and social atmosphere of a single London locality. As this chapter will discuss, Baron drew on personal and literary sources to reconstruct the look and feel of a place that had undergone dramatic transformation since the early twentieth century but where patterns of social life and class identity had left deep traces in the present. His research for and revisions of the novel, moreover, suggest a preoccupation with the meaning of place both in his own family history and in the history of east London's working class.

King Dido begins with Baron's earliest childhood memories. In his memoir, *Chapters of Accidents*, Baron recalls his grandfather's cobbler shop in Hare Street (now Cheshire Street), Bethnal Green, in the 1920s which, he gathered from snatches of adult conversation, was "under the protection of 'them', a family of hard cases somewhere down the street." His grandfather "did not pay for this" Baron added, "they had taken a liking to him."[1] From this single remembered detail Baron was to build the masterful tale of the rise and fall of Dido Peach, a Hare Street gangster, and his nemesis, the ambitious detective inspector William Merry. The novel undoubtedly took inspiration, too, from contemporary Bethnal Green. Beginning in May 1968 (after several inconclusive trials for extortion and police corruption) until their conviction in March 1969, the Kray twins, notorious local protection racketeers, were front page news daily.

But *King Dido* emerged from historical sources too. Although it is informed by Baron's recollections, the novel's action begins in a period before he was born — in 1911, a year of political unrest in east London with the police siege of anarchists in Sidney Street in January and the docker's strike in August. This atmosphere of antagonism is echoed in

---

1 Alexander Baron, *Chapters of Accidents. A Memoir*, unpublished final typescript, August 1997, p.36.

the protagonist who, despite having no class solidarity and disdaining radical politics, maintains a fierce resistance to authority. Finally, *King Dido* also draws from Baron's long immersion in Victorian fiction, looking in particular to a late nineteenth-century precursor, Arthur Morrison's *A Child of the Jago* (1896). Set in the same area, Morrison's novel thrilled its Victorian readers with a portrait of a world in which respectable bourgeois values were inverted. Revisiting Morrison's urban realism, I will argue, gave Baron a narrative form for exploring the relationship between individuals and their environment.

Alexander Baron's East London

Alexander Baron's writing returned repeatedly to the east London of his youth, not through the blurred vision of nostalgia but with a sharp eye for the distinctive character of its different neighbourhoods. In *The Lowlife* (1963) the narrator observes contemporary Dalston returning to its original identity as a respectable working-class suburb, in which new Caribbean immigrants, "the Victorian residents of this street, come back a century later, with black skins," embody the hardworking, churchgoing ethos of the locality.[2] Baron's autobiographical story "My Grandmother's Hands" (1963) remembers his two grandmothers who lived in Spitalfields and Bethnal Green. The Spitalfields grandmother sat in a kitchen chair in front of her house, a home that was always full of children, while the Bethnal Green grandmother "sat alone in a silent back room behind her husband's shop."[3] The personalities of the two grandmothers — the warm conviviality of one and the chilly austerity of the other — are also closely associated with the places where they live.

Geographical realism is never merely setting in Baron's fiction. In *King Dido*, memories of East End markets are transformed into interpretive descriptions of place. The bird market in Sclater Street where Dido wanders with his younger brother Shonny "echoed with the din of singing birds, crowing poultry and screaming parrots," pointing to a feral presence in the urban environment.[4] A walk through

---

2 Alexander Baron, *The Lowlife* (London: Black Spring Press, 2010; first publ.1963), p.12.

3 Alexander Baron, 'My Grandmother's Hands' in Gerda Charles, ed., *Modern Jewish Stories* (London: Faber and Faber, 1963), pp.151-157 (p.151).

4 Alexander Baron, *King Dido* (Nottingham: New London Editions, 2009; first publ. 1969), p.223.

Whitechapel market, where crowds surge and trading continues despite a snowstorm, suggests the vigorous entrepreneurial energy at the heart of the East End. "Rabbit Marsh", where Dido lives, is also drawn from memory: "a narrow ravine whose floor consists of worn cobbles running between pavements of uneven flags." The walls of the buildings on either side, blackened by soot from the railway and interrupted by bare windows "which stared blind, black and grimy against the sunlight", are "dark cliffs…leaning forward with age, cleft by an alley here and there or pierced at the base by a porch leading into a yard." Baron's description of Rabbit Marsh adapts his early impressions of Hare Street, still imprinted with the child's perspective in which three-storey buildings appear as giant cliffs hanging over a deep ravine. But while *Chapters of Accidents* records the excitement that the sight and smell of Hare Street inspired in him, the fictional Rabbit Marsh is an oppressive landscape inscribed with menace, an abyss too deep to climb out of, "cleft" and "pierced" as if with violence. These touches of the urban gothic situate Baron's novel in a tradition of London writing that begins with Reynolds' *Mysteries of London* (1845) and culminates in the nineteenth century's

Hare Street (now Cheshire Street), King Dido's 'Rabbit Marsh'.
Courtesy of Tower Hamlets Library and Archives

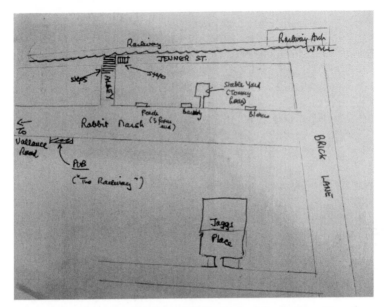

Baron's sketch map of 'Rabbit Marsh' in Bethnal Green, the setting of
King Dido (with thanks to the Alexander Baron archive)

most notorious slum novel, Arthur Morrison's *A Child of the Jago*
(1896).[5]

Return to the Jago

The history of the East End remained a rich source for Baron's writing
throughout his career. One of his earliest film scripts, *The Siege of Sidney
Street* (1960), fictionalised the true story of an anarchist cell besieged by
the police in a Whitechapel tenement in 1911.[6] In 1966 he read widely
and prepared extensive notes on the great East London dock strike for
a novel entitled *London 1889* (which remained unwritten). In 1982 he
prepared a treatment of *A Child of the Jago* that elicited keen interest
from the BBC, although among the many Victorian novels he
successfully adapted it was not ultimately produced. But Morrison's

---

5   Robert Mighall, *A Geography of Victorian Gothic Fiction: Mapping History's
    Nightmares* (Oxford: OUP, 2003).

6   Jon Cleary and Alexander Baron, *The Siege*, 1958.

novel had been in Baron's mind since the 1960s when he began to compose *King Dido*. In a 1992 interview he acknowledged that *"King Dido* was very much influenced by *A Child of the Jago*. A wonderful novel by Arthur Morrison, set in... an area which was finally wiped out by slum clearance. Social historians believe that the inhabitants of the area which was called 'The Old Nichol' were dispersed throughout the whole neighbourhood — and perhaps they sowed the seeds of the lawless and rough elements who infected the surrounding areas. They were soon interspersed among a great population of peaceful and law-abiding citizens."[7] Victorian fiction often provided the reference point for Baron's descriptions of the world of his parents: his father had missed the opportunity to become a pupil teacher like Bradley Headstone in Dickens' *Our Mutual Friend*, and his mother grew up in a court in Spitalfields that resembled Bleeding Heart Yard in *Little Dorrit*.[8] Similarly Baron saw *A Child of the Jago* as the prequel to the story of his grandfather's Bethnal Green.

Morrison's novel was widely read and discussed in the 1890s, but not reprinted in the twentieth century until 1969. It is a bleak melodrama, narrated with a dark wit and a good measure of slapstick violence, depicting life in a fictional slum — the "Old Jago", closely based on Morrison's observation of the Old Nichol area in Shoreditch. The novel's pessimistic message is carried by the central character, Dicky Perrott, a small and hopeful eight-year-old who is born into a society ruled by vicious feuding clans where casual violence is ubiquitous and the only livelihoods are earned through robbery. His one chance at honest employment in a shop is sabotaged by the local dealer in stolen goods (also a police informer), with the intention of forcing him into a life of crime. Although Dicky battles against these forces he is ultimately brought down by them, and concludes: "Who was he, Dicky Perrott, that he should break away from the Jago habit, and strain after another nature? ... Why should he fight against the inevitable, and bruise himself? ... His bed was made in the Jago, and he must lie on it."[9] At the end of *A Child of the Jago*, the slums are being cleared, but the

7 Transcript of a 1992 interview with Alexander Baron for the film The Cardinal and the Corpse, by kind permission of Iain Sinclair and Chris Petit.
8 Baron, *Chapters of Accidents*, p.13, p.45.
9 Arthur Morrison, *A Child of the Jago* (Chicago: Academy Chicago Publishers, 1995; first published 1896), p.96.

novel's verdict, delivered by two authority figures, the local vicar and a young middle-class surgeon, is that, nonetheless, "the Jago rats bred and bred their kind unhindered, multiplying apace and infecting the world."[10] While the novel appears at some points to espouse the late-Victorian environmental determinism that was associated with reformist politics, it gives more weight to a eugenicist analysis of urban poverty.

In *King Dido*, Baron frequently references *A Child of the Jago*. From the outset, the Nichol casts its long shadow, providing the backstory for the Murchison family, who, at the beginning of the novel, run a brutal protection racket in the Rabbit Marsh area. The family originated in the Old Nichol, described by the narrator as "a thieves' kitchen so notorious, dangerous and insanitary that it had been demolished by the authorities. But the clans of roughs, who for generations had lived by terror and easy pickings, only scattered into the surrounding streets." Displaced to nearby Bethnal Green, the Murchisons now live in a crowded, dilapidated court whose name, Jaggs Place, recalls Morrison's literary slum. Like their forbears in the Jago, they revel in the squalor: "They lived here because they liked it... the stink and the filth were those of an animal den, a comforting lair; and the crowding kept their bodies warm as it warmed their spirits in a hubbub of shared life." There are echoes here, too, of the *fin de siècle* fear, dramatized in *A Child of the Jago*, that city life had sent evolution into reverse, producing a loss of civilisation and a degenerate underclass. Dicky Perrott's stunted physique, a sign of hereditary degeneration, is reproduced in Baron's Cockeye Keogh, "a wizened, sickly creature" and his uncle Harry Murchison, "tall and skeletal, with a skin pale as the underside of a toadstool and sunken, melancholy eyes". The inviolable kinship bonds, intense local patriotism and disregard of physical pain mark the people of Morrison's Jago and Baron's Jaggs Place as urban primitives.[11]

Yet Baron's novel eschews narrow caricature for a wider geographical and social perspective than Morrison. As Sarah Wise has pointed out,

---

10 Ibid, p.127.

11 John L Kijinski, 'Ethnography in the East End: Native Customs and Colonial Solutions in A Child of the Jago', *English Literature in Transition, 1880-1920*, 37.4 (1994), pp.490-501.

the real Nichol was more socially varied than *A Child of the Jago* implied.[12] This mixed population is evident in *King Dido*, where the Rabbit Marsh neighbourhood includes not only the parasitic poor but also the respectable railway and dock workers like the well-scrubbed, chapel-going Peach family. Baron also steps away from Morrison's degenerationist model with an insistence on bringing historical context to an understanding of the flourishing of lawlessness in Bethnal Green. The characteristically local form of crime practised by the Murchisons, extortion with threats of violence, is not solely the effect of their inherited savagery. It is also facilitated by a local ethos that has its roots in the traumatic population movements of the nineteenth century:

> Wherever they came from, descendants of dispossessed country folk, refugees from foreign persecution or Irish famine, seekers after work on many brutal waterfronts or in many pitiless streets, often-evicted tenants, they accepted that there must be victims and victimisers, that someone must assume authority over them and take tribute from them. (*King Dido*)

The heritage of migrancy in the Bethnal Green population has ingrained habits of pragmatism and resignation that readily incorporate the protection racket as a necessary evil in their lives.

On the other hand, however, Baron's approach to Bethnal Green shares the meticulous ethnographic eye of *A Child of the Jago*. Morrison observes the Jago with a particular fascination in the rules that govern its subculture, from the prohibitions against narking to the police, or against accusing another of theft, to the organisation of a "break" or collection to fund a neighbour's defence counsel if arrested and brought to trial. In *King Dido* there is a similar interest in the shared social rituals of the Bethnal Green working class. One example, undoubtedly startling to the reader, is after the death of Ginger Murchison from the injuries inflicted on him by Dido for insulting his mother, when Dido, now the new ruler of Rabbit Marsh, dutifully fulfils his obligation to attend "the brick — the traditional collection and tribute to the dead," and to make the largest contribution. At a number of points the narrator makes this ethnographic perspective explicit, switching to a detached, authoritative tone. This enables the novel to convey something of the interior experience of characters who cannot articulate it themselves:

12 Sarah Wise, *The Blackest Streets: The Life and Death of a Victorian Slum* (London: Bodley Head, 2008), pp.225-35.

159

> The Peach brothers were like workers of primitive "magic" who are astonished at what they seem to have achieved but believe in it because the evidence of their own eyes is not to be denied. The tribe believes in it too, and offers them gifts and leadership. So chieftains and kings once came into being, in return for their protective powers.

The coronation of the new king at the beginning of the novel, coinciding with Dido's conquest of Ginger Murchison and his assumption of the crown of local protector, is thus understood as part of a ritual system that preserves social order. Rabbit Marsh is a "primitive" society but its practices are a local version of the structures of belief and power that have survived into modern national life too.

What links *King Dido* to *A Child of the Jago* most profoundly of all, however, is its use of environment to convey a claustrophobic sense of determinism. When the narrator describes the daunting prospect of the "narrow ravine" of Hare Marsh early in the novel, this image follows directly after a sketch of Dido himself. The sketch reveals little. Dido is laconic and enigmatic: "a strange intensity in his face as if ceaseless thoughts churned inside him, but what they were no one could know. He could not express himself". Yet if Dido is unreadable, the weighty presence of Hare Marsh offers some kind of explanation of a man in battle with forces much greater than himself. This narrative orchestration of individual and landscape indicates that Dido must be understood as formed by the place he inhabits.

At other points in the novel, the external environment is similarly magnified in relation to the minuscule individuals who act in it. When for the first time Dido accompanies the tea-shop waitress Grace Matthews home to her working women's hostel in the City Road, the foggy street she walks through is sensorially overwhelming. Narrated from Grace's perspective, this brilliant passage of literary expressionism suggests an experience of blurred perception that intimidates her.

> Great shire horses loomed out of the fog, sparkles of moisture on their backs and manes, high-laden wagons from docks and rail depots rumbling behind them, carters huddled, grotesquely wrapped, on their perches. The clash of the great hooves on cobbles, the iron rims of wheels mingling their noise in a thunder, the wide road a jam of wagons, here and there the gawky, coloured upper deck of a bus among them, all in a pale yellow cavern of light that blurred away into fog. Her voice and

his were small, senseless sounds among all the noise and movement.

Grace's consciousness of the limits of her physical power anticipates her later walk with Dido through the backstreets of Shoreditch after their evening out at a music hall, when she feels "like a prisoner with rifle-muzzles behind her" and senses that the walk will end in him raping her. Both these descriptions of place were added to the first draft of the novel, suggesting that Baron wanted particularly to augment the reader's impression that these are characters shaped and limited by their environment.

In this vein, in a passage later cut from the end of Chapter Three, the narrator reflects ominously on the series of events which has turned the respectable Peach brothers into reluctant mobsters: "Like all human beings, they lived in the illusion that they were in command of their situation, unaware that they were the puppets of agents natural and human invisible to them, not to speak of forces equally invisible within themselves."[13] In deleting this paragraph, Baron presumably sought to let his point be made by the plot, rather than the narrator. Thus, later in the novel, Dido finds himself in the position of Dicky Perrott, his legitimate employment as a milkman deliberately jeopardized by Inspector Merry so as to force him back into crime, and thence to punishment. He grasps, then, that it is not only Merry's manipulation but "all Rabbit Marsh which had brought him to his plight." Although the clean-living Peach family pride themselves on their difference from their Jaggs Place neighbours, they are no more in control of their destinies. It is as Dido gradually comes to consciousness of the forces that constrain his agency, but struggles to the end against them, that he becomes the protagonist of a tragedy.

The policeman and the gangster

In contrast to Morrison, who eschews a political analysis in favour of a hereditarian one, Baron maintains that the key force that structures lives in Bethnal Green is class. This is brought to the foreground of *King Dido* in the existential conflict between Dido, whose only wish is to be "respectable", and the aspirational middle-class Inspector Merry, who holds "a placid confidence in his own right and ability to order the game

---

13 Alexander Baron, *King Dido*, TS, n.d.

of people's lives." Merry's pursuit of Dido begins after the first bloody encounter between Dido and Ginger Murchison, who had attempted to bring the Peach family under his rule. This incident begins a vendetta between Dido and the extended Murchison clan as Dido's battle to maintain his autonomy becomes a competition for territorial control. Despite his distaste for taking money from his neighbours, Dido finds himself the ruler of Rabbit Marsh. The Murchisons fight back with an arson attack on Dido's house. Surviving this, he retaliates with a fire in Jaggs Place that kills seven people including Murchison's son-in-law Keogh and grandson Cockeye. Eventually understanding that there is no escape from the cycle of revenge, he plans to emigrate with Grace, but, deprived of his job, he can only do so by obtaining money through a robbery. However he is caught in the act by Merry.

All the time that Dido imagines his adversary is Keogh, it is in fact Merry. From early in the novel, Merry has an indirect hand in everything that happens, "not interfering, of course, but making sure that events ran his way. Not the way of justice, which was one of those abstractions that he never thought about; but the way of Inspector Merry, an ambitious man, a man of authority." Like a kind of omniscient narrator, he has an overarching view of those under "the illusion that they were in command of their situation." Having decided, in Chapter Two, that Dido shall be brought down, Merry proceeds with restraint and patience to lay his traps and await his prey. At the novel's climax he is alerted to Dido's presence by a watcher stationed behind one of Rabbit Marsh's opaque sooty windows. Thus Dido's fate comes to meet him from the street that presented such an ominous aspect at the novel's opening. His final confrontation with Merry plays out across the multi-level terrain behind the houses, alongside the railway embankment, over the wall, up the steps to the platform and finally down into the alley off Rabbit Marsh — a struggle over who has the fuller mastery of the topography.

The germ of the novel's plot came from the tales Baron was told as a child by his Bethnal Green grandfather.[14] In his preparation for King Dido, Baron assembled a list of memories including "That 'legend' I once heard, always wanted to use, of the classic fight between the policeman and the gangster, who knew each other so well, right through the house and out the back... that ended the reign of the gangster."[15] (That he

---

14 Ken Worpole, 'Introduction' to Baron, *King Dido*, p.13.
15 Alexander Baron, *King Dido*, research notes.

believed the legend must be based in fact is indicated by the strenuous efforts he went to while researching the novel to ascertain that there was no detective inspector named Merry at the time the novel is set, which could have rendered the novel libellous.) There is a hint of Baron's interest in this trope in his script for *The Siege of Sidney Street*. Here, the focus of the story is the adversarial Inspector Mannering, a fictional figure (possibly based on Frederick Wensley, Divisional Detective Inspector for Whitechapel, who was involved in the case) who infiltrates the anarchist cell in order to lead the police to the whereabouts of those who are in hiding. The idealism, albeit violent, of the youthful anarchists is contrasted with Mannering's resort to mendacious methods to gain access to their private lives.

The intimate familiarity between the detective and the quarry is a recurrent theme in the celebrated autobiography of Frederick Wensley. It's possible that Baron consulted Wensley's *Detective Days: the Record of Forty-Two Years' Service in the Criminal Investigation Department* (1931) on its reissue in 1968. In the book, Wensley, who was promoted to detective chief inspector in 1912, describes his lifelong devotion to the task of catching the rogues of Whitechapel, and asserts that new technology cannot replace human knowledge: "The only real method is to employ detectives who know rogues by direct contact, know their habits, their ways of thought, their motives, and above all, know their friends and associates." Wensley has a contextual understanding of crime, noting that the East End presented particular incentives in the location of the highest concentration of valuable goods in the country in the area around the docks and the City, and the close proximity of common lodging houses. His career in the CID, he concludes, has enabled him to understand the humanity of criminals: "It is not always their fault that conditions have moulded them wrongly. With very few exceptions criminals are made by environment and circumstances." Throughout the memoir Wensley emphasises the uniquely comprehensive understanding that the detective has of a suspect, "his mentality, his domestic circumstances, his motives in taking to crime, his difficulties, his reaction to punishment."[16] For his own part, he also professes intellectual admiration for the skill and

---

16 Frederick Porter Wensley, *Detective Days: The Record of Forty-Two Years' Service in the Criminal Investigation Department* (London: Cassell, 1931), p.12.

intelligence of burglars and the patient research conducted by safebreakers.

In east London, according to the sociologist Dick Hobbs, the detective and the criminal have a particular reason for mutual understanding as they share a common culture. The East End, with its distinctive "deviant identity and economically determined traditions that stress autonomy and entrepreneurship," Hobbs argues, shaped the style of local detective work. This culture has its roots in the situation of the worker in nineteenth-century east London, where the prevalence of small workshops and casual contracts resulted in an ethos of independence and resourcefulness. The rule of the Kray twins in the 1960s, Hobbs contends, must be understood in these local terms: "The class solidarity that had emerged from centuries of poor housing, casual work, unemployment and individual entrepreneurial endeavour, … served to structure an informal but pervasive form of social control that by definition had tended to exclude representatives of society's master institutions." Within and because of the cultural isolation of the East End, the Krays functioned as "integral agents of the indigenous social order," an order that included respect for the elderly and conservative gender values. For this reason, they co-existed with the local CID and their activities were considered, for nearly two decades, as "normal and unremarkable."[17]

This is the ethos, too, of Baron's historical Bethnal Green, where the local detective inspector, William Merry, tolerates the Rabbit Marsh protection racket: "He did not regard petty extortions of the Murchison kind as crime, but as part of the normal life of the riff-raff over whom he, Merry, watched. They could do what they liked to each other as long as they did not infringe on what Merry regarded as law and order." He is sanguine, too, about police corruption: "'Dropsy' [bribery] was an institution. Constables on the beat took their weekly half-dollars from bookies' runners as they took the pay from their packets. Inspectors took their banknotes from bookies, brothel-keepers and race-gang bosses in the same spirit; perquisites of office." Policing, like protection, is a feudal arrangement. Intimacy with the perpetrators of low-level organised crime facilitates the successful pursuit of serious offenders, thus it is held by some officers that dropsy

---

17 Dick Hobbs, *Doing the Business: Entrepreneurship, Detectives and the Working Class in the East End of London* (Oxford: Clarendon, 1988), p.2.

is in fact "beneficial to law and order." Published at a time when the Metropolitan Police detective branch was facing increasing exposure — with evidence of widespread corruption emerging in the late 1960s and new disciplinary procedures punishing practices such as bribery and giving false evidence that had previously been regarded as routine — *King Dido* excavated the deep historical roots of police-criminal collusion in east London.

In Baron's early twentieth-century Bethnal Green, social order is maintained by the co-existence of the gangster and the policeman — an ecosystem challenged by Dido Peach, whom Merry can neither control nor read. But with the narrator's insight into the domestic lives of these men, the reader can see that their identities are shaped by similar moral values. Although he considers himself a liberal father and employer, William Merry exerts firm patriarchal control over his household, insisting that his children address him correctly and eat their greens before pudding. In the Peach home, similarly, small details indicate Dido's rigid adherence to forms of domestic order and signifiers of respectability: his prohibition of his brothers' drinking; his exclusive use of the breakfast mug as man of the house, his fastidious refusal to venture outdoors, even when injured, unless clean-shaven. Merry, who has "made something" of his De Beauvoir Town villa in the same way that he intends to make something of himself, shares the disciplined, fiercely independent sensibility of Dido Peach. Authoritarian in their private lives, they both see themselves as the guarantor of local stability. After Dido drives Keogh from Rabbit Marsh, Merry warns him that this violence will not go unpunished: "There's going to be law and order round here," to which Dido responds: "I believe in law an' order, Mr Merry." In his notes on the character of Dido for the novel, Baron wrote:

> How he upholds the "law" (his conception of it)
>
> This shd bring him into active conflict with Merry — not crime.
>
> His resentment.
>
> Whose law runs here?[18]

Underlying the antagonism between the gangster and the policeman, the novel suggests, is a likeness. As Dido resents Merry's interference in

---

18 Alexander Baron, *King Dido*, research notes.

Baron with his paternal grandparents, Simon and Leah Bernstein

local governance Merry too resents the intrusion of the superintendent and "all the higher-ups who were trampling over his patch." Yet Merry's law is alien to Dido. It is not a system of justice or honour but a manifestation of middle-class power. For Merry, Bethnal Green is a fiefdom to be used in the cause of his professional advancement. The conflict is not one of law versus outlaw but a battle over territory.

The End of Dido

In the final chapter of the novel, set in summer 1918, Dido, his proud body permanently damaged and disfigured from his fight with Merry, has recently been released from prison. His wife and daughter have left the country, his younger brothers have died on the battlefields and his mother has lost her mind. Dido sleeps on a mattress in a hovel in Jaggs Place and does odd jobs for the stallholders of Rabbit Marsh. Here, penniless and degraded, he encounters Merry, whose triumphant subjugation of "his province" has resulted in his promotion to superintendent.

In Baron's first draft of the novel, Dido has been completely crushed. He looks "[c]rookbacked like a conqueror's menial" as he "peered up adoringly at the policeman" and assures Merry that he is causing no trouble. Merry humiliates him further by tossing a coin to him, telling him to keep his nose clean. He replies, obediently, "Much oblige, Mis' Merry."[19] There is a suggestion that he is now in Merry's pay, and part of the network of informers through which the neighbourhood has been successfully subdued. Baron later added an internal monologue by Merry, in which the detective "noted the way the man bore the inspection, patient as a donkey. It was the way with these hard cases. Break their spirit and no-one was meeker. Look at this one — he had come back to the scene of his rise and fall as if nothing had happened. He lived on the charity of those who had cringed to him."[20]

Later still, Baron radically altered the novel's ending. This time, Merry's coin falls to the pavement; instead of craning his neck subserviently towards the detective, "Dido's head came up and for a moment his eyes looked directly at Merry, astonishingly alive and clear." Rather than replying to Merry, Dido returns his gaze, inscrutable as ever.

> Dido was silent. Only his eyes answered, looking directly into Merry's; clear, grey, unfathomably patient. He had lost everything except the place he knew, the familiar place in which to die. In silence he would endure anything, from this man and from the others, rather than be driven from it (*King Dido*).

Replacing Merry's scorn for Dido's return to "the scene of his rise and fall," Baron makes Dido's love of "the place he knew" the source of his vitality. While Dido remains unreadable to the end, he also remains unconquered, driven by the fierce and deep clarity of his sense of purpose.

---

19 Alexander Baron, *King Dido*, first draft, p.346.
20 Alexander Baron, *King Dido*, TS, n.p.

In his notes for King Dido, Baron makes it clear that he wanted the novel to capture the unique ethos of the urban working class of the pre-war period:

> These are people with special qualities —
> probity
> intelligence
> pride
> ambition
>
> But their imagination never takes them out of the milieu or little world in which they are born
>
> They may struggle, climb, enact dramas of utmost and universal intensity -- but it simply does not occur to them to overleap the low walls of the small arena in which they perform[21]

If Baron initially conceived the novel to illustrate the limitations of Dido's imagination, his final draft suggested something more subtle and less condescending. In this final glimpse of Dido's subjectivity, the narrator does not adopt the omniscient ethnographic voice as earlier in the novel; rather he expresses something more like awe. In the extraordinary image of Dido's clear-sighted gaze, his attachment to "the familiar place" has become both his tragedy and his redemption.

The Barsky Novel

Dido's unacknowledged potential surfaces at one earlier point in the novel too, when he is waiting in the dark behind the houses in Rabbit Marsh, having challenged Keogh to settle their feud with a bare-knuckle fight in the street. His gaze falls through the kitchen window of his neighbour, the "Jew cobbler" Barsky, "a man he felt inexplicably at ease with," who is "as tough and taciturn as Dido," and whom Dido has never asked for protection money, feeling that "Barsky's black-button eyes could see through him." In the kitchen, Barsky is celebrating the Sabbath with his wife and two sons. There is a "dazzling white cloth" on the table and "two brass candlesticks, polished to a high gleam," "an enormous plaited loaf of shining deep brown," and wine that "caught the candlelight in a ruby gleam." The watcher is "held by vague wonderment... Dido knew these people but they looked like

---

21 Alexander Baron, *King Dido*, research notes.

strangers; a tableau around the pure flames of candles." Shortly afterwards, Keogh refuses the challenge, and Dido understands that instead of a fair fight he must instead live in fear of an imminent and brutal attack. At night in bed the tableau of Barsky's family returns to him "like a vision of unknown people. It disturbed him. It awakened in him drifts of longing which he could not follow. It made him feel lost and sad, something that drew him but was infinitely out of reach behind the panes of glass." Watching through the window has provoked a sudden moment of self-consciousness. Witnessing Barsky's Friday night brings home to Dido that he is trapped in a world in which the sole purpose of existence is the struggle for survival.

Captured in the midst of a private ceremony not usually visible to others, the Barsky family emit radiant light amongst the sooty grime of Rabbit Marsh. The scene is more significant, however, for what it reveals about Dido: his deep but inchoate longings. But because Dido remains enigmatic to himself as much as the reader, the exact meaning for him of Barsky's Friday night is unclear. He is, perhaps, stirred by the image of a cohesive family, bound together in a shared ancestral ritual — a contrast to his own restless family whose origins are obscure and uncertain. He is also struck by how unrecognisable his neighbours appear, as if their religious practice lifts them out of the mundane existence in which he knows them. In the first draft of the novel, the narrator intrudes into the last sentence of the scene to reflect on the mystery and prompt the reader to understand that Dido's vision, "though he could not identify it, was civilisation."[22] Dido's imaginative response to the Barsky family, his vague apprehension of something beyond his familiar world, marks him out from those around him. In particular it is the novel's clearest indication that whatever the cultural affinities between Dido and Merry, Merry remains a self-satisfied materialist, motivated above all by self-interest, whereas Dido has the capacity for idealism.

The tableau Dido observes, framed by the window, is Baron's own childhood memory of Friday night with his family, which he records in his memoir together with joyful recollections of other Jewish festivals celebrated while his grandmother was still alive. Although only this fragment appears in *King Dido*, at the same time as writing the novel, Baron was also planning another, labelled in his notes as the "Barsky

22 Alexander Baron, *King Dido*, first draft, p.276.

Novel".[23] It would tell the story of Barsky's two sons, apprentices to a cabinet-maker, who are glimpsed through the kitchen window in *King Dido*. In the plan for the "Barsky Novel", one son, Abie (renamed in other notes as Mo) enlists in the army and hits an officer who insults him, for which he spends six months in prison. Later, he is wounded at Passchendaele and lives subsequently as a drifter, sleeping rough and returning home only when he is too cold and hungry. The main focus of the novel, however, is his brother Louis, who knows nothing of Mo's experiences, and who becomes a rich and successful painter, but suffers bitter conflict with his own son, a "smoothie businessman" with no emotional connection to his father's generation.

The "Barsky Novel" notes indicate alternative directions for Baron's meditations on Bethnal Green. The notes include a list of memories of Hare Street, including "The market", "The interior of the shop" and "That 'legend' of the classic fight between the policeman and the gangster," all of which he used for *King Dido*. Other topics in the list, like "The railwaymen in their old 1914–1918 tunics" and "Sroulka and the carter", were later developed into anecdotes in *Chapters of Accidents*: the story of the war veterans who worked at the Shoreditch goods yard and gathered at Baron's grandfather's shop, and the story told of his grandfather's tough older brother Sroulka who was once flicked in Brick Lane by a carter's horsewhip, which he caught, pulled, and used to drag the carter off his horse. Also listed is "Hymie as hero's brother." In *Chapters of Accidents* Baron recalls Hymie, his "mysterious uncle" who appeared intermittently at his grandparents' house, laconic and apparently dim, and evoked "a tug of strange feelings" in the youthful Baron. Only later he learned that after losing all his money gambling, Hymie had enlisted in the army where he was imprisoned for hitting an officer. He repeatedly took on casual work as a cabinet-maker only to gamble away his earnings and return home when he was destitute.

It is this subject, "Hymie as the hero's brother," that is the focus of the majority of Baron's "Barsky" notes. He grapples compulsively with the character of Abie/Mo and his motivations:

> Why does MO leave home again and again. Are his hungers, although sharp and clear, not articulated in thought? E.g. he is stifled, it becomes unbearable, the oppressive combination of contempt and kindness, the lack of reproach, the care he

23 Alexander Baron, *King Dido*, research notes.

receives... and he goes... And he enjoys the keen bite of cold air, the darkness of the doorway in which he sleeps, the night, the changing light to dawn, the noises and passing, mysterious figures of the street, the menace of the passing policeman with his lantern... freedom...

Until freedom in its turn becomes physically unbearable and he slinks home.[24]

Of course, Baron had once before used the story of Hymie — as a source for his tormented anti-hero Harryboy Boas in *The Lowlife* (1963). Harryboy represented the defiant negation of the myth of immigrant self-betterment, repeatedly resisting opportunities to make money and leave east London. In the "Barsky Novel" plan, Baron returned a second time to his fascination with this "family outcast". Here, through the story of the Barsky brothers, he explored two opposing trajectories of Jewish immigrant history — one towards success and wealth, the other always dislocated, rejecting material prosperity. Just as Baron later recognised in Hymie *"mon semblable"* [my double], so does the artist, Louis, eventually understand that the luftmensch Mo is "the missing part of himself". In his notes, Baron debated the meaning of Mo's urge to wander and sleep rough in the streets, asking: "this man without ideas, is he driven by the unformed thought that man does not live by bread alone?"[25] Mo's yearning for the spiritual stretches back to the tableau that Dido observed in Bethnal Green, when "the pure flames of candles" teach the Barsky boys to look beyond their flawed world.

In the third and final part of the "Barsky Novel", Louis "wanders back to Bethnal Green after visiting his own Retrospective at the Whitechapel Art Gallery," where he comes upon the aged Dido Peach.[26] Dido, now in his eighties, has outlived William Merry. But the story of the Jew cobbler and his family, as it unfolds in the "Barsky Novel", has turned out not to be the shining alternative to Dido's life as it appeared on that night in 1912. It too is full of longing, loss and bewilderment. At the end of the "Barsky Novel" both sons, one wealthy and one destitute, find themselves in "the familiar place" that similarly drew back Dido. Each of these characters is compelled to return to Bethnal Green for reasons they cannot explain.

24 Alexander Baron, *King Dido*, research notes.

25 Alexander Baron, *King Dido*, research notes.

26 Alexander Baron, *King Dido*, research notes.

Conclusion

In *King Dido* Baron captured in careful detail the interior and public spaces, the streets, markets and railway lands around Hare Street in the early twentieth century, and a parochial social world bonded by ritual and codes of honour, and shaped by cultural traditions of independence and resignation. There is a radical edge too to *King Dido* that takes it beyond pastiche Victorian slum fiction. This local ethos is embodied in the novel's protagonist — inflexible, emotionally repressed and conservative, with none of the bolshy charisma of the working-class heroes of 1960s fiction — who is nonetheless a figure of undaunted resistance. He defies the forces of social control, whether in the form of the bullying gangsters of his neighbourhood or the institutional power of the police who control them. If he only gradually understands that his life is determined by his place in the social hierarchy, he nonetheless finds a way to survive on his own terms.

Baron's novel is also a complex layering of intertextual reference and personal memory. In *King Dido* and in his unpublished and planned writing on Bethnal Green, Baron reflected on his own family's relationship to place. It's for this reason that the scene in which Dido watches Barsky's family through the window is so poignant, because Dido's distanced perspective was that of Baron himself, looking back through the years on his grandfather's home in Hare Street. Like many Jewish writers of the period, Baron was expressing through his character a fascination with the lost world of ritual and belonging that his subsequent secular upbringing left behind in the East End, "something that drew him" but was now "infinitely out of reach." In the unwritten "Barsky Novel", however, Baron planned to subject such nostalgia to scrutiny. His narrative brought together the Jew cobbler's sons and the small-time gangster to suggest that the source of their vitality, creativity or spirituality is not religion or art, but "the familiar place" of Bethnal Green.

In *Chapters of Accidents*, there is an uncanny repetition of Dido's surreptitious glimpse into Barsky's window. At the end of Chapter Six, following his account of Hymie's troubled life and squalid death, Baron writes of revisiting Cheshire (formerly Hare) Street more recently only to find that "most of the buildings were boarded up, as if awaiting demolition." His grandfather's house is fire-damaged and covered with corrugated iron, denying entry. However, "[f]rom the other side of the street I could see into the first-floor front room… The faded wallpaper was the same that I had known as a child, with diagonal rows of light blue rosettes enclosing chains of pink roses" (*Chapters of Accidents*). Baron's last glance through a window into a scene from his childhood is not overtly nostalgic, even with the prospect of the imminent erasure of this key site of personal memory. Unlike many East End writers who revisited the scenes of their childhood in the late 1960s and early 1970s when demolition and rebuilding was transforming the landscape, his sentiment is restrained. Instead, the survival of the blue and pink wallpaper, which has persisted despite the Blitz and arson, arouses a faint but distinct sense of wonder.

Chapter 6
Ground Level
Questions of How to Live and Where to Live in Alexander Baron's London Novels

Anthony Cartwright

A Lonely Traveller

The burnt tower looks out over the city: its blackened skeleton stands mute over motorway flyovers and shopping centres and homes worth millions of pounds in which no one lives. Much of this architecture did not exist when Harryboy Boas made the journey west from Hackney to White City in the 1960s in search of fast and lucky dogs, but Grenfell, and all that the word has come to suggest since the disaster, does seem to me a symbol of why Baron's London novels have gained a twenty-first century readership. This is not an essay about the Grenfell disaster, but my reason for starting with that image is that the wider issues of housing, class, power and powerlessness, questions of how to live and where to live, are central themes in his work. Baron would have understood the anger about the burnt tower, and the bodies that burned within.

The original title of this essay was to be *Slow Burn City*, from Rowan Moore's 2016 book about London in the twenty-first century, its architecture and urban-planning specifically, which I shied away from for obvious reasons. "Ground Level" could also be read as grimly ironic, but my suggestion is that the people in the tower, and those who went to their aid, are in some ways the heirs of Harryboy Boas and Dido Peach and Jack Agass. So too are those who attacked the Finsbury Park mosque five days later, on the edge of Baron's literary terrain and, again, those who went to help. They were, and are, representatives of the city's "horizontal forces", the city at ground level, to borrow an image from Iain Sinclair, to which I will return, regardless of how many floors above the streets people might live or might have lived. That is, part of a local, grounded, vulnerable, vanishing, working-class city (with roots elsewhere: in London it was ever thus), in contrast to the "vertical" city of grand projects and white elephants, the "global" city of, to quote from Jonathan Meades' review of Moore's book, "class clearances; the betrayal by central and local governments of the most easily betrayed; the blurring of public and private; the absentee proprietors; the greedy planners … the tangible inequalities you trip over in doorways; houses as currency; the market, always the market…"[1]

I use this quote as an exemplar of the rage generated by the way London has developed over the last forty years or so, in the period since Baron stopped writing. Not that this rage — which seems to erupt in many forms, from articles in *The Literary Review*, to the summer riots of 2011 — has been able to do much to stop it. Urgent contemporary questions of how to live, and the more prosaic, although in today's London it might be the more difficult question, where to live, are central to Alexander Baron's London novels, in the way they sketch out patterns of twentieth-century working-class life, with echoes, at least, in the twenty-first.

In a surprising way, given the subject matter, the war fiction too, addresses some of these same questions and patterns of behaviour, in the creation and dissolution of communities, the waiting, patience and relative powerlessness involved in much working-class experience, the small gradations and qualifications of social class, and the over-riding sense of "making the best of a bad job" (the final lines of *Rosie Hogarth*). The novels *Rosie Hogarth*, *The Lowlife* and *King Dido* address the questions of how and where to live most directly, concentrating on post-war experience, from the 1940s into the 1960s, bookended by a long past at one end, reaching back to the Edwardian era in which *King Dido* is set, and further, to the slum novels of the 1890s which inspired it, and at the other end, the present-day of when that novel was published, 1969.

It is in the opening pages of *Rosie Hogarth*, Baron's first London novel, where he sets out a vision of how London functions:

> London, for all its reputation and its civic institutions, is an archipelago of life, not an island. Its boroughs are like separate towns; people who live in one may spend their whole lives without venturing into more than a couple of the others; to those who live on one side of the river the part of the town beyond the opposite bank is as remote and unknown as San Francisco. Even the boroughs are not communities. The millions of Londoners are really broken up into tens of thousands of little clusters of life. Each is gathered round some centre, perhaps a street, perhaps a block of buildings, perhaps a market, perhaps a public house or a Working Man's Club or any one of a thousand different organizations. Within each of these

---

1   Jonathan Meades, "Capital Gains", *The Literary Review*, March 2016.

little hives people live for each other as well as for themselves, and life generates a comfortable warmth. But the man or woman who tries to settle in London without gaining admission to one of these little communities (and it is not easy, for the more closely-knit each is the more hostile it is to the stranger) is like a lonely traveller wandering, as night gathers, across the vast deserted moors, mocked wherever he looks by the clustering lights of villages. He is on his own, and he can go mad or die for all anybody cares.

There is a terrible fear of outsidership in Baron's novels: "that's the mark of an outsider" to call Hackney part of the East End, as Harryboy Boas explains to the reader early in *The Lowlife*, and yet there is something of the "lonely traveller" in all his central characters. Harryboy is alone for so much of that novel, a solitary figure at the dog-track or lying on his bed reading Balzac. In *Rosie Hogarth*, Jack Agass is an orphan, his childhood home destroyed by a German bomb (which is true also of Harryboy, his mother killed by a V2 which hit Cable Street), and Jack returns to a post-war London in 1949 (after staying on in the army in the Middle East), too late for the celebrations, with cynicism about the Labour government already setting in, a man at the start of the novel, out of time and out of place. Dido, too, is a young man uncertain of his place in the world, his heritage is unclear, exemplified by his name: in Baron's London a Queen of Carthage becomes the king of a scrap of Bethnal Green; there is the suggestion of a Gypsy father we read nothing else about. The person with whom Dido identifies most in the novel, even as he rises in prominence and influence, is Barsky, "the old Jew", and it is tempting, of course, to see something of Baron's own Jewishness in this theme of "outsidership" and "wandering", not least in the way he answered the questions he was posed of how and where to live: his family came from the Russian Empire via the East End to the street in Stoke Newington on which he grew up to the suburbs of Temple Fortune. This is the archetypal pattern of Jewish movement through London in the twentieth century, increasingly secular, materialist, suburban. Baron too, is the "lonely traveller", among many thousands of others on similar trajectories.

But in his novels, Baron's is the view of the insider, an advantage he has over many of the novelists who had covered his terrain before, whom he wrote either in argument with or in homage to, accordingly: George Gissing, Arthur Morrison, Jack London, and, of course, Dickens.

It's this uneasy ground between being an insider and outsider, between homage (to Dickens, to Gissing) and revision (of "Darkest London", of Arthur Morrison's *A Child of the Jago*), and the odd mixture of stability and flux which is working-class London, that is Baron's city.

The Lowlife begins with Harryboy musing on questions of how and where to live, following a visit to his sister's and the arrival of new neighbours. Harryboy Boas lives on a road called Ingram's Terrace in Stoke Newington (closely modelled on the street on which Baron grew up, Foulden Road), and looks back "to the other side of Commercial Road" and his parents' lives in the East End. Harryboy also looks forwards, to one possible future in the suburbs, where his sister Debbie has settled "in Finchley, the smart part." In Baron's work, the East — whether the East End or further afield — is always equated with the past; Hackney and Islington with a specific working-class, post-war present; whereas at least one kind of future belongs to the north-western suburbs, Finchley and Golders Green.

But suburban comfort is not Harryboy's only possible destiny, of course, in fact is not his preferred outcome at all. He flirts with the idea of a career as a Rachman-style slum landlord.[2] Harryboy, a professional gambler, at one point wins — and then loses — a row of derelict houses in an East London dice game. "I'm in property," he tells his new neighbour, Mrs. Deaner, who is, in turn, at pains to tell him that her family used to live in Ilford, and intend to return to the suburbs as soon as possible. Harryboy wants to stay where he is, "I like it here," he says. And Baron too liked London, loved it, in fact, "I have always loved London," he told Ken Worpole in an interview in June 1983. "A city should be accumulated memory," he added, wondering if contemporary Londoners loved the city in the same way he had.[3]

The London Baron loved and whose patterns of life he recorded follow a familiar template in *Rosie Hogarth*, *The Lowlife* and *King Dido*. There is the immediate locality, a little "cluster of life", such as Lamb Street and Dido's Rabbit Marsh. Harryboy remains apparently more solitary, but the house on Ingram's Terrace itself, with the Deaners and De Souzas and the owners and landlords, the Siskins, offer their own

---

2　Peter Rachman was the most notorious inner-city London landlord of the 1950s and early 1960s — the period in which the novel is set, and I will raise his legacy again in part three of this essay.

3　Ken Worpole, "Introduction", *King Dido* (Five Leaves, 2009), p.12.

Foulden Road, the Hackney street where Baron grew up and which features in *The Lowlife*

tiny, admittedly dysfunctional, community. Then there is Harryboy's pride in the street itself and Stoke Newington High Street and other lowlifes and members of "the fraternity of the doggies and the ponies" on the street corners all the way from "Stamford Hill to Aldgate", plus the dog tracks themselves — Haringey, Hackney, White City — with all their rituals and hierarchies, and the lure of sudden wealth.

Allied to the immediate locality, with neighbours, the pub (The Lamb in *Rosie Hogarth*, The Railway in *King Dido*) the market (Chapel Market in *Rosie Hogarth*, Hessel Street, "the last ghetto market", in *The Lowlife*), contained within the arc of a few streets, Baron's template of life in London offers a few other patterns. One is the dream of the suburbs, one which Harryboy half-dreams himself on his journey home from his sister Debbie's house. Debbie's life with her husband Gus, ironically a successful bookmaker, in suburban Finchley is contrasted with Harryboy clinging to Hackney. Likewise, in *Rosie Hogarth*, a new council flat on the edge of Hackney (possibly the Woodberry Down estate, built on either side of Seven Sisters Road in the late 1940s) "doesn't seem like London... so clean and — oh, all that grass and flowers... it must be like living in fairyland". Dido dreams of an escape to Walthamstow, is keeping an eye open in the neat streets of Clapton for a pair of respectable rooms; a house he is involved in robbing is in well-to-do De Beauvoir Town, on the borders of Hackney and Islington.

Escape is often considered, but never realistically attempted. Escape from what? In an image that seems off-key, Baron describes London as a "prison" early in *Rosie Hogarth*, but it is hard to take this seriously and this image is not sustained until it re-appears in Rosie's speech about a communist future near the novel's end, which is equally unconvincing. Harryboy dreams of a kind of escape through a big win and a boat to the Canary Islands if nuclear war breaks out, the novel's opening image. Jack's escape is out to the Surrey hills, themselves being swallowed by London's expansion, or to Hampton Court, or to visit a cousin of Joyce's in Twickenham. Dido seeks to escape through status, material wealth, and seems, if not aware beforehand, then certainly not surprised, in the way this proves futile.

And then, of course, there are the ruins. Both Harryboy and Jack dwell on the bombs — and the rubble they have left behind — that have destroyed parts of their lives. In *Rosie Hogarth*, the site of the house at the end of Lamb Street in which Jack grew up is just "a rough expanse of waste ground, bounded by ragged ends of wall," the legacy of the bomb which killed "Mrs. Hogarth and a score of his old friends." On Cable Street, Harryboy visits a bomb crater, "patches of diseased weeds, black puddles, rusty bedsteads, sodden newspaper, old prams, smashed packing cases and the turds of tramps — this is where my mother died." Not far away is where Dido dies too, destitute, defeated by his nemesis, Inspector Merry, in the "back alleys of Spitalfields", which are invoked in all three novels as the very bottom of the pile (all three novels highlight the sharp gradations of social standing, and the attitudes of a "respectable" working class towards those perceived as less so). The photographs by Don McCullin (born in Finsbury Park in 1935, a generation after Baron) taken around Spitalfields in the late 1960s and early 1970s give a sense of the dereliction Baron seeks to convey; perhaps most notably the "Homeless Irishman" portrait of 1971, who could almost be Dido, "only his eyes answered". At heart, there is an unease at the provisional nature of existence, perhaps, the flux and vulnerability of working-class London life certainly, the sense that everything might suddenly disappear: "In the rain I stood and cried," Harryboy laments, "Not even a body, not even a gravestone."

How to Live

The physical geography of Baron's London fiction centres on Stoke Newington, of course, the Hackney in which he grew up, with Foulden

Road, re-imagined as Ingram's Terrace in *The Lowlife*, at the heart of it, a sweep of the north-eastern inner suburbs from the Angel round to Limehouse. There are fixed boundaries in the south and east, formed by the River Thames and the Lea and the marshes; and more porous borders in the north and west (it is unclear, for instance, why Baron ventured to Angel for the very specific setting of *Rosie Hogarth*, other than a distancing from Jewish East London, and the quixotic, yet apparently accurate, idea that Lamb Street is Baron Street, which runs off the market towards Pentonville Road). Jack Agass walks this territory one Sunday morning, "through the back streets of Islington and Stoke Newington, down to the banks of the Lea, along the river and back homewards through Dalston and Highbury."

"From childhood I used to roam about," Baron explains in the Worpole interview. The things Jack observes — narrated in that same, removed omnipotent voice as the description of London as "an archipelago": almost the authorial interjection of the Victorian fiction which formed Baron — show how curiously London has changed and yet somehow remained so much the same:

> Thousands of people are at work on their allotments and ten times that many in their gardens. Flights of cyclists swoop through the streets. The football teams are clattering off to the parks in hundreds, the morning swimmers off to the pools. Young couples are on their way to railway stations carrying rucksacks on their backs and two-handled carry-cots between them from which prodigious babies bellow. From backyards comes the roar of motor-cycles being tuned for afternoon excursions. On the public athletics track astonishing numbers of young people, liberated from shop and factory, are sprinting, hurdling, vaulting, flying through the air in high jumps, charging doggedly at the sandpits in long jumps, proudly lifting fantastic weights, and hurling discuses about. Beefy young dockers, builders, metal-workers and clerks skim their racing shells along the barge-cluttered, factory-lined dirty River Lea, while their coaches wobble along the towpath on bicycles bawling bawdy and indefatigable exhortations at them. It is all very beautiful: a reminder that humanity still clings to its capacity for happiness. (*Rosie Hogarth*)

It would be easy to dismiss this passage as a description of a world that has gone, that may even have been fading when it was written, which explains the sentimental tone, but what is surprising is how much of it is, at least partly, recognisable in today's London, and how on a Sunday morning walk following the same route today you might see much the same. Certainly "flights of cyclists swoop through the streets", although whether "the mad pumping rush of the peloton"[4] on the Hackney towpaths has quite the same "blissful lightness of spirit" Baron describes in another cycling passage in the prologue to *The Human Kind*, of kids cycling north out of London to a camp site in the Lea Valley, is questionable.

The pitches on Hackney Marshes, a landmark of grass-roots football, still host the biggest concentration of Sunday morning matches in the country, although it is true that lower level football faces its own crises of participation and funding (as elsewhere in the economy the money awash at the top, in the Premier League, never does seem to trickle down to the bottom, in spite of all the promises). The pitches are home to the fifty-eight team Hackney & Leyton Football League on Sunday mornings, as well as the Marshes' senior club, Sporting Hackney, in the Middlesex Premier League on a Saturday, along with tournaments such as the African Nations Cup UK: one of the country's biggest community football events. All of these teams and events provide the "little hives" of community Baron observed. The pitches today belie the marshes location, of course, and the "Wilderness" ground name of the Eton Manor club who played at the marshes in the early twentieth century, in that they are built on much of the rubble created by the Blitz, and are thus so robust and well-drained that matches are rarely called off here. Eton Manor followed the route of many East London families of the era and moved eventually to Broxbourne and a place in the Essex Senior League.

Rowing on the Lea has a long history of working-class participation — something which may seem a contradiction in terms, given the sport's elitist reputation. In 1899, of the thirty-nine registered rowing clubs on the Lea, nineteen were those of tradesmen's organisations. At its height in the late Victorian era, the banks and boatyards were lined with rowing clubs with names typical of the cult of "muscular Christianity" and its obsession with classical physicality, such as Alpha and Spartan, as well as the more geographically-specific Clapton United, and the more politically minded Gladstone Radical. All of these, as with the numerous football clubs associated with the Marshes, are examples of the "little clusters of life", of which Baron's London is comprised. There were

---

4   Iain Sinclair, "The Last London," *London Review of Books*, 30 March 2017.

sixteen rowing clubs still registered on the Lea in 1953, four years after Jack's walk, with a cluster of boathouses at Radley's boatyard, which was subsumed into what became Springfield Marina in the 1970s. Rowing on the Lea never quite died out — although with depopulation and changes in working practices (many of the rowers had been river workers or the "beefy young dockers" of the description) the culture was disappearing by the time Baron was writing *King Dido* in the late 1960s. But the Lea Rowing Club, with its new boathouse opened in 2016, has its home on the edge of Springfield Park today, and embraces the legacy of the clubs that came before it.

As for the athletes, again it might be easy to bemoan their ironic disappearance in the shadow of the white-elephant Olympic development at Stratford, to suggest they have all gone shopping at Westfield, except that it would not be true, because to walk through any of the area's parks on a Sunday morning would be to witness numerous "parkruns" and people of all shapes and sizes "proudly lifting fantastic weights" in the outdoor gyms or with their trainers "bawling bawdy and indefatigable exhortations" at them. On this walk Jack might have skirted Finsbury Park, where at the track at its centre, scores of children and adults train every Sunday with the London Heathside club. Likewise, the swimmers — at the lido at London Fields, Hackney Baths, Clissold Leisure Centre, Highbury Pool (which burnt down during the editing of this essay), the swimmers that share space with the canoeists and sailing club at the Stoke Newington West Reservoir — flourish in these "little hives" of community, around which people organise their lives.

The waiting lists for allotments in Islington and Hackney are closed due to high demand, community gardens and projects such as Organic Lea and the Dalston Eastern Curve Garden, thrive, young couples are always on their way to railway stations with "prodigious babies" between them (the birth rate has climbed steadily in the early twenty-first century, and this is particularly true in London, contradicting all projections of increasingly declining fertility — London is a youthful city today in a way it has not been for generations), young men tinker with and then ride around on motor-scooters (and some join street gangs), as these heirs of Dido and Ginger Murchison play out the inevitable result of clinging to a "little hive", gang, postcode posse, honour, too tightly, perhaps one more outcome of such an economically unequal city. These patterns of life, as described by Baron in his "archipelago" image, continue, for all the upheavals that London has been subject to in the intervening years.

There are, of course, no "beefy young dockers" or "metal workers" any more. London, the great industrial city, has disappeared almost entirely, leaving remarkably few traces (the train line north from Baron's territory is one of the last London landscapes left with even a vestige of industry, small manufacturing and light engineering units and factories line the track through Edmonton and Enfield). This re-making is recent, of course. Docklands, the Olympic Park and Westfield at Stratford, the huge swathe of land behind King's Cross Station, much of Shoreditch and Hoxton, the "dark alleys of Spitalfields", all had — or were — huge areas of dereliction and abandonment, not to mention local residents trying to "make the best of a bad job." They continue to do so, not least in the confrontation between the mayor of Newham, Robin Wales, and the campaigners who occupied the Carpenters Estate in Stratford in 2014 in protest against "class clearances", to use Meades' term. Certainly, there is still something recognisable in Iain Sinclair's description of Hackney as an "unresolved hinterland, between canal, gas-holders and half-built flats"[5] but not much, and not for much longer. And this, perhaps, is where we start to hear a more discordant note, because if many parts of the infrastructure of how to live are lost — around places of worship, sports clubs, hospitals, libraries, parks, pubs, markets and so on, the "little hives" of communal, urban life — then the question of where to live becomes increasingly difficult. If you are the heir of the "dockers" or "metal workers" or "Hoffman-pressers" (Harryboy's trade when not loafing) or "fur-cutters" (Baron's father's occupation) or shop-fitters (Jack's job) or "milkmen" (Dido, for a while) or any of thousands of jobs that have disappeared, but instead are a delivery driver or shop worker or warehouse operative or street cleaner or council official or even teacher or nurse or police officer or fire-fighter (or do any of the innumerable jobs required to keep a city functioning) then you are going to struggle to afford to live in any of the sweep of Baron's city in a way that is perhaps unimaginable in the novels, although may be hinted at in the dereliction Dido faces, and in the dice game where Harryboy gambles for, wins and then loses, a row of houses in East London, worth millions of pounds today.

---

5 Iain Sinclair, *Ghost Milk: Calling Time on the Grand Project*, (Penguin, 2011).

A cynic might suggest that the people Jack observes on his Sunday morning sojourn are generally working-class, and on the same walk today those you would see are overwhelmingly middle-class. And on first reflection there might be something in that, except not at the football on the marshes, or on any observation of the parks, or any close observation of the boroughs at all, in fact. It is worth noting, that council tenancies still account for just over a quarter of all housing in Islington and Hackney (way above the national average), with housing association tenancies accounting for a fifth. This compares with owner occupancy of just under thirty per cent in both boroughs, with private renting making up the rest.[6] Nationally, the number of properties rented privately has doubled in the last twenty years. And it is the simple fact that the rate of return on rent is greater than the rate of economic growth, as investigated by Thomas Piketty in *Capital in the Twenty-First Century*, and discussed explicitly with regard to the London property market by Anna Minton in her book *Big Capital*, that has hastened the current crisis.[7] The point is that the issue of who lives (or doesn't live, in respect of absentee landlords) in these inner-London boroughs is very much a contemporary question; and currently, whoever they are, counter to the idea that people live increasingly atomised lives, plugged into machines, where one place becomes much like the next, many of the people are still, to a great extent, following patterns of living Baron observed in his mid-twentieth century novels. I write this as a note of optimism, that for all the iniquities, that London endures.

Yet maybe not for long, and surely only in a city which has given itself over so totally to the concept of "houses as currency", to "the market", can the question of where to live be more difficult to answer than how to live.

Where to Live

A novel called *Ironopolis* by Glen James Murray, published in 2018, opens with an epigraph taken from a speech by Aneurin Bevan in 1948: "I believe that if we have a few more years at our disposal, we shall have the best housing record of any nation in the world."[8] The novel tells the story of the fictitious Burn Estate, on the edge of Middlesboro, the hopes for the future

---

6 All data for Islington and Hackney taken from national census data 2011.

7 Anna Minton, *Big Capital: Who is London For?* (Penguin, 2018).

8 Glen James Murray, *Ironopolis*, (Parthian, 2018).

when it is built, and the hopeless years before it is torn down for "regeneration", which shows, at least, that the current housing malaise does not just apply to London. In an as-yet unpublished novel called *Wretched Things*, Scarlett Parker writes about a council block off City Road, in Islington, with residents about to be "decanted" to make way for gentrification, and what happens when an existing resident decides to stay put (in an echo of the Carpenters Road stand-off in Stratford, referred to above). John Lanchester's 2012 novel, *Capital*, concentrates on a single London street that for most of its one-hundred and fifty-year history housed "respectable" lower-middle class families, whereas now: "Having a house in Pepys Road was like being in a casino in which you were guaranteed to be a winner. If you already lived there, you were rich. If you wanted to move there, you had to be rich."[9] The casino analogy is one Harryboy would have appreciated, about a road which might have excited Dido's attention. The plot is built around the idea every house on the street receives a note one morning which states simply, "We want what you've got."

The stock themes of nineteenth-century realism — property, heredity, marriage and social status — loom large in Baron's work, but it is that of property (and the social status it gifts) which seems to correspond most fully with any contemporary reading of Baron, and of contemporary London itself. Murray's use of the Bevan quote is ironic, of course. Even by 1949 Jack Agass has the following experience when standing in front of "a great stack of new bricks, red and bright":

> He asked one of the workmen, "What's up, nob?"
>
> "Building job. Block of flats. For the council. Why? Lookin' for a place to live?"
>
> Jack grinned. "I might be soon."
>
> "Well, you won't get one of these. If you hurry up round the Town 'All and put your name down, you might get one before your youngest great-grandson gets wed."
>
> "Don't give him hopes," grunted another labourer as he passed, "I wouldn't like to see 'im wait a 'undred years and then die of disappointment." (*Rosie Hogarth*)

---

9 John Lanchester, *Capital*, (Faber, 2012).

A major factor in the post-war Labour government losing the 1951 General Election, and entering one of its periods in the political wilderness, was the perceived slow pace at which it was building houses and the kind of frustration expressed in Jack's conversation. The Tories promised to build houses more quickly: "a Conservative and Unionist Government will give housing a priority second only to national defence. Our target remains 300,000 houses a year. There should be no reduction in the number of houses and flats built to let but more freedom must be given to the private builder. In a property-owning democracy, the more people who own their homes the better" (*Conservative Party Manifesto*).

"It doesn't seem like London, does it?" Joyce says to Jack on a visit to a friend who has moved to a new council flat. She looked around her.

> "It's all so clean, and — oh, all that grass and flowers. I told Nancy last time, it must be like living in fairyland. All sunlit. If I lived here I'd be afraid it was a dream, and that I might wake up any minute and see dirty black walls again." (*Rosie Hogarth*)

Delores and Alexander Baron with their son, Nick, 1972

Because the hopes, at least, were real enough. Jack and Joyce, and Nancy and Craddock in Baron's war novel, *There's No Home*, when he imagines what peace-time will be like from the streets of Catania in 1943, are representatives of the people whom the "cradle-to-grave" ethos of the welfare state was to benefit most. Residents of a communal, ordered, modest, working-class city. Not least, "respectable", as the residents of Lamb Street are keen to think of themselves (in comparison with places like Hoxton and Shoreditch, certainly). As John Boughton points out in a recent history of council housing: "council estates in their earlier years, and well into the post-1945 era, were the home of a (relatively) affluent and aspirational working class. Indeed, their success to a significant degree rested on just that."[10]

It is worth noting that the housing shortage in inner-London has not been continuous. Harryboy gambles for derelict houses in the East End. On his Sunday morning walk, Jack might have zig-zagged through the streets between Holloway and Hornsey Roads, where Islington Council took vacant possession of scores of houses in the 1970s and 80s in order to prevent the dereliction going on in the east. London emptied out and then filled back up again. If the Siskins had someone to pass the house on Ingram's Terrace on to, their heirs might also have felt they had arrived in a "casino in which you were guaranteed to be a winner". An equivalent house on Foulden Road today would sell for over one million pounds. Joe De Souza breaks the news one morning that they are moving, have "taken a small house over in Stoke Newington, sharing the deposit." The "taken… over" phrase is ironic. The De Souzas possibly feel forced into this move partly through the racist complaints of Evelyn Deaner, and Siskin's anxiety about the coming and going of various friends and family (although Siskin calls them "lovely people," and is delighted by the rent being paid on time, he remains "demented with fright" regarding his Black tenants). The De Souzas, then, are significant for two different reasons — as a very early depiction of an African Caribbean family in London fiction, and as an example of the way ordinary, working-class families of any background or ethnicity might have come to own a house in inner-London at a particular point in the city's history, and to somehow gain entry to "a casino where you are guaranteed to be a winner".

---

10 John Boughton, *Municipal Dreams: The Rise and Fall of Council Housing*, (Verso, 2018), p.47.

Woodberry Down itself is in the process of being "regenerated", or "gentrified", depending on which term you prefer, part of it (the most expensive part) being re-named Woodberry Park. A new three-bedroom "penthouse" in one of the blocks overlooking the reservoirs costs even more than a house on Foulden Road. That term, "gentrification", is identified by Anna Minton as being coined by the sociologist Ruth Glass in 1964 to describe the process of middle-class families buying up Victorian houses in Islington, Barnsbury specifically, on the edges of Baron's terrain. Minton goes on to argue, after Piketty, that the difference between the 1960s and today is that the rate of return of the London property market far exceeds the percentage growth of the economy, and that this has both created and worsened the housing crisis (and made a small number of people rich beyond comprehension) at a terrifyingly fast rate.

In a poem called "Eviction Day", in the collection *Koestler Voices: New Poetry From Prisons*, a poet called Nick writes,

> We're all Rachman's children now
> Digging out new basements
> To bury the homeless deep…

He concludes,

> Clean bricks hide dirty money.
> We're all Hoogstraten's children now.
> Buy-to-rent. Buy off-plan.
> Dying for a home.[11]

Peter Rachman, as mentioned above, was a notorious London landlord of the 1950s, his crimes even leading to the term Rachmanism being included in the *Oxford English Dictionary* as a definition of behaviour exploiting vulnerable tenants; Nicholas van Hoogstraten is a property developer and convicted criminal (most notoriously for manslaughter, and also for an attempt to kill a business associate in a grenade attack). He once boasted: "I'm a Fascist, and a Nazi, didn't you know that? If I wanted I could pay £50 to men in London to get every Jew in Brighton bumped off."[12]

---

11 Nick, "Eviction Day", *Koestler Voices: New Poetry from Prisons*, (Koestler Trust, 2017), pp. 53-54.

12 "Explosives man was like one of the family", *The Times*, 15 December 1967.

"And what do you do Mr. Boas?" asks Mrs Deaner. "Me? I'm in property," Harryboy says, disingenuously, but there is something in his grasp of how the city is shifting (back) towards this exploitation of property (and people), schooled in part by Marcia, his middle-class prostitute sometime girlfriend; by Gus, his brother-in-law, and in gossip at the dog tracks; something also in Dido's striving for new wallpaper and belt buckles and a house in Clapton, that foreshadows the Thatcherism of the 1980s which unleashed all that right-to-buy, Long-Good-Friday, financial deregulation, and the promotion of the individual at the expense of the common wealth.

Iain Sinclair writes an account of a public meeting expressing objections to yet another east London housing development: "Most of the development will be buy-to-let investments," a lawyer friend of his claims, "Huge amounts of Russian and Saudi money. Tenants will move in and out constantly. There will be no community at all" (*Ghost Milk*). Certainly, if whole swathes of the capital further west are the future, with up to forty percent of residences being left empty for much of the year across the West End, and areas such as Knightsbridge and parts of Kensington, then the days of Baron's "little hives" of community truly are numbered, this really is "The Last London". Later, Sinclair visits the boarded-up statue of Clement Attlee on Commercial Road. The statue "was receiving a compulsory makeover and not being prepared for removal, like Lenin and Stalin… Perhaps Clement was, as a courtesy to the dream of the welfare state, being shielded from the self-regarding towers of Canary Wharf" (*Ghost Milk*).

Attlee's statue (which is there to commemorate that he was once Mayor of Stepney) is not far away, half a mile or so, from the streets to which Harryboy Boas returns and weeps in the rain over his mother's death, about the same from where Dido lives out his last days in dereliction. And somewhere within the patterns of life described in Baron's novels there are warring alternative visions of a city, alternative answers to the questions of how and where to live. That of Clement Attlee and Aneurin Bevan on the one hand, of post-1945, and that of Margaret Thatcher and Peter Rachman on the other, of post-1979. And there, of course, are other visions still, those of Mosley and his Blackshirts in the 1930s streets on which Baron grew up, and also of the Communist Party he served so enthusiastically as a young man, chronicled in Andrew Whitehead's chapter of this volume. One reason for the enduring quality of Baron's work is how these warring visions are represented or pre-figured in characters such as Jack, Dido and

Harryboy. And perhaps something else, the "horizontal energies" of which Sinclair writes, "democratic, free-flowing, uncontained", opposed to the "vertical thrust of a single structure", both metaphorical (ideology such as that espoused by Rosie Hogarth at the end of the novel, the communism Baron grew away from, but also the worship of "the market", and "top-down" administration of any sort) and literal (Canary Wharf, the Olympic Stadium and Village, the numberless towers of steel and glass), seeking to dominate place "by overlooking it" (*Ghost Milk*).

There is a homeless man who sits on the bench in Haggerston Park in Sinclair's book, unmoving, a personification of "Last London", and also of Dido at the end of the novel, and of Don McCullin's portraits of Spitalfields' homeless, "the invisibles… the people who are left in the bushes… the ones who disappear…"[13] It's hard to know what Jack Agass and Dido Peach and Harryboy Boas might make of the city's current inequalities. One the one hand, a returning soldier, a gangster and a professional gambler, all relatively young, fit and healthy white men, are hardly representative of today's working-class London, although they — their descendants, at least — have their place within it still. Jack would no doubt shrug, bemused, try to "make the best of a bad job"; both Dido and Harryboy might shrug too, see more of an opportunity, though whether that would end happily or not is another story. "Such is my luck," Harryboy might protest.

"Everything is provisional here. Nothing is grounded…" runs Sinclair's commentary on today's Hackney. And that is something that in different ways, Jack, Dido and Harryboy already understood: it is perhaps a hard truth of working-class London life through the years, hence the clinging to both the idea and the reality of "little hives [where] people live for each other as well as for themselves", patterns of life, observed on Baron's part, and lived by many of his characters, quietly and calmly at ground level, all "making the best of a bad job".

---

13 From Iain Sinclair: *The Last London*, a short film for *The London Review of Books*, March 2017. https://www.youtube.com/watch?v=B05mdDG8k2s

Tenement flats in Coronation Avenue, Stoke Newington, subsequently re-built and still in use, opposite Baron's family home in Foulden Road. This was one of the worst civilian disasters of the Second World War, and is referred to in *With Hope, Farewell.*

A Walk Round Baron's Manor

Alexander Baron was brought up in the streets where Stoke Newington shades into Dalston — and he returned to the family home after his wartime years in the army. It forms the backdrop to the most successful of his London novels, *The Lowlife*, published in 1963, in which the central character, an inveterate gambler and chancer called Harryboy Boas, explains to the reader why he lives in Hackney:

> Me? I want to live where I grew up. ... Also, I like it. ... Here, all sorts live. The Cockneys are of the old breed, sharp-faced , with the stamp of the markets on them. The young Jews either look like pop singers or pop singers' managers. The old ones - it's funny, the pious old men with yellow beards I remember from my childhood seem to have died off, all of them, but the old women survive. Among the crowds, you can see the old women, women you might have seen in the East End fifty years ago... schlapping [swinging] their big shopping bags.

But this is not the East End, Harryboy insists: "That's the mark of the outsider, when you hear someone call Hackney the East End. The East End starts two miles down the road, across the border with Bethnal Green."

This short walk — it should take you no more than an hour — guides you round the places where Baron grew up and that feature in his writing: a synagogue, a church, a factory, a market, a school, a housing estate, a bomb site... and starting at his old home.

START AT THE CORNER OF STOKE NEWINGTON ROAD AND FOULDEN ROAD, AND HEAD ALONG FOULDEN ROAD

Before 1965, in the days when Stoke Newington was a borough in its own right, Stoke Newington Road was the eastern boundary. Alexander Baron was brought up a few yards into Hackney and his street, Foulden Road — he recalled — always "aspired to Stoke Newington gentility".

The street dates from about 1880 and has survived wars and clearance drives almost unscathed. Alexander Baron (his surname at birth and until he became a published novelist was Bernstein) grew up at 6 Foulden Road (1) — and this was the model for the boarding house where Harryboy lives in *The Lowlife* on a street given the name of Ingram's Terrace:

Locations

1 6 Foulden Road
2 Somerford Grove Estate
3 Shacklewell Primary School
4 Ridley Road market
5 Olympic House / Simpson's factory
6 Stoke Newington Baptist Church
7 Walford Road Synagogue
8 Coronation Avenue

Map designed by Nancy Edwards

It was probably named after the Victorian spec builder who ran it up; mostly two-storied houses, with basements; some bigger like old-fashioned vicarages; and the end houses with passages at the sides from street to back garden. ... When I was a boy, these houses were occupied by superior working-class families, who kept them in beautiful condition. Every year, when the fresh gravel and tar was laid on the road (I can still smell the tar) the houses were bright with fresh paint. Now most of them are tenements.

The street's residents — as Baron recounts in the novel — were Cockneys and Jewish families along with newcomers from Cyprus and the Caribbean:

The people in Ingram's Terrace don't mix, but they all say "good morning" to each other. I never smelt any hatred between one kind and another, not even an ember that might flare up in the future. Of course, they all have good jobs. The children mix. The children all play in the street together. I love to watch them. The children are the only real common ground of the grown-ups. The Yiddisher mumma who comes out with a cake for her boy will bring cakes for the kids he's playing with, black, Cypriot, gentile, the lot.

FROM FOULDEN ROAD TURN RIGHT ONTO AMHURST ROAD, THEN RIGHT ON SHACKLEWELL LANE, AND RIGHT AGAIN ONTO SHACKLEWELL ROAD

You are now among Hackney's post-war council housing estates — the Shacklewell Road estate and just beyond it the Somerford Grove estate (2). Hackney decided in the 1940s that it would build only low-rise estates and stuck to that until the mid-1950s. The Somerford Grove estate in particular consists largely of two- and three-storey buildings, with hidden away closes and courtyards giving it a very different feel from the later high-rise developments. It was designed by the architect and town planner Frederick Gibberd and completed in 1949. A gable wall still has a plaque recording that the development won an award for merit in the 1951 Festival of Britain

In Baron's novel *Rosie Hogarth*, published in 1951 and set mainly in the crowded Chapel Market area of Islington, Joyce and her fiancé Jack come to take a look around a "modern housing estate in Hackney", hoping that one day they may be able to live in a place as green and spacious as this:

"It doesn't seem like London, does it" Joyce said. She looked around her. "It's all so clean and — oh, all that grass and flowers. ... All sunlit. If I lived here I'd be afraid it was a dream and that I might wake up any minute and see dirty black walls again."

"Ah," said Jack, "it's like the bloody pictures or something." ...

They walked hand in hand , like a pair of wondering children ... On their left rose blocks of buildings overlooking plots where lawns and gardens were being laid out. The flats had big sun windows and private balconies, each with a built-in flower bed projecting. On their right were rows of cottages, their frontages consisting mainly of glass and harmoniously-coloured tiles, each house with its private garden and many with neat porches.

It's a good fit for the Somerford Grove estate.

LOOP ROUND SOMERFORD GROVE, WALKING ALONG THE IMPOSING SIDE ELEVATION OF OLYMPIC HOUSE HEADING AWAY FROM STOKE NEWINGTON ROAD, AND THEN HEAD DOWN AN ALLEY WITH A 'SCHOOL' SIGN ON TO SHACKLEWELL ROW

Cottage terrace called Seal Street next to new flats opposite Shacklewell Lane School, Stoke Newington. This tiny locale features in several Baron novels, including *Rosie Hogarth*, in which Jack Agass and his fiancée admire the new post-war council flats.

Seal Street terrace, workers' cottages built in 1881, with rear of Simpson's garment factory in view. This once employed more than 2000 workers, and is where the fictional Harry Boas may have worked as described in *The Lowlife*.

The school at the end of the alley is Shacklewell Primary School (3) which Baron attended — now entirely rebuilt. Baron liked it here and recalled that on his last day he wept — he said it was the last time he ever cried. He went on in 1929 to Hackney Downs School (still then known to many by its old name of the Grocers' School), which the playwright Harold Pinter also attended and which closed in 1995.

To your left is Seal Street, a particularly attractive terraced street from the 1880s now pedestrianised and part of a conservation area. Take a glance, but head down Shacklewell Row past the Merchant Taylors' School Mission — founded by the public school of that name — and hidden behind it, the church of St Barnabas, Dalston. Both date from about 1890, and as the church website comments: "It was very much the done thing at this time for public schools and Oxbridge colleges to establish frontier outposts in the London slums, partly to do good works spiritually and socially, and partly to give their privileged students a glimpse of how the other half lived."

CARRY ON ALONG SHACKLEWELL ROW AND FOLLOW SHACKLEWELL LANE AS IT CURVES ROUND TO THE MAIN ROAD — TURN LEFT ON TO STOKE NEWINGTON ROAD / KINGSLAND HIGH STREET AND CONTINUE TO THE JUNCTION WITH RIDLEY ROAD

As you join Shacklewell Lane, opposite is the public wash house with the inscription "PUBLIC WASHING BATHS" which opened in the early 1930s and helped keep Shacklewell clean for half-a-century. On the right just before Kingsland High Street is a commanding brick building — this is Shacklewell Lane Mosque, the first mosque to serve the local Turkish Cypriot community, which was built in 1903 as Stoke Newington Synagogue and remained in its original use until 1976. As you pass Nando's on the corner of Kingsland High Street take a peep through the window and admire the decorative tiling — a remnant of when this was a pub, "The Castle".

On to Ridley Road (4) — one of London's liveliest food markets, dating back to the 1880s. It reflects the diversity of the area, with many stalls specialising in produce from Africa and Asia. In the years immediately after the Second World War, Oswald Mosley — founder of the British Union of Fascists — held open-air meetings here, leading to

Foulden Road

198

clashes with anti-fascist demonstrators including the 43 Group of Jewish ex-servicemen.

In Baron's 1952 novel *With Hope, Farewell* — a bleak account of post-war anti-Semitism — the young couple at the heart of the story, Ruth and Mark Strong, are trapped in a bus on Kingsland Road, surrounded by rival groups of protestors and ranks of mounted police:

> In the street missiles were flying. From the rear of the compartment came the sound of breaking glass and the hysterical screaming of a woman. Two men crushed together in the gangway were cursing each other and exchanging blows.

Amid the tumult, Ruth has a miscarriage — providing a tragic ending to a sombre novel.

CROSS THE ROAD AND RETRACE YOUR STEPS UP KINGSLAND ROAD WHICH BECOMES STOKE NEWINGTON ROAD, UP TO OPPOSITE THE JUNCTION WITH SOMERFORD GROVE

The marvellous art deco-influenced building across the road on your right (5), now a kind of Retro superstore, was built in 1929 as Simpson's men's clothing factory. It was one of the biggest in London and was particularly well-known for making trousers with a self-supporting waistband, so making braces redundant. It's now called Olympic House — you walked along the side of it a little earlier, so you can get some idea of its immense size. Its workforce once numbered in the thousands.

In *The Lowlife*, Harryboy — when down on his luck at the dog tracks — turns to his trade as a Hoffman Presser, a specialist role in the clothing trade, working at factories much like Simpson's:

> I like the machine roar from the big shops and the bray of music while you work. The factory was also very convenient for women. ... It's a kind of sex war all the time. There's this tribe of girls at their machines. Each time you go past, to the lav or the foreman's cubicle, you can feel them all sizing you up as if you are a bull in the auction ring, and sometimes they give you a razzing.

CARRY ON ALONG STOKE NEWINGTON ROAD PAST THE JUNCTION WITH BRIGHTON ROAD

You can't miss the Aziziye mosque with its beautiful Turkish tiling, which was built in 1913 as a cinema and at one time screened Yiddish language films. Just next to it is Stoke Newington Baptist Church (6), which features in *The Lowlife* as a focus of the area's Caribbean migrants, a community of "marvellous respectability" who made a point of looking their smartest for Sunday morning service. "They are the Victorian residents of this street," — Baron wrote — "come back a century later, with black skins."

If you look across Stoke Newington Road at the far side of the petrol station, you can see some old workshops and light industrial buildings which would once have given work to Harryboy's neighbours.

TURN LEFT ALONG WALFORD ROAD

At the far end is Walford Road Synagogue (7), an independent orthodox synagogue with a history stretching back to 1912 though the building dates from the 1930s. In *With Hope, Farewell*, the central character Mark Strong stands guard, a gun in his pocket, over a back-street synagogue to stop it being defaced or burnt down by anti-Semites. One evening,

Walford Road Synagogue, Stoke Newington, featured in the final scene of *With Hope, Farewell.*

Main entrance to Walford Road Synagogue, Stoke Newington.

he is alarmed when two gruff, well-built men, one carrying a jack handle, loom menacingly out of the dark:

> "This is the Jews' church?" asked the burly man. His voice matched his face; it was like a growl gathering in the chest of a bulldog.

They are not fascists, however, but rail workers and trade unionists come to take their turn ensuring that the synagogue is protected — an act of solidarity rather than desecration.

RETRACE YOUR STEPS, HEAD ALONG BEATTY ROAD THEN TURN LEFT ON TO STOKE NEWINGTON ROAD AND LEFT AGAIN ON TO VICTORIAN ROAD

As you walk along on Stoke Newington Road you are passing the frontage of Coronation Avenue. On your left as you turn into Victorian Road are the entrance arches to the buildings, with striking iron gates and ornate signage (8). Coronation Avenue — along with adjoining Imperial Avenue — opened in 1903 to provide housing for those moving out of the East End. This was the site of one of the worst civilian tragedies of the Second World War. Baron makes allusion to it in *With Hope, Farewell*:

> along the Stoke Newington Road, a parachute-mine had caused
> an entire block of flats to collapse into the communal shelter
> underneath, killing hundreds of people.

Local residents had taken refuge during an evening bombing raid in a three-room shelter underneath ground-floor shops. At about nine on a Sunday evening six weeks after the start of the all-out German air offensive know as the Blitz, it took a direct hit.

A plaque records: "In memory of over 160 people who died when a high explosive bomb fell on this building during the Blitz on 13th October 1940". It was put up in 2011, and the following year that same initiative to honour and remember those who perished led to the publication of a marvellous book, *Just Like the End of the World: stories of the Coronation Avenue disaster*, which offers a personal and human dimension to the tragedy.

The shelter was used not simply by residents of the blocks above but by many of those who lived in nearby streets. Five people from Baron's street, Foulden Road, were among the dead. Many of those killed, some unidentifiable, were buried in a mass grave at Abney Park cemetery. After the war, Stoke Newington Borough Council erected a memorial there to all those who died in wartime bombing raids. The explosion left a gaping hole in the Coronation Avenue buildings. The flats were eventually renovated and residents moved back in from 1949.

This is the end of the walk — if you want to visit Abney Park, one of London's "magnificent seven" garden cemeteries dating from the first half of the nineteenth century, it's a ten minutes' stroll away... if the bookshops, cafés and bars of Stoke Newington's High Street and Church Street don't claim you first, that is!

Thanks for making the journey.

Notes on Contributors

Anthony Cartwright is a writer and teacher, whose recent work includes the novels *Iron Towns* (2016) and *The Cut* (2017), both set in his native Midlands. His interest in Alexander Baron began on reading the London Fiction Series edition of *The Lowlife*, published by Harvill Press in 2001, and has grown through years of living and working in north and east London. His essay on Baron's work, "'The Young Men of the Nation': Alexander Baron and Urban Working Class Masculinity" appeared in *A History of British Working Class Literature*, published by Cambridge University Press (2017).

Sean Longden is an author and historian specialising in the untold stories of World War II. For his first book, *To the Victor the Spoils*, a social history of the British Army in World War II, he was given access to the personal archives of Alexander Baron which helped to develop his interest in Baron's work. He has provided the foreword and notes for recent publications of Baron's novels *From the City, From the Plough* and *The Human Kind*. These give the reader historical context to the novels and allow readers to understand which elements of the stories were taken directly from Baron's experiences.

Dr Susie Thomas has taught Baron's London novels on her literature courses to American undergraduates in London for many years. The students always say the same thing: "*The Lowlife* is awesome. Why isn't Baron better known?" It is difficult to know how to answer. She has published articles on British Literature from Aphra Behn to Martin Amis. She edited *Hanif Kureishi: A reader's guide to essential criticism* and she was the Reviews Editor for the *The Literary London Journal*.

Dr Nadia Valman is Reader in English Literature at Queen Mary, University of London. She has published widely on British Jewish literature, including a survey of the postwar British Jewish novel in the *Oxford History of the Novel in English*, editing *British Jewish Women Writers* and co-editing the *Routledge Handbook of Contemporary Jewish Cultures*. She is the creator of Zangwill's Spitalfields, a walking tour app using Israel Zangwill's classic novel of Jewish immigration, *Children of the Ghetto* (1892) as a guide to Spitalfields, east London, where the novel is set. She is currently researching the literature of east London.

Andrew Whitehead is a journalist and historian and the creator and moderator of the London Fictions website:www.londonfictions.com. He co-edited, with Jerry White, *London Fictions* — published by Five Leaves — in which twenty-six authors, scholars and enthusiasts each write about an exceptional London novel. He has written or co-authored *Curious King's Cross*, *Curious Kentish Town* and *Curious Camden Town* — transgressive explorations of the urban landscapes of north London where he lives. He has a longstanding association with *History Workshop Journal* and is an honorary professor at the University of Nottingham. Once upon a time, he was the Editor of BBC World Service News.

Ken Worpole is a writer on architecture, landscape and public policy (www.worpole.net), and was Emeritus Professor at the Cities Institute, London Metropolitan University. He has a particular interest in the literature of east London and Hackney, where he and his wife, the photographer, Larraine Worpole, have lived and worked since 1969. Ken's 1983 interview with Alexander Baron formed the basis of his pioneering re-appraisal of Baron's fiction in his first book, *Dockers & Detectives, a study of post-war British working class fiction*, published in 1983 and re-issued in an updated edition by Five Leaves in 2008.

Acknowledgements

The editors and contributors would like to thank the following for their help in bringing this project to fruition: The Barry Amiel and Norman Melburn Trust for their generous grant towards the costs of production, and the the the staff at the Museum of English Rural Life, Reading University — where the Alexander Baron archive is now located — for consistent help and advice to researchers. Many individuals have also given time and support, notably: Nick Baron, for advice, thoughtful comment and provision of family photographs and other documents; our publisher, Ross Bradshaw; long time Baron enthusiast, Iain Sinclair; and Liz Vater, director of the endlessly inventive Stoke Newington Literary Festival. Finally we would also like to thank Matthew Cowley, Nancy Edwards, Laurie Elks, Pippa Hennessy, Rachel Kolsky, Rebecca Taylor, Nicolas Tredell, Muriel Walker and John Williams, for help and support in a myriad of other ways. Parts of Chapter Four have previously appeared in the *Literary London Journal*.

Names and bylines

Readers may find some confusion as to the names Alexander Baron was known by at different times in his life. He was born Joseph Alexander Bernstein, known to his family as 'Joe'. When he left school to became a political journalist he wrote under the name of Alec Bernstein, remaining 'Alec' to his friends for the rest of his life. However, just prior to the publication of his first novel, *From the City, From the Plough* in 1948, Jonathan Cape, his publisher, suggested he change his surname. This he did — to Baron — and Alexander Baron became the name by which he was known as a writer ever after.

Alexander Baron titles in print or due to be reprinted in 2019

From the City, From the Plough (Black Spring/Imperial War Museum)
King Dido (Five Leaves)
The Human Kind (Black Spring)
The Lowlife (Black Spring)
Rosie Hogarth (Five Leaves)
There's No Home (Sort of Books)
The War Baby (Five Leaves)
With Hope, Farewell (Five Leaves)